A FACE IN THE CROWD

A FACE IN THE CROWD

My Life As An NFL Wife

Nicole Berti

Copyright © 2004 by Nicole Berti.

Cover Photos by Audrey Dempsey/Infinity Photo

Library of Congress Number: 2004091243
ISBN :   Hardcover   1-4134-4950-6
              Softcover   1-4134-4949-2

All rights reserved. No part of this book may be reproduced or transmitted in any form or by any means, electronic or mechanical, including photocopying, recording, or by any information storage and retrieval system, without permission in writing from the copyright owner.

Note: This book has not been approved, licensed or sponsored in any way by the National Football League.

This book was printed in the United States of America.

To order additional copies of this book, contact:
Xlibris Corporation
1-888-795-4274
www.Xlibris.com
Orders@Xlibris.com
24136

Contents

Chapter I	: In The Beginning	9
Chapter II	: The NFL Draft	15
Chapter III	: Rookie	27
Chapter IV	: Off-Season Highlights	43
Chapter V	: A Real Start	50
Chapter VI	: First Team Wives' Club	60
Chapter VII	: Celebrity-ism	75
Chapter VIII	: Groupies, Cheerleaders and Infidelity	84
Chapter IX	: Starting on the Wrong Foot	89
Chapter X	: Travel Secrets	106
Chapter XI	: Down But Not Out	111
Chapter XII	: Fumble	128
Chapter XIII	: A Season To Remember	154
Chapter XIV	: Politics As Usual	205
Chapter XV	: Walking Away	216
Chapter XVI	: XFL Extreme Football	219
Chapter XVII	: Financial Yardage	228
Chapter XVIII	: The Final Score	232

For My Boys

Tony, you are my rock! Thank you for your unending patience, eternal commitment and unconditional love. Thank you, too, for giving me something to write about, supporting me in everything I do and always seeing the positive side of things. I'm always passionately yours!

Brennan and Easton, you are the reason I put this story to paper. You two monkeys give me reason to appreciate every day, every laugh and, of course, every mess. You make me a better person and constantly remind me love is the stuff dreams are made of. Always follow your dreams, but let your hearts be your guide!

Chapter I

In The Beginning

1994

Prior to meeting Tony, I was seeing a guy I'd met through an old college friend. But things weren't especially working out and when he failed to make an appearance at my 25th birthday party, I was put off by the blow-off and the previous eighteen months I'd spent wading through the muck of the dating pool. The compulsive search for Mr. Right was truly distracting and the mere fact I felt my life wasn't complete without someone in it was terribly annoying. After all, established in my career and independent, living alone in a home I owned, I didn't need anyone dictating my decisions or making things complicated, right?

I decided my single girlfriends' tireless complaining and belief all men were selfish and egotistical jerks was, perhaps, warranted. In the past, I'd ignored their whining and rebuffed their skeptical attitudes. But, by the time I met Tony late in January 1994, I was just as jaded and my sniveling and hateful attitude was certainly reflective of my negative state of mind. Guarded with my emotions and determined not to waste time or energy on one more meaningless relationship, I vowed to immediately wade through the traditional dating crap and pre-qualify anyone of potential interest before getting too involved. To get through my defensive posturing, the next guy interested in my affections would have to be Superman or at least a close facsimile. Fortunately for me, Tony and Superman had much in common.

People frequently ask us how we met and I often get the feeling they're using the question to ascertain whether it was before Tony was a professional ball player or after. As if our answer will shed light on the type of relationship we have or what kind of person I might be based on the timeline of our courtship. I suppose the questions stem from the many preconceived notions people have regarding professional athletes, their wives and their lives, in general. The number of times I've been asked, "What's it like being married to a professional ball player?" alone suggests a certain mystique and prestige associated with our union. But, while Tony provides sports commentary to his often asked question, "What's it really like playing in the NFL?" I never really know what to say to mere acquaintances who openly inquire of our personal life. So, the answers often depend on who's doing the asking.

When asked how we met, Tony and I routinely tell people we met through mutual friends, which is the truth. But, if we want to mess with them and ingratiate their thirst for some lurid tale about how the professional athlete and his wife came together, then we tell them we met in a hotel room at 3:00 in the morning, which is also true.

The whole truth of the matter is Tony and I met through mutual friends in a New Mexico-based country band called Redneck, which regularly performed at a Denver bar both Tony and I frequented called the Grizzly Rose. I met the band through one of my girlfriends who supposedly attended high school with the guys and Tony met them through his sister, Lori, who, at one time, followed the band to various locations throughout Arizona and Colorado as they tried to make a name for themselves.

In January 1994, Redneck returned to the Rose for a week-long stint during Denver's National Western Stockshow and while my friends and I didn't attend their shows early in the week, we were sitting directly adjacent to the dance floor on Friday night. Always attracted to big and tall men, Tony instantly garnered my attention after I noticed him moving through the crowded bar and standing a full head above most. He was very good looking and, though my friends and I proclaimed to be having a girls' night out, I periodically found myself scanning for him in the crowd. By the end of the night, I'd spotted him several times looking very comfortable with a tall redhead on the dance floor. Assuming she was his girlfriend, I reminded myself I wasn't looking for romance and tried to forget about the attractive cowboy!

Around closing time, my girlfriend, Tracy, suggested we go to Redneck's hotel, following their last set, to attend a party. I was reluctant. Their parties routinely didn't start until 3:00 a.m. and I was already tired from my 50-hour work week. But, after she teased me about my recent birthday, I was convinced to meet her at the Travel Lodge off Interstate 25.

It was already 2:30 a.m. when I pulled into the hotel's parking lot and noticed Tracy's car was no where to be found. But, I parked my car anyway and headed into the lobby for a brief look around. It was quiet and I decided to wait no more than a few minutes before calling it a night. After acknowledging the lone desk clerk with a half-hearted wave, I moved toward the front door just as the rambunctious group of band members, drunken cowboys, groupies and my girlfriends burst into the lobby. Joining the fray, I headed upstairs.

Several rooms were being used for the impromptu gathering and Tracy and I briefly mingled in one room until she suggested we go to another, down the hall, where the party overflowed into the tiny hallway and several attractive girls were surrounding the band mates. We pushed through the crowd in the doorway and I took an empty seat on one of the two double beds. The garbage cans were piled high with ice and beer, the windows were steaming up from all the heated bodies in the small space and the sound of the television was overshadowed by the intense chatter of people bullshitting and the sudden jeers from the table of cowboys in the corner downing multiple rounds of shots. Packed in elbow to elbow, the scene was reminiscent of more than a few underage hotel parties I attended in high school.

The bustle of more people attempting to make their way into the congested room forced me to turn toward the door and the tall cowboy edging his way through the entry. As he took a seat on the corner of the dresser, his giant frame moved to reveal the redhead and a brunette standing close behind. I was disappointed he had company, but I couldn't keep myself from eyeing him. He caught me looking his direction and I quickly smiled and looked away. I continued talking to Tracy and a few others but I couldn't help looking back at him. When I did, he smiled at me and we played a quaint game of cat and mouse for a while. During a lull in the conversation, I turned to him again and this time he got up and walked over. Taking a seat on the bed next to me, he introduced himself. We began the conversation by talking about the cold weather and our musical tastes and fondness for the band. But, soon enough, we were talking about how I'd seen him earlier at the bar, how we were both single, and what I did for a living. He seemed genuinely interested when I told him I was the Director of Marketing for DC Marketing, a small marketing office representing several restaurants and nightclubs in Denver.

Throughout the conversation, I was mesmerized by his blue eyes; they sparkled. He was so big and imposing and yet his smile, encircled by a thick goatee, was warm and charming. He was sexy as hell and once I discovered the redhead was his sister and the brunette her friend, I quickly lost track of the time until I noticed many of the party patrons leaving. A quick glance at my watch and I couldn't believe it was 5:30 in the morning. Tony and I were both surprised by the time and he commented on having to be at work-outs in three short hours. I must have looked puzzled because he followed up by explaining he had to lift weights first thing in the morning at school. Confused further by the details, I reluctantly asked him how old he was and he replied, "Twenty-one." My enthusiasm for the cowboy suddenly waned as he continued to say he was a student at the University of Colorado where he played football.

He then asked my age and, full of attitude, I arrogantly blurted out "Twenty-five" and added I'd graduated from Colorado State in 1991. Tony looked to be 25 or 26 and he was so interesting, intelligent, attractive, and seemingly mature. I couldn't believe how old he was. Terribly disappointed by his age and the knowledge he was still in school and a football player to boot, I discounted the previous two hours of engaging conversation. Suspect of his intentions, I made him for a young stud out on the make and I wasn't interested in that type of guy. They had a propensity to drink too much, fool around too often and commit too little. Uninterested in a one-night-stand, I took it as my cue to head for the door.

Waiting for the elevator, Tony joined me in the hall. We rode down together and he asked if I was going to the Rose again Saturday night. I told him I wasn't sure because, as a spokesperson for Miller Beer, my side job had me spending most of the day manning a Miller booth at the Stockshow giving away free samples of their Sharp's non-alcoholic brand. As a Tecate beer girl, I often earned extra money by making appearances for Miller at local bars and events, signing posters and giving away related promotional items.

By the time we reached the lobby, I told him I would consider going to the Rose even though I had no intention of going to the bar again that night or allowing myself to get all fluttered over him. Following me all the way to the front door, he caught me off guard when he said he held Stockshow tickets for the afternoon rodeo and would try to stop by the Sharp's booth to say hello.

Needless to say, Tony never came by the booth that day and I chalked up the no-show to his unsuccessful bid to get laid the night before. Working the booth until it closed at 9:00 p.m., I was on the fence about actually going to the Rose again. Tony was at such a different stage in his life and I wondered why in the hell I was even thinking about it. But, something inside kept urging me to go and when I couldn't stop thinking about him, I considered stopping at the Rose for one drink on the way home.

I arrived at the bar solo knowing my girlfriends would be there for Redneck's closing night. But, the minute I walked through the door, I found myself scanning the crowd for Tony and, to my surprise, he was waiting near the entrance and approached me as soon as I was in the door. He was eager to tell me, he and his friend, Derek West, visited the beer booth earlier in the day but I was talking with one of the beer reps and didn't notice them. He claimed he didn't want to disturb me so he just walked on. Annoyed by my internal giddiness at the news he'd actually come by, I tried to contain myself. But, hiding my obvious attraction to him was difficult and we were soon settled into a cozy table talking further. At the time, I never would have guessed going to the bar that night would change everything in my life.

Four months later, Tony and I agreed he should move into my two-bedroom town home. I'd lived alone since June of 1993, and I liked the idea of having someone to come home to. Besides, it seemed silly for Tony to continue paying rent on his apartment in Boulder when he'd been virtually living at my place, in Denver, since our fifth date. We'd become inseparable since meeting and our relationship just kept getting stronger. I liked everything about him. As my boyfriend, he was supportive, honest and caring. But, there was more to it than that. We'd become best friends and our relationship was very different from the two, previous long-term commitments I'd experienced. His upbringing as the only boy in a house with three sisters and a strong-willed mother made him very respectful of women. His mother, Phyllis, and father, Charles, divorced when Tony was six and his estranged relationship with his father and his sometimes tumultuous relationship with his stepfather, Vern, made Tony fully aware of the importance of male responsibility within a family unit. Early on, he knew what type of man he wanted to be and every one of his actions was built on that foundation. I learned quickly he was nurturing, always true to his word and exceptionally dependable. The notion his family would always come first was deeply engrained in him. My dad always made family his first priority and I found that same quality in Tony very endearing. Early in our relationship, I knew I could love him for the rest of my life and formally moving in together seemed like the logical progression of our relationship.

Chapter II

The NFL Draft

1995

Tony worked very hard his senior season to establish his name in the world of college football. His accomplishments in the fall of 1994 included a very impressive 4.68 second, 40-yard dash, an important statistic to NFL teams, and a number of University of Colorado weight lifting records including a 365 lbs. power clean lift and a 465 lbs. bench press. He was fast and he was strong. Throughout Tony's final collegiate year, the sports media paid close attention to all of the CU Buffs as they marched their way toward what they hoped would be a National Championship. Unfortunately, the disappointing 24-to-7 loss in game eight to big rival Nebraska effectively ended CU's championship quest. However, the weekly radio and newspaper interviews continued despite the loss, in part, due to CU tailback Rashaan Salaam's bid for the Heisman Trophy, which seemed imminent after he ran over the 2,000 yard rushing mark joining the ranks of Barry Sanders, Mike Rozier and Marcus Allen. Tony, as the starting left tackle, was an integral member of the powerful offensive line, which made that accomplishment possible and when Rashaan actually took home the Heisman, the o-line's memorable play and the team's overall success parlayed Tony and his name into the national sports spotlight. He was named to the Associated Press' All-Big Eight Conference and All-American college football teams. The acknowledgements were outstanding athletic honors and the media attention was steady.

But, he wasn't alone in the field. Tony was joined by eleven other outstanding CU seniors who would all find their way into the NFL in the spring of 1995 including the likes of Kordell Stewart, Christian Fauria (Big C), Michael Westbrook, Ted Johnson and Derek West (D West).

The '94 Buffs won virtually every game during the season and Tony's confidence was at an all-time high. During his five seasons at CU (he red-shirted his freshman year giving him an extra year of football eligibility) the team lost fewer than eight games. It was a Cinderella story of a powerhouse football team. The media loved them, the fans loved them and the city loved them. They were on top of the world. Then, to everyone's surprise, Coach Bill McCartney announced he was retiring as head coach of Colorado to spend more time with his family and pursue his founding role in the Promise Keepers religious organization.

Tony couldn't believe McCartney would leave the Buffaloes behind. Only a few years earlier, Bill McCartney played an integral role in Tony's decision to continue playing football. Tony was recruited to CU as a strong, high school defensive player but, as a college sophomore, struggled with the game and the time constraints of his classes as a pre-med major. He was relinquished to a back-up role on the team and was frustrated with his own progress. He weighed the relief of walking away from football against the burden of disappointing his mother. She was extremely proud of his heavy recruitment out of high school by the University of Arizona, Arizona State, the University of Colorado, Colorado State (my alma mater), and a number of other Division 1A schools. Growing up on a farm in South Dakota and having worked difficult blue-collar jobs in construction, she made higher education an important issue in the family. She wanted Tony to receive a top-notch education and leaving the football program had the potential to end his full-ride scholarship. With his mother in no position to provide any financial assistance, thoughts of losing his scholarship and putting his education in jeopardy weighed heavily on his mind.

However, after much consideration and regardless of the financial fall-out, Tony felt his role on the football team was providing little sense of accomplishment and he made the difficult decision to tell McCartney he was leaving the team. During their meeting, McCartney told Tony changes would be made and convinced him he had a bright future as both a CU athlete and student. Shortly after, McCartney switched Tony to the offensive side of the ball where he quickly found a home on the offensive line. He dropped the time-consuming organic chemistry class giving him difficulty and switched his major from pre-med to psychology. With his study schedule lightened, his academics fell into a rhythm and his football outlook improved. McCartney always took care of his players and encouraged them to be the best they could be as individuals and athletes. He took seriously his responsibility to take over where his players' parents left off when they turned them over to his program.

Tony and I discovered just how committed Coach was to taking over when we decided to move in together in the spring of 1994. Tony knew Coach McCartney's strict team policy would require him to approve of our living arrangement and Coach wouldn't do that until Tony's mother, Phyllis, called him to say she was aware of the situation and approved. Phyllis seemed to like me fine and while we weren't close, she trusted Tony's judgment and placed the call.

Coach then summoned Tony to his office to have a little discussion about the responsibility of moving in with a woman. He quoted some scripture and made darn sure Tony was committed to the relationship. I didn't necessarily agree with the process but it did prove just how much Bill McCartney cared about his players. There is no doubt in Tony's mind that without Bill McCartney, he would not have had the opportunities, as a senior in 1994, to experience the "Miracle In Michigan" where CU beat Michigan in the final four seconds of the game on a Hail Mary pass, the success of assisting Rashaan Salaam win the Heisman Trophy or the honor of being invited to the East-West Shrine All-Star Football Game at Stanford and the Hula Bowl All-Star Classic in Hawaii. Bill McCartney kept Tony in football and for that he was eternally grateful.

Much had happened since that fateful day when McCartney convinced Tony things would work out. Tony's college football career was such a success he felt compelled during his final season to interview and "hire" Ken Ready of Prudential Securities as his financial advisor in anticipation of potentially turning pro. And, once Tony's college football career officially ended in January of 1995 following the Fiesta Bowl, Ken assumed the daunting responsibility of screening the twenty-five or so agents calling our home daily seeking the opportunity to meet with Tony and discuss representation. Based on criteria Tony set forth, Ken narrowed the enormous field to five potential agents with extensive experience representing professional athletes, a relatively small number of clients and legal backgrounds. Tony then planned to personally interview the top three based on their qualities and experience. To my surprise, he wanted my input and asked me to sit in. We narrowed the choice to Neil Schwartz in New York and Brad Blank in Boston. We really liked Neil but Brad was more experienced in dealing with higher round draft picks. Swayed by the difference and eager to end the interviewing process, Tony selected Brad Blank.

Despite not selecting Neil Schwartz for representation, Neil helped Tony secure his first endorsements. Signature Rookies and Superior Pix inked deals with Tony to produce trading cards featuring him in action as #50 at the University of Colorado. Excited about the idea of having his own trading cards, Tony reveled in the opportunity to spend hours in front of the television signing thousands of finished cards for each company. By the end of each 1000 card sitting, his signature was virtually illegible. But, Tony was too thrilled with the process to be concerned. The cards were a bench mark in his dream of becoming a professional football player.

The next hurdle on the road to the draft was the two-day National Invitational Camp (commonly known as the Combine) in February, where the National Football League invited prospective players to Indianapolis, determined by their playing position. Everyone with hopes of being drafted attended the Combine for the opportunity to showcase their talent, promote themselves and meet the participating NFL teams' position coaches, medical staffs, player personnel directors, general managers and head coaches.

On the first day of the Combine, the players received comprehensive physical examinations conducted by team physicians and athletic trainers. Tony was given a red jersey with the NFL logo and an "OL" (Offensive Line) and the number 2 printed on the front. Berti and the number 2 appeared on the back. The physicals were exhausting. The players spent the entire day walking from room to room where each team had an opportunity to examine medical records, poke, prod and basically give them the once over twice. They were weighed and measured, flexed and pulled, pushed and stretched and even x-rayed. At one point, Tony was directed to stand on a podium while a gentleman measured the size of his hands and then announced the results to the crowd. It was like cattle going to auction.

On the second day, the players went to the RCA Dome for non-contact skill workouts, agility drills, and timing in the 40-yard dash conducted by members of the coaching and scouting staffs of the participating NFL teams. Tony ran a 4.95 second 40-yard dash, making him the fastest lineman in the draft—a rare feat for a lineman topping 287 pounds. He was touted as a high-round draft pick with great strength and fast feet and he returned to Colorado feeling optimistic about his Combine evaluations.

The closer we got to Saturday, April 22nd, 1995, the more we were asked if we were having a draft day party. Tony's uncertainty of the draft's outcome initially curbed his interest in a public celebration. But, with each passing week, our friends, families and the media kept asking. The request by two local Denver news stations to join us at our home on draft day finally convinced Tony he would be selected in the first three rounds. Before we knew it, we were swept up in the excitement of it all and planned a party for twenty-five of our friends and family. We informed everyone we knew not to call the house on draft day because that's how the teams would contact Tony regarding his selection. However, still nervous about the media hype, the invitations read, "Party Rules:

1) Fun is to be had by all, 2) No food is to be left over and 3) No one is to feel sorry for Tony if he is not drafted on the first day."

Once the invitations were mailed, Tony got into the spirit. It would be taxing to seat and feed that many people in my small two-bedroom town home, but the challenge added that much more excitement to the day. For the once-in-a-lifetime occasion, Tony wanted to splurge on the food. As a poor and unemployed college student, he decided prime rib sandwiches would be easy to serve and eat while adding a bit of flair to the festivities without too much expense. The head chef at the Diamond Cabaret Steakhouse, one of my marketing properties, ordered us a large, ten-pound prime rib. He sold it to me at cost, seasoned it perfectly and slow-cooked it the day before. All we had to do on draft day was finish it up in the oven at home.

Neither Tony nor I slept well Friday night in anticipation of the next day's activities. When Saturday morning finally arrived, we busied ourselves by cooking and rearranging the living room and dining room furniture to accommodate the crowd. Tony even set up an additional television out on the deck so everyone could watch the draft action.

The smell of prime rib permeated the neighborhood as the first round of the 1995 NFL Draft got under way at 10:00 a.m. Mountain Daylight Time. Each of the 30 NFL teams, selecting in reverse order of how they finished the previous year's season, had up to fifteen minutes to make their first round draft pick. The Jacksonville Jaguars and Carolina Panthers, as new expansion teams, would make the first and second selection as well as the final two selections, #31 and #32, in the first round. Allowing the expansion teams to pick twice in the first round gave them the opportunity to add new talent and depth to their roster, build the franchises more quickly and enabled them to compete with already established teams.

Usually, the players projected to be selected in the first ten picks are present at the draft's broadcast headquarters. Once a team selects them, they join the team owner on stage and have a photo-op sporting their new team's jersey and cap. The draft is broadcast live so during the long pauses between selections, the commentators talk about the next pick, who it's likely to be and any relevant statistics that apply. After they get through the first ten players or so, the announcers just talk football and highlight the players as each team makes their selection. The first round is a long drawn out process taking hours to complete. The second and third rounds follow the first on Saturday with the remaining four rounds held on Sunday. As each round passes, the teams get less and less time to make their selections. By the fourth round, there is only five minutes between each pick and the commentators simply read off the names of the selections with little fan fare. Since Tony was touted to go sometime in the second round, we suggested our guests arrive around 1:00. But, to our surprise, the doorbell started ringing before noon. It seemed everyone was excited and ready to celebrate.

The two crews from rival stations Channel 4 and Channel 9, each with a cameraman and reporter, added four more people into the fold. They arrived before the second round began to interview Tony about his impending selection and supplement their draft day coverage. With so many University of Colorado players touted for the draft, the local media was in a sports-induced frenzy. They did several live "cut-aways" from our home during the day's news coverage. During one of the brief live interviews, Tony's five-year-old niece, Audrianna, couldn't figure out how her Uncle Tony was right there but was also in the TV. We got a kick out of her reaction as she glanced back and forth between Tony and his image on the television.

The mood at our house was jovial. At the end of the first round, everyone started paying closer attention to the television as each team made their selection. Midway through the second round, the phone rang and everyone erupted with excitement. The cameramen jumped up from their plates of food and were set to catch Tony's reaction. After extensive hushing, Tony picked up the phone in anticipation. Within seconds, the color drained from his face and he handed me the receiver. To my embarrassment and Tony's anxiety, it was my cousin, Sherry, calling from Florida to see if

Tony had been selected yet. I briefly brushed her off and reminded her not to call the house again. We would contact everyone as soon as he was selected.

Late in the third round, sometime after 6:00 p.m., the tension at our house was getting very heavy. The day was almost over and everyone, especially Tony, was feeling uncomfortable. Highly-rated wide receiver Michael Westbrook and Heisman Trophy winner Rashaan Salaam were selected early in the first rounds as predicted. But, few of the other outstanding Colorado Buffaloes who had been given such high hopes for the draft heard their names called. Tony and Derek West, his good friend and fellow CU teammate, kept phoning each other on their cell phones attempting to calm each other's obvious anxiety.

The month before, Tony and Derek decided to spend an afternoon looking at new trucks in anticipation of being drafted and having the money to pay for them. As soon as they stepped foot onto the lot, the dealerships, familiar with their names and NFL potential, were eager to help them. Before they knew it, they were signing on the dotted line without a dime for a down payment. Tony showed up at the house in a new Ford F250 extended cab diesel pick-up. It was his first new car and he was so excited to show it off. I was excited too! It was a far cry from the $50.00 Chevy Citation he'd been driving with the front seat propped up by a broom stick, the smashed dash board and the back seat full of snow in the winter because the rear window wouldn't roll up. He "sold" the Citation for an egg burrito and now he and Derek were wondering if buying the trucks was a good idea. They joked about the dealership's return policy. But, their half-hearted bantering only intensified their anxiety. If they weren't drafted, neither one of them had the money to pay for the new trucks.

Several of our friends left before the end of the third round, each attempting to make some comments to lighten the mood as the situation darkened. One of the camera crews packed up and I began cleaning the dining room to take my mind off the situation. I went so far as to vacuum the floors in the kitchen and dining area while the remaining guests were still watching the final third round picks, which would bring the first day of the draft to a close. When it was over, the last of our guests and the remaining camera crew moved toward the door. I quietly phoned my parents, who had been watching the draft from their home in northern California, to let them know we didn't know what happened and we hoped for the best the next day. Tony spoke to his mom and made it clear he did not want anyone to come over on Sunday. He preferred to ride out the remaining four rounds quietly.

That day was one of the most excruciating experiences of our lives and I'd never seen Tony so disappointed and down. Neither of us slept that night; both lying awake but not talking. I felt so bad for him and I didn't know what to say to offer comfort. He didn't want to hear about the rounds remaining. He was emotionally shocked and upset he'd allowed himself to be sucked into the publicity and the hype regarding his selection. He felt embarrassed about the party and severely frustrated with its anti-climactic ending.

The next morning, before the draft began, the New York Jets called to inquire about Tony. They said they were interested in selecting him in the fourth round. The call breathed some life back into him and he turned on the TV as the selections began. But, the New York Jets' pick in the fourth round came and went and they selected someone else. It was another blow. Tony nearly wore a path in the carpet pacing between the kitchen and the living room.

Midway through the fifth round and with the 149th pick, the Indianapolis Colts selected Derek West. At 6'8", 300 lbs., Derek, as the Buff's starting right tackle, had size and talent. It was no surprise he was drafted. But, many analysts were confounded when Tony wasn't drafted first. Local Denver draft analyst, John Riegel, said many teams projected Tony, the fastest offensive tackle in the draft, to be taken in the early rounds. Having only played offensive tackle for two seasons, John believed Tony still had some minor technique problems but was smart and gifted. Nationally-renowned draft expert, Mel Kiper Jr., called Tony "a sure-fire No. 1 draft choice on paper."

Emotionally drained, Tony crawled into bed upstairs without turning on the television; he was beside himself. He couldn't bear to watch any more. I reminded him there were still a few rounds remaining. But he thought his chances of playing in the NFL were over. I felt completely helpless. He was hurting so bad and nothing I could say would make him feel better. I turned on the bedside television and put on the draft. They were making picks five-minutes apart and the draft was moving fairly quickly.

At the end of the fifth round, the Arizona Cardinals called and asked if Tony thought he could play for Head Coach Buddy Ryan. Tony, trying to regain his composure and contain his excitement, said he could play for anyone; he just wanted to play. The Arizona Cardinals wanted to know why he was still available that late in the draft and if there was anything wrong with him physically they should know about. Tony explained he was in excellent shape and he was in the dark as to why he hadn't yet been selected. On that note, the Arizona Cardinals said they would take him with their next pick in the sixth round. Tony beamed as he hung up the phone. We clapped and cheered and excitedly discussed the mild winters and lack of snow in the city of Phoenix. He was grinning ear to ear and I just hoped the Cardinals would actually follow through with their pick, unlike the New York Jets.

We turned up the sound from ESPN as they were coming out of a commercial. The announcer then said, "During the break, the San Diego Chargers selected CU offensive lineman, Tony Berti with their pick in the sixth round." Tony and I stared at each other and questioned what we'd just heard. I repeated it and Tony agreed he'd heard the same thing. San Diego never contacted us, but they held the draft pick before Arizona. Tony had finally been selected with the 200th pick.

A few long minutes later, the phone rang and Bobby Beathard, the general manager of the San Diego Chargers, informed Tony of his selection and welcomed him to the team. While he was on the phone downstairs, I went out on the deck for a breath of fresh air. Our neighbors were standing on their deck and clapped and cheered as I came outside breathing a gigantic sigh of relief. They, too, had been watching the draft and wished us well after two grueling days of uncertainty. I phoned my parents on the cell phone to inform them of the good news and asked them to please contact everyone so they wouldn't be calling the house. Tony was tied up on the phone with what would be the first of many newspaper and magazine interviews over the next few hours.

Everyone asked the same question, "Why were you selected so late in the draft?" Neither Tony nor his agent, Brad Blank, could ever figure out what happened on that day. There was speculation a rejected agent could have black-balled Tony by starting rumors about a non-existing knee injury. John Riegel thought maybe some of the teams questioned Tony's on-field aggressiveness. But these were just guesses and we never heard any concrete reason as to why Tony slipped so far down in the standings. All we could ever come up with was, once the third round began, perhaps the teams thought the other teams knew something regarding his health that they didn't. The situation snowballed until the teams were afraid to take him and he slipped to the lower rounds in a fit of conjured rejection. Even Mike Shanahan, head coach of the Denver Broncos, was mystified. "I thought Berti would go a lot quicker," Shanahan was quoted as saying in the *Rocky Mountain News*. "He was very strong in our evaluation."

Monday morning's *Rocky Mountain News* featured several articles about the draft and its unexpected results. They, too, questioned what happened to Tony and some of the other CU Buffs as their stock seemed to tank over the draft weekend. There were no definitive answers and while Tony was quietly tormented by his experience with the draft, he was determined to prove he had what it takes to play in the National Football League.

Tony flew to San Diego the weekend following the draft and joined the other Chargers' draft picks for a full-team, mini-camp. There, he was subjected to yet another physical and five grueling practices in three days. He received an abridged version of the team's playbook and was expected to start mastering the plays as quickly as possible. That first introduction to the NFL was followed by another two-week mini-camp in June where Bobby Ross, the

San Diego Chargers head coach, evaluated players in practice and implemented additional plays to the ever-expanding playbook. When back home in Colorado, Tony continued to work out and condition daily at the Dal Ward athletic facility on the University of Colorado campus. In addition, he completed the one-credit class he needed to secure his Bachelor of Arts Degree in Psychology.

Chapter III

Rookie

1995

On July 11, 1995, about ten days before the start of most NFL training camps, Tony signed his first professional contract. The two-year deal certainly wasn't representative of the contract he'd hoped for prior to the draft debacle. But, after thinking he might not get a shot in the NFL at all, he was happy just to have the opportunity.

Upon agreeing to the League's minimum rookie salary of $119,000 for the 1995 season, he received a $25,000 signing bonus, an amount basically predetermined by a sliding scale based on his selection (#200) in the draft. Of course, he had to make the club's 53-man active roster at the end of training camp to see any of the negotiated salary. But, once that was accomplished, two addendums, outlining $30,000 in performance-based incentives, made additional compensation in 1995 and 1996 possible.

If Tony participated in 50% or more of the offensive plays, excluding special teams, and the team ranked among the top 5 in the NFL in total offense (net yards) during the regular season, or if he participated in 50% or more of the offensive plays, excluding special teams, and, the team ranked among the top 5 in the NFL in average net yards gained per rushing play during the regular season, or if he participated in 50% or more of the offensive plays, excluding special teams, and, the team ranked among the top 5 in the NFL in fewest sacks allowed during the regular season, he would receive $10,000 for each accomplished goal.

The second year of the contract, 1996, featured a minimum base salary of $149,000 and included the same three $10,000 performance-based incentives. I didn't really understand the particulars of the statistics-driven addendums but I knew enough to understand Tony had to play and the offensive line had to do extremely well to secure the additional compensation. His two-year contract with the Chargers would terminate on February 28, 1997.

A few days after signing the contract, Tony packed two suitcases of clothing, a blanket and pillow, a stereo, a television I gave him for his birthday in June, his cell phone and a lamp, which was everything he owned, into the back of his new pick-up and headed for training camp at the University of California, San Diego campus in La Jolla. We kissed goodbye in the driveway amidst tears. I was in love with him but I was uncertain of our future. As he waved goodbye and his truck vanished into the distance, I thought about the first night we met and the initial disappointment I felt after discovering he was so much younger than me and still in college. The differences seemed so inconsequential now. And, I thought about my surprise when the words "I love you" unexpectedly fell out of my mouth for the first time while we were laughing and talking one night in the living room. They came so naturally it really caught me off guard. Tony had surprised me in so many wonderful ways since we met I sometimes wondered if it was all too good to be true.

As I walked across the deck, where I breathed that gigantic sigh of relief following his ordeal with the draft, and back into the empty house, I felt very alone. I tried to find consolation by reminding myself that, before I met Tony, I was independent and my life was relatively full. At 26, I owned my own home, held a good paying job and felt secure and content with the life I'd built for myself. But, talking about my strengths and abilities out loud to no one in particular didn't change the fact I already missed him. The past 18 months had passed so quickly and I was happier than I'd ever been before. My relationship with him was one of mutual trust, respect and admiration. I'd come to rely on him emotionally more than I ever thought possible. He was my best friend and I couldn't imagine my life without him in it. But, I also couldn't stop wondering if the NFL would change him and the distance would force us apart.

Throughout training camp, we spoke on the phone twice a day; once during his break at lunch and each night before he went to bed. As a sixth round draft pick, it was essential Tony stand out in order to get noticed. In a profession where salary numbers can substantiate a person's value, Tony's minimum contract and relatively small signing bonus of $25,000 would do little to instill a sense of vested interest by the team. The San Diego Chargers had little at stake if Tony failed to make the grade. If he became a casualty of the slimmed down roster, he would only cost the team the meager bonus and few in San Diego would take note of his departure. On the other hand, if he played well, he was signed to a two-year deal for the minimum rookie salary and that might make him more attractive than an older player with a bigger paycheck. In the high stakes game of sports, it's all about being in the right place at the right time.

I looked forward to Tony's brief but daily phone calls. At work, he invaded my every thought, making it difficult to focus on my job. I'd look at my watch and wonder what he was doing right then and I couldn't wait for the phone to ring just to hear him say hello. I knew he was working really hard and despite the fact he was very tired at the end of each day, he always called to say goodnight. During his nightly phone calls, we often talked about the rigors of training camp, how he was playing, how I was faring and how much we missed each other. The conversations were usually brief but on one particular night, he began telling me about some of the team shenanigans going on. It seems many of the players rented golf carts during training camp to get around the campus from the dorm apartments where they were staying, to the practice field, to the workout facility and to training table where their meals were served. This unique mode of transportation lent itself to golf cart drag racing as well as "four-wheeling", sometimes with three and four 225-pound plus guys weighing so heavily on a cart's frame it flattened the tires. That day, several of the rookies finished the afternoon practice and found their golf carts had been "stolen" by the veteran players. The rookies were forced to walk up the steep hill from the practice field. They were tired after the extremely demanding, two-hour practice and not happy about the walk. But, it could have been worse. Tony was relieved that as a rookie, the mild hazing was more for laughs than harm. Tony found the humor in it because it was reminiscent of some of the pranks perpetuated on the freshman players at CU. He was never involved in any of those activities, of course!

At the team dinners, many of the rookies found themselves the night's featured entertainment. Whenever a veteran player tapped his glass, the designated rookies had to stand up and sing either their college fight song or one designated by a vet. When Tony was anointed to sing, veteran offensive lineman Stan Brock put a stop to it. Stan had befriended Tony during the spring mini-camps because he, himself, had been a CU lineman as had his older brothers, Willie and Pete. Stan felt obligated to take Tony under his wing and he wasn't going to let anyone get over on a fellow Buffalo. He was quick witted and fast with a quip. If someone started in on Tony, Stan would take him down a notch with just a few words. If someone started hassling Tony, Stan was right there to defend. And, with fifteen years in the League, no one was going to argue with him. Tony respected Stan's longevity and team leadership and was very happy about never having to sing for his supper. It was good to hear him laugh and the stories he shared with me about training camp made me feel close to him despite the distance.

Tony's dedication to our relationship seemed unwavering and I believed we had a future together. Early in our relationship, when Tony and I started spending all our free time together, I realized I no longer wanted to work 60-hour weeks or dedicate myself solely to my career. For the first time in my life, I found myself more interested in a long-term relationship and its possibilities than climbing the corporate ladder.

Late in July, the team broke camp at UCSD and the rookies and players yet to secure residences in San Diego moved into the

Town and Country Hotel for the remainder of training camp. Shortly thereafter, the team made its first cuts to get closer to their allotted 53-man roster. At 5:30 in the morning the phone rang in Tony's hotel room. He sat straight up in bed reluctant to answer it. After a deep breath, he picked up the receiver expecting the worst. But, the voice on the other end asked to speak his roommate, Kent Call. Kent had been cut and arrangements had been made for him to leave immediately. Tony was extremely relieved to have made it through the first round of cuts. But, with the final cut still remaining, he was still cautious about his chances of making the team. I tried to reassure him based on some of the things I'd been reading about him in the Denver papers.

The Denver Post had been following his progress in San Diego. Joseph Sanchez, a Denver Post sports writer, quoted Head Coach Bobby Ross as saying, "Tony Berti has been a very pleasant surprise. I mean I was very surprised that he was still sitting there in the second round. A guy that big, who had played so well on such a good team. I mean, I had seen him, and I thought he was very athletic, so when he was still there I couldn't believe it." The article continued that with a couple of the veteran linemen (Harry Swayne and Courtney Hall) in questionable health, Tony looked even better. "We definitely like what we see in him," said Coach Ross. I relayed the information in the article to Tony. He was pleased to hear the head coach thought he was doing well. But, he was still wary. The draft taught him not to believe everything he read.

While Tony was away at training camp, my company opened a new restaurant, Mama Mia's in the Denver Tech Center, and I worked twenty-one straight days preparing for the grand opening. I used to love the challenge of opening a new property but over the past weeks, with Tony so prevalent in my thoughts, I lost interest in the process. Adding fuel to my priority shift, the company's Chief Financial Officer informed me I would not be receiving my usual pay raise following the opening of a new property. I made very good money and when he told me I was basically at the top of my pay scale, I can't say I was surprised. But, every aspect of my life seemed to be indicating it might be time to make a change.

After making it through the first round of cuts, Tony asked if I could come out and scout apartments for him in the event he made the final roster. He didn't have the time during camp and the team would only put him up in the hotel for a few days once the final roster was announced. He had to be prepared in the event he made the team.

I called my mom and dad to tell them of Tony's good news. They liked Tony very much and my mom offered to fly down from northern California and help me in the apartment search. Within a week, we flew into Las Vegas from our respective cities and then onto San Diego together where we spent the weekend looking around the Chargers facility for a nice apartment near by. The three apartment complexes with units available for move-in within the next few weeks were all in the same price range. But my favorite was La Mirage overlooking the stadium. The location was ideal and their sales representative said many of the players held leases there. With Tony's checkbook in hand, I wrote out the deposit for a one-bedroom apartment and filled out the paperwork to be signed by Tony later. If Tony didn't make the team, the deposit would be refunded.

Having lived in Colorado the majority of his life, Tony was surprised by the high cost of apartments in San Diego. His take home pay during training camp was a little more than $300 a week and at $975 per month, the rent for the one-bedroom apartment seemed overwhelming. I assured him his regular season football checks would more than cover the monthly expenditure.

Though my mom and I stayed the weekend at the team's hotel, Tony's schedule hadn't permitted us to spend much time together. When I returned to Denver, I missed him more than ever.

Near the end of August, the coaches told the team the second and final group of players to be cut would receive phone calls before noon the following day. All morning long, Tony sat in his hotel room waiting for the phone to ring. But, it didn't. At 1:00 p.m., Tony phoned General Manager Bobby Beathard and asked if he'd tried to call him. Bobby told him he'd made the team and to go find an apartment. He was excited and relieved to know for certain he had indeed made the 53-man roster.

Tony called me at my office and I was so thrilled for him. He deserved this chance and I was so glad they were giving it to him. His professional football career had officially begun. As I told the ladies in my office the news, it sunk in that by Tony making the team, he wasn't coming back. I'd always believed in his abilities, but that was a strange epiphany.

A week went by and I thought about quitting my job and moving to San Diego. It was something I swore I would never do without having a ring on my finger. Uprooting my whole life for a guy without any firm commitment for the future seemed ludicrous. I couldn't figure out if I was actually unhappy with my job or if missing Tony was making my job seem that much more miserable. My mind's constant wandering and lack of focus was making my ten-hour days seem even longer and my usual clashes with the three on-site managers over their inability to accurately execute a promotional event was wearing thin. The general manager's excuses for their incompetence were getting really old. At that day's management meeting, I passed out a memo on an upcoming Jack Daniel's sponsored promotion outlining the event and what needed to be done. When the meeting was over, several of the memos were left on the table, irritating me and only adding to my thoughts about leaving.

When Tony phoned that evening, I was sitting at the kitchen table going through the mail. The tone of his voice was different, more serious than usual. He asked me how my day was and then said he needed to tell me something. A lump swelled in my throat and for a brief second, I was afraid he was going to tell me our relationship was over. But then, his voice softened and he said he couldn't imagine his life without me. And, while he wasn't exactly ready to get married, the commitment was there and he wanted us to be together. He said he knew I'd be making sacrifices to be with him but he was now in a position to move forward in our relationship. I hung up the phone in awe of his ability to be so honest and articulate. Now, I was really in a quandary. My heart said to go for it but my mind was playing scenarios in my head and some of them didn't end happily. What if I gave up my job and house, moved to California and things didn't work out? It had taken me years to establish my career, independence and security and I would be putting all of it at risk. If the relationship failed, the move would set me back emotionally and financially.

I spent the entire Labor Day weekend mulling over the decision. I realized hitting the glass ceiling at my job probably would facilitate a change of employment in the near future. But, did I really want to move to California and face proving myself to a new employer there? Did I want to move to California, period? Should I sell my house? Leave my friends? I asked myself a hundred questions over the next few days. I wondered why I was willing to risk so much just on Tony's word. My girlfriends said I was crazy if I didn't go. They'd never seen me so happy and they thought Tony was the catch of a lifetime. I didn't ask my parents for their input because as much as they liked Tony, they would never have encouraged me to give up what I had worked for without a formal commitment. Three days after he moved in with me I told them we were living together. When prompted, they said they weren't happy about it but I was an adult with my own home and it was my decision. I was certain this bigger leap would definitely bring about a negative response.

In the end, I decided Tony had always been forthright with me on everything. So on Tuesday morning, I put my house on the market and turned in my letter of resignation. The owner of the company, Bobby Rifkin, was floored and all he could say when I handed him the letter was "Why?" I wasn't ready to divulge my plans so I just told him I wasn't happy with some of the management and I was looking for another opportunity. I was petrified I was making a mistake which would haunt me. I reluctantly phoned my parents and my mother was mortified by my decision. I was the first person to graduate from college in my family and, as I expected, my parents were concerned I was risking a lot without at least being engaged. I listened to my mom's rationale and I can't say I didn't agree. It was a scary thing for me and I needed some reassurance I was doing the right thing.

After expressing my concerns to Tony over the phone, I bought an airline ticket to see him face-to-face in San Diego that weekend.

On Friday, I was just walking out the door to the airport shuttle when my real estate agent phoned to inform me I had three potential offers on my home. The news was rattling. I thought it would take some time to sell the town house and I had given a generous 60-days notice in order to train a replacement at work. In the whirlwind, I accepted one of the offers over the phone and completed the paperwork via fax from California over the weekend. The closing was scheduled for the second week in October. Tony was ecstatic. I worried it was all happening too fast; but, it was too late to back out.

For the next six weeks, I traveled to visit Tony every other weekend. He purchased a California King mattress and box spring the day he moved into the apartment and ordered a custom-made, heavy-duty leather couch with his first paycheck. Each time I visited, I arrived with my suitcases packed with items I intended to leave in San Diego. I was slowly moving via United Airlines. Because I planned on moving little from Colorado, Tony and I spent much of his free-time during the visits picking up things we needed for the apartment.

I closed escrow on October 11th and the moving van came on October 13th. That night I said goodbye to my best friend Bunny Reid and a few other friends and colleagues with a small celebration at Comedy Works before departing for San Diego the next morning. It was shear insanity and it happened just that fast.

Upon arriving in San Diego, I was overwhelmed by the recent changes in my life. To calm my anxiety and celebrate my move, Tony surprised me with a brief getaway. During the regular season, each NFL team has a week in which they don't play a game. The off week is known as the bye week. How much time the players have off during their bye week is left to the discretion of the coaches. The Chargers bye week happened to coincide with my arrival in October and Coach Ross had given the guys several days off.

Tony booked an ocean-view suite at my favorite hotel, Hotel Del Coronado, on Coronado Island. Our room was spectacular and the view incredible. French doors on the balcony opened to allow in the sea breeze and the gentle sound of waves breaking on the shoreline. It was very romantic. The management sent up a complimentary bottle of champagne along with a cheese and fruit assortment welcoming Tony Berti of the San Diego Chargers to the hotel. It was an unexpected gesture and the celebrity perk made us feel pretty cool. We enjoyed the extended time together and we were happy Tony's career and our relationship were all falling into place.

After the idyllic holiday, Tony and I tried to make the best of the limited space in the small one-bedroom apartment my mom and I had found for him months earlier. But, while I'd sold the majority of my large furnishings in Denver, moving even a portion of the contents of my two-story, two-bedroom town home into a one-bedroom apartment was a real challenge. The day the truck arrived, Tony was at work and I really wanted to surprise him by getting the majority of the delivery put away. I worked my ass off opening boxes, organizing, reorganizing and trying to find a place for everything. By the time he got home, there wasn't a box in sight and the floor had even been vacuumed. But he wasn't happy. Instead of being pleased everything had been unpacked, all he saw was that every corner of the 900 square foot space had stuff in it from floor to ceiling. For the first time in his life, he'd set up his living space exactly as he wanted it and in one fell swoop I'd come in and rearranged everything. He felt his space had been violated and we had our first argument in California. I recalled what it had been like when he first moved in with me. While he didn't have much stuff, I didn't want him changing things around either. We'd talked out our feelings then and, with the tables turned, it wasn't difficult to see how each of us had been affected by the moves. The town home had been my place and this apartment was his. We needed to find a new place where we could start from scratch together. We resolved the issue by agreeing we would look for a new, larger place at the end of the football season.

Only a week after leaving my job, the company called me with a request. They wanted to know if I would consider flying back weekly to work on the new restaurant, Mama Mia's. Things hadn't been going well and they wanted me to take over the sales department to handle corporate party bookings. I would maintain my salary and they would cover all of my expenses. It was too good an opportunity to pass up and it offered a little security should things go awry in San Diego. By accepting, I felt as though I still had my foot in the door and Tony thought the connection might make my transition a little less worrisome. So, for the next six months, I flew out every Wednesday morning on the 5:30 a.m. flight from San Diego to Denver and returned every Saturday evening in time for Sunday's football game. It seemed like an odd schedule to most but, during football season, ball players only get Tuesdays off. I would see Tony after the game on Sunday, then on Monday when they finished watching the game film around 2:00 and then all day Tuesday.

While I was enduring my grueling schedule, Tony was busy learning the fundamentals of being a rookie. With that said, he and two other offensive line rookies took turns buying two dozen donuts every Friday, accompanied by two gallons of whole milk and one gallon of orange juice for the veteran players on the offensive line. But not just any donuts would do. They had to be donuts from a certain place and each lineman had his favorite kind. In addition, one day a week, Tony had to buy McDonald's breakfast sandwiches for the line. He hated going into McDonald's and ordering those 22 sandwiches. It was embarrassing standing in a busy breakfast line and ordering that much food, effectively making everyone behind him pissed off. Once, a McDonald's employee even asked him if they were for there or to go. Tony wasn't amused by the teenager's inquiry but he knew the mild form of hazing would end with his rookie year. It was a rite of passage and it was going on elsewhere in the League too!

As an Indianapolis Colts rookie, Derek West was also buying donuts for his offensive line. On his first day, unaware of the veteran players' preferences, he purchased donuts from the wrong donut shop. When he returned from practice, a note on his locker informed him the line only ate Krispy Kreme donuts and to drive home their dissatisfaction, all of his clothes, including his shoes, were found floating in the team whirlpool. Needless to say, Derek only purchased Krispy Kremes from that day forward. We laugh about the donuts and the breakfast sandwiches now, but as a rookie it was a tiresome rite of passage.

Another rite of passage on many teams required a rookie take all the veterans playing his same position to dinner and pick up the tab, which could be a very expensive proposition. First, football players can eat a lot of food and second, the veterans got to choose the restaurant. Our financial advisor, Ken Ready, said the most expensive rookie dinner receipt he ever received came from one of his Denver Bronco players and totaled more than $13,000. I don't care who you are or what kind of money you make, that's an expensive meal. Luckily for Tony, his fellow lineman preferred breakfast to dinner and the tab for the entire season ran only about $1500.00.

Despite the mild hazing, Tony was relatively unscathed by his rookie experience at San Diego. Stan Brock's creed "A Buff's a Buff forever," afforded Tony a certain degree of "protection" and Stan's knowledge and experience proved to be invaluable to Tony his rookie year. All locker room stunts aside, Stan taught Tony some of the ins and outs of the game and helped Tony adjust to the level of the NFL, which was very different from college not only in terms of the level of talent but also in the social workings of the team. At CU, no one was getting paid so everyone was on even ground. Winning was all about the team. The guys gave their all because they'd worked together for the past four or five years and they wanted to win for the sake of hard work, dedication and team pride. The guys were close and part of a unique brotherhood which encompassed, first and foremost, education, then team and finally individual.

The dynamics of the NFL were different. New guys were not necessarily welcomed with open arms. In almost every case, the new guy was there for someone's job and that notion always had someone on the defensive. Rookies suffered from isolation during training camp because most of the veteran players didn't want to know them. They were a threat and vets didn't want to waste their time getting to know someone who could potentially take their job or not be there in a few days or weeks. It was cruel but the competition at that level is fierce. Players can't help being standoffish at the beginning.

Once the final cuts were made, the tension eased a bit. The rookies who made the team proved their talent and the depth chart, outlining who's a starter (first string) and who's a back-up, emerged laying out the pecking order for the season. For most players, their rookie year is a year for learning and adapting. Of the 53 men on the team's active roster, only 47 are activated to suit-up for each game. The inactive list is determined by many factors including injuries, position depth and the team's particular strategy for that week's game. Many times rookies developing into the system were placed on the inactive list because their overall contribution to that week's game was considered minimal. Tony was no different his rookie season and found himself inactive for most of the games in 1995. But he still got to travel with the team to away games and he enjoyed the opportunity to stand on the side lines in plain clothes.

Back in San Diego, he took it all in, practiced hard, watched vets like Stan Brock and Harry Swayne carefully and learned the game. At one of the practices late in the season, Tony got into a pushing and shoving match with starting defensive tackle John Parrella. Practices could be intensely competitive and when the offense practiced plays against the defense it wasn't uncommon for the heat of the moment to take over. Tony always called the fights tiffs because they were like those of husbands and wives. On the field, fellow teammates and even friends could get pissed off and exchange heated words. Other players would step in and break it up before it ever really came to blows and, when it was over, the guys always "kissed and made-up."

Determined to play with the big boys, Tony was awarded his first game day opportunity when he was added to the active roster on Saturday, December 9th, 1995, for the last home game of the season. He was nervous but he looked forward to putting on the #61 jersey, a number he'd been assigned, and hitting the game field for the first time during his rookie year even if it was only for one offensive series late in the game.

I didn't care if Tony's participation was only for four or so plays. I could hardly contain my excitement. It was a total rush sitting in the stands, listening to 62,000 screaming fans, and knowing Tony was in the thick of it. I was so proud of him. And to top it off, my parents, Dwight and Joy, and sister and brother, Audra and Marc, happened to be visiting us that weekend and they were delighted to have the opportunity to watch Tony play in his first professional game. It was the first time they'd ever been to any of his games and my dad, donning a new Chargers cap, was so proud you would have thought Tony was his own son.

Tony subbed for Stan Brock, did everything he was supposed to do, and the Chargers defeated the Arizona Cardinals 28-to-25 thus keeping their playoff hopes alive by winning their third consecutive game and bringing their record to 7-and-7. With two regular season games remaining, the Chargers hit the road and defeated the Indianapolis Colts 27-to-24. Then, in the final week of the regular season, they defeated the New York Giants 27-to-17 in New York, despite almost having that game called due to unruly fans aggressively hurling snowballs at the Chargers players and onto the field. Tony had never seen anything like it. Inactive and standing on the sidelines in street clothes, he was being pelted with a constant barrage of snowballs. Sid Brooks, the equipment manager, took a direct hit to the side of the face and fell to the ground in an Oscar-winning performance meant to garner penalties against the home team. The incident incited several arrests and made for interesting fodder on sports radio.

The Chargers closed out the 1995 post-season by losing the AFC Divisional Playoff Game to Indianapolis 35-to-20 on New Year's Eve. Despite the loss, Tony wasn't disappointed with his rookie season. His first professional appearance in game fourteen against Arizona was a defining moment for him and he knew he was gaining momentum with the team. He'd learned a lot over the past six months and he wanted a starting spot on that offensive line.

I, too, learned a few things over the last half of his first season. I learned the Chargers front office wasn't very good at providing information to those of us making the transition to a new city and life in the NFL. The team didn't make any attempt to introduce the families to one another and when I first got to San Diego in October, I didn't know anyone inside or outside the Chargers organization. I wasn't familiar with the city or Tony's day-to-day activities as part of the team. I was eager to learn the inner working of being affiliated with the Chargers but I felt a little intimidated not knowing anyone to show me the ropes. It was like starting a new job without someone showing me to my desk and telling me what I needed to do. I wasn't sure what was expected of me and definitely didn't know my way around. I had assumed there would be someone from the team to take an active role in introducing me to this unconventional way of life.

In addition to football related questions regarding game day procedures, ticket purchases for guests, and how I might get involved in any upcoming community events, I also had general questions regarding insurance and benefit options, recommended doctors and dentists, and where to go in San Diego and how to get there. At Tony's suggestion, I made an initial call to Robyn Walters, one of the public relations staff, and was disappointed to learn the organization had no family point person, no welcoming packet outlining procedures regarding Charger activities and not even as much as a typed list identifying contacts within the organization. Robyn said, however, I could contact her for any of my administrative questions and she would point me in the right direction.

Feeling isolated and insecure as an uninformed new-comer, Tony picked me up during his game-day break and took me to the stadium with him for the first two home games I attended. But I didn't like the idea of sitting in the stands for three hours before game time so I elected to drive myself to the next home game. Tony carpooled with another player from the apartment complex and gave me his parking pass. I left our apartment one hour before kick-off and discovered I couldn't get anywhere near the stadium, even with the pass Tony had given me. I didn't realize the players' parking lot would be inaccessible when the outer parking areas were full and the stadium gates closed. I drove over two traffic cones, begged and pleaded with parking attendants at no less than ten check-points and sweet-talked two security guards at the F1 lot, who didn't know me from Adam, into allowing me into the players' parking area. Everything was new and unfamiliar.

My introduction to the NFL was coming via baptism by fire. Arriving late in the season, I felt my best hope to get a handle on things would be to align myself with the veteran wives and follow the crowd. The first wife I met was Lori Brock. I think she took pity on me as a rookie and at Stan's urging began to teach me the ropes. She explained everything from the best time to get to the game to the finer points of a good post-game tailgate. She answered my many questions about how things worked and what to expect. Before she welcomed me and I got comfortable with the situation, I felt very disconnected. Lori's input was as important to me off the field as Stan's was for Tony on the field. I, too, had to make the transition to life in the NFL.

Chapter IV

Off-Season Highlights

1996

We were feeling confident about Tony's future in the NFL and with his first season officially behind us, we made last minute plans to take advantage of the two Super Bowl XXX tickets we'd purchased for $250 each. Every year, each NFL player is allowed to purchase two Super Bowl tickets at face value and corporations, familiar with that process, start hitting the players up early with offers to purchase them for upwards of $1000 each. Players often sell them at a profit even though they sign a paper saying they won't.

While we hadn't sold our tickets to the game, making the decision to attend the Super Bowl so late made finding a place to stay in Phoenix nearly impossible until Tony's Aunt Mary, a resident of Tempe, graciously offered for us to stay at her home. We drove the short four-hour trip from San Diego to Phoenix where we were met, as planned, by Tony's sister, Lori, Derek West and his friend Sandy, and a couple of my friends from Denver. As luck would have it, Redneck, the band through which Tony and I met, was also in Phoenix during the Super Bowl week playing several nights at a popular country bar.

Our first night in town, we jump-started the hellacious week of partying by kicking it at the bar where Redneck was appearing. We hadn't seen them since the draft party fiasco the previous April and we were determined to make up for the frustration of our last meeting by drinking the night away. In the middle of Redneck's last set, a country star, Tracy Lawrence I think, showed up with a small contingent of people. Our cocktail waitress mentioned one of the guys with him was an NFL ball player. After a few more cocktails, Tony went over to introduce himself. The guy, whose name I can't remember, was a second or third year pro. He thought himself pretty cool and gave Tony the brush-off. Tony wasn't impressed and returned to the table and our circle of friends. He said, "If I ever act like that slap dick, one of you needs to kick me in the ass." We all laughed and ordered another round of drinks.

Throughout the week, every night was the same. All we had to do was show Tony's NFL Player's Association ID card and we were in every party, bar and club in the city without waiting in line or paying cover charge. Because of Tony's NFL affiliation, we were automatically invited to several private parties including one hosted by former big-name player and quarterback Jim Kelly. The party was designated for players and their guests only, so I was amused to see Deion Sanders sitting in a booth, alone, shielded by a contingent of muscle-bound, gold-adorned bodyguards. They stood with their backs to him and their beefy arms crossed. They were eyeballing everyone in the place. It was a riot. After all, we were at a players' party. Everyone there was either a player or the guest of one. Was it really necessary to have bodyguards encircling him and protecting him from, well, the guys he played with? It was quite a show.

At another party, which I was told was hosted by Michael Jordan, we ran into fellow CU teammate and Pittsburgh Steeler, Kordell Stewart. He was cordial but distant. He and Tony had been friends on and off the field at Colorado, so Tony was annoyed by Kordell's cold shoulder. Scanning the crowd and slinking away during the brief exchange, Kordell obviously had more important people to see. Maybe he was preoccupied with thoughts about the upcoming big game. Or, maybe, his successful rookie year playing running back, wide receiver and quarterback lending itself to media hype and the nickname "Slash" and culminating in a Super Bowl appearance, had gone to his head. Regardless, after a few brief words, he darted into the crowd. We never did see Michael Jordan.

But, we did run into Chargers punter, Darren Bennett and his wife Rosemary, at the press center prior to NFL Commissioner Tagliabue's big party. Media from all over the world had set up interview booths and satellite feeds for radio and television. Darren, unique to American football, hailed from Australia where he played Aussie Rules football for a number of years before landing in the NFL. Aussie Rules is more rugby or soccer than American football and their kickers are truly talented. The San Diego media was fond of an Aussie clip of Darren kicking a ball through the goal posts as he stood in the end zone facing away from the uprights. The ball was like a boomerang and elliptically sailed out and then returned to pass right through the posts. It was the most unnatural looking happening. Darren had an amazing leg and a wonderful demeanor, which made him a natural to explain the game to fans and listeners of the international media covering the event.

While interviewing with one of the radio stations, Darren invited Tony to sit down and join in the conversation. Tony sat right down, pulled up the microphone and wallowed in the moment. It was thrilling to be part of such an enormous spectacle. The entire city of Phoenix was abuzz with activities surrounding the game. No wonder cities vie so hard to win the Super Bowl bid.

By game time on Super Bowl Sunday, we were exhausted from all the late nights. Rather than attend the game, we elected to drive back to San Diego. We sold our tickets about ten minutes before kick-off to two very happy souls standing on a street corner and listened to the game on the radio on the way home. I won't say how much the tickets sold for but that piece of paper Tony signed promising not to sell the tickets for more than face value was discussed quite a bit on the ride home. D-West and his friend Sandy made the return trip with us to California and stayed for a few days to tour the sights of San Diego before returning home to Denver.

The following month, Tony and I made the much anticipated move to a larger apartment. Now familiar with the city of San Diego, we moved further inland to La Mesa. Apartments were less expensive and we secured a spacious two-bedroom for the same price we'd been paying for the one-bedroom at La Mirage. The new complex didn't have as many amenities but we were pleased to finally get out of the confines of the smaller place.

Two days after moving, we took a brief trip to northern California to visit my parents in Livermore. With the passing of Christmas, my birthday and Valentine's Day, I'd been giving Tony a hard time about not yet being engaged. My continual off-handed remarks were getting to him and we had a small tiff on the flight. He said I was pushing too hard and if I'd just cool it, things would work out. I'd moved to California five months earlier and despite our rock-solid relationship, I needed the ring to solidify my decision was the right one. With each special occasion I really thought he might ask. But, he didn't.

Then, on February 24th, while we were sitting on the couch watching TV with my parents, Tony got up and disappeared. When he returned, he stood in front of me and told me to pick a hand. We always played that guessing game with candy, rented movies, and what have you so I didn't think too much about it. I picked a hand and he started to give me something. But, I accidentally dropped that something between the couch cushions. When Tony retrieved it, I saw it was a ring. The first thing I said to him was that it wasn't mine. I often left my jewelry on the side of the sink and I thought he'd found a ring in the bathroom and assumed it belonged to me. He just stood there smiling and handed the ring to me again. I looked at my parents and they looked very confused too. A few more seconds and the realization of what was happening finally took hold. I looked at the ring again. I was so surprised I just didn't get it right away and I had to ask him, "Is this what I think it is?" Tony simply said, "Yes." My heart started thumping nearly out of my chest and I stood up and hugged him. My eyes welled up and my hand shook as he placed the ring on my finger. My parents, also in the dark, finally got it too! The living room erupted into laughter and tears. I, of course, said yes even though he never actually said the words, "Will you marry me?" It didn't matter. I was just so happy to finally know for sure we were going to spend the rest of our lives together. As it turned out, he had the ring for almost two months but knew, with each occasion, I was expecting and hoping he'd pop the question. He really wanted it to be a surprise so he just kept waiting.

My parents were both thrilled and relieved at the announcement. They were finally comfortable with the decision I made to move to San Diego and enthusiastically welcomed Tony into our family. In celebration of the occasion, they took us on a Hornblower Yacht Cruise around San Francisco Bay the next day.

When we returned to San Diego at the end of February, Tony resumed his daily off-season workouts of lifting weights and conditioning. I commuted to Denver from San Diego two additional times before informing the company I could no longer endure the rigors of traveling back and forth on a weekly basis. The CFO returned the second resignation with a request for consulting services via telephone. I obliged by working through the month of April when I finally cut the apron strings. It was time to stop holding onto my job as a security blanket and fully commit to my new life with Tony in San Diego.

I racked up nearly 40,000 frequent flyer miles over the previous six months and the extensive traveling burned me out. I wasn't ready to dive into yet another demanding marketing position in San Diego but I didn't want to just sit home either. Tony wanted me to do whatever I wanted and suggested I get a "fun" job to keep me busy while he focused on football. I liked the idea of taking a break in my career and feeling less pressure. So, at the end of May, I went to work at SeaWorld California in their education department. The presentations I'd given in earning my degree in speech communication assisted me in landing the position and, fortunately, I didn't find the training, an intensive ten-day biology class, difficult. Though, I'm certain Tony was tired of listening to me enthusiastically spew an exorbitant number of marine mammal facts at the end of each of my ten-hour training days.

As an animal educator in the park, I rotated from exhibit to exhibit giving informational talks and answering guests' questions regarding any and all of the park's animals. It was a terrific job! I worked outside and wore shorts and tennis shoes to work each day.

I interacted with people from all over the world and the animals were fascinating. The other education department employees were mostly young, college students and the environment was a far cry from my high-stress, high-pressure position in Denver. It was exactly what I need to get re-energized and it kept me occupied while Tony was working on football each day.

In June, Tony came home one afternoon with a new, three-passenger jet-ski. He was a big water enthusiast and he was delighted with his purchase. I was excited but I wondered where we were going to keep it; our apartment didn't have a garage. Tony said he'd figure out something as he began packing the truck for a trip to Lake Comanche, near my parents, in northern California. We drove up the coast, stopping at Hearst Castle in San Simeon and the Ventana Country Inn Resort in Big Sur. When we pulled up in front of my parent's home, Tony couldn't wait to show off his new toy. With little prompting, my parents packed up their motor home and jet-ski and we were off to the lake.

We spent a relaxing weekend camping, eating and breaking in our new water toy. While there, we decided to set the date for our wedding. Based on the off-season mini-camp schedule, we thought we'd like to get married the following May, which would give us plenty of time to plan. My family lived in northern California and Florida, so they would have to travel regardless of our selected location. Since the majority of our friends and Tony's family resided in Colorado, Denver seemed like a logical choice for the 1997 nuptials.

The weekend trip to the lake was great but I couldn't wait to get home to San Diego to start working on the wedding. After surfing the Internet and asking friends about weddings they'd attended, Tony and I made a brief trip to Colorado to scout potential locations for ourselves. The Chief Hosa Lodge in Golden was perfect for what we had in mind. The outside deck overlooked the Continental Divide and pine trees and snow-capped mountains, even in the month of May, provided the perfect backdrop for the ceremony. The old hunting lodge with its log cabin beams and oversized, rock fireplace was quaint and would easily accommodate the small number of guests we wished to invite. Based on their limited availability, we selected Saturday, May 24th as our wedding day.

At the end of June, Gina and Junior Seau sent us an invitation to attend the MVP kickoff of Junior's new restaurant, Seau's. I'd never met Gina before, but Junior had always been very friendly on the few occasions I'd actually spoken with him. His incredible athletic talent and down to earth demeanor made him a natural team leader and his invitation seemed like a welcomed chance to get together with the team before training camp began in the next few weeks. Other than during the team's spring mini-camps, we had seen very little of the other players during the 1996 off-season.

The opening of Seau's drew quite a crowd of media and celebrities alike. The parking lot looked like a luxury car dealership. Players arrived at the restaurant to red-carpet fanfare as fans cheered from bleachers set up in the parking lot. Photographers snapped photos and security held back autograph seekers. Tony and I felt as if we were arriving at the "Academy Awards". Once inside, we were escorted upstairs to a private landing where we were able to look down at the shoulder-to-shoulder crowd. Most of the team turned out to show their support and, of course, take part in the free food and drinks. I met more players and wives that night than at any other time during Tony's rookie season. I also saw an NFL parade of hobnobbing athletes, extremely attractive and provocative female "fans," expensive clothes, jewelry, cigars and alcohol, completely engendering exactly what people perceive the NFL to always be.

Chapter V
A Real Start
1996

Standing in the grocery store magazine isle just weeks into the 1996 off-season, Tony and I were positively gleeful when we discovered a February issue of *The Sporting News*, which profiled the San Diego Chargers upcoming season and speculated Harry Swayne, the starting left tackle, might be cut from the roster to make additional salary room. If he was cut, the article said, "The team would be banking on Tony Berti, a second-year player with a lot of potential but little experience." The find assured Tony his rookie season had garnered some attention and he was already eager for football season to begin again.

While some players choose not to condition very hard during the off-season, Tony dedicated himself to a rigid off-season workout program to ensure he would enter the 1996 football season in the best of shape. At one of the team's scheduled off-season workouts, Tony out lifted all of his teammates by bench pressing 225 pounds, 39 times. The official feat designated him the Chargers' strongest man and earned him recognition in *Muscle and Fitness* magazine. Following that article and just prior to training camp in July, the Topps Company released another of Tony's trading cards featuring him in assigned Chargers uniform number 61. The national media attention during the off-season was definitely a good sign and helped Tony maintain his positive attitude going into his second year. He was now more focused on securing a starting position on the offensive line than ever before.

In my opinion, securing a starting position in the NFL is 50% talent, 25% luck and 25% politics. With that in mind, there are only three ways to become a starter in the National Football League. The first is probably the easiest. A player is absolutely heads and tails above the rest. They have more talent in their little pinky than most players have in their whole body. Guys like John Elway, Junior Seau, Ray Lewis and Tony Boselli come to mind. They're 100% talent and they usually come to the NFL as high round draft picks with big money contracts from the beginning. They are icons of the game.

The second way a player becomes a starter in the NFL is if the guy in front of him on the depth chart has one of two strikes going against him. The first strike is if the starter is a veteran player, while outstanding in his prime, is on the downhill slide and just not cutting it anymore. It's difficult for a person in any field to acknowledge they've lost their game and, certainly, no professional athlete wants to lose their starting job to a back-up. Unfortunately, in the NFL, there is always a back-up waiting in the wings, which is the primary reason veteran players are slow to accept the rookies. Every one of them is a potential threat. And, if the threat of them being younger or better isn't enough, there is always the threat that they can do the same job for less money, which brings me to strike two. There is a very fine line between being paid and being over-paid as a veteran in the NFL. When a team lands a solid back-up player, the organization almost always starts to question the veteran's higher salary. Once this happens, the back-up has the advantage and can quickly become the team's next golden goose. The vet may still have what it takes to play in the NFL, but the organization is going to key in on that up-and-comer. And, if the media jumps on the band wagon, it's only a matter of time until the veteran finds himself on the way out.

The final way to step into a starter's shoes doesn't involve politics or salaries, but it does involve luck. For every starting player that finds himself unfortunately sidelined by an injury, a back-up player finds fortune in the opportunity to step in, showcase his talents and steal the thunder. It only takes one good game or one great play to make an impression and that's the reason many players play even when they're hurt. Injuries can easily shuffle the depth chart and the slightest appearance of weakness can be detrimental to a starter's career. Regardless of how a player gets to the top of the depth chart, everyone, of course, wants to be a starter in the NFL.

Tony reported to his second Chargers training camp on July 23, 1996, with an additional fifteen pounds of muscle and a sense of job security. He changed his number from 61 to 75 claiming a big guy needed a big, well-balanced number. By the time training camp actually opened, numerous articles about Tony appeared in the *San Diego Union-Tribune* sports section. Each time the media quoted Head Coach Bobby Ross, General Manager Bobby Beathard, or the new offensive line coach, Jack Henry, positively mentioning Tony's athletic abilities and intelligence, Tony was assured the team was looking to him as the future of their offensive line. Articles entitled "Battle on the Line" and "Can Berti Tackle Crucial Line Job?" began to appear on a regular basis touting Tony's battle with Harry Swayne for the starting left tackle position. Even *The Denver Post* ran an article highlighting Tony's talent and potential to be "No. 1 In Year No. 2."

Returning from off-season knee surgery, Harry and his five-year tenure as the starting left tackle looked to be in jeopardy. The Chargers wanted him to take a pay-cut from $1.8 million to the League minimum base salary of $300,000. He chose to first test free-agency. As a free-agent and vested veteran with more than four active seasons, he was able to freely market himself to any team without restriction. But without an overwhelming offer from another team, he elected to stay in San Diego despite the heavy pay cut. Tony hoped Harry would sign with another team, which would significantly improve his chances of securing a starting line position. But, when he didn't, Tony took the competition in stride. The mere fact the Chargers were willing to let Harry go worked in Tony's favor.

Tony was disappointed, however, when the one veteran offensive lineman he hoped would remain with the team did not. After sixteen years in the League, Stan Brock reluctantly retired. The Chargers showed little interest in re-signing him and he didn't want to move his family to another team. Tony and I knew we were going to feel the loss of Stan and Lori's friendship. Their support was essential to our introduction to the NFL and we knew the offensive line would miss the chemistry they tried to foster via their leadership both on and off the field.

During Tony's rookie year, when we didn't have any family in town for Thanksgiving, the Brock's opened their home to us and other players who had no where to go for the holiday. When the Chargers organization didn't schedule any type of Christmas party for the players, the Brock's planned an event at a local restaurant to celebrate the season. They took it upon themselves to foster team chemistry and their departure was going to be felt, one way or another, by the whole team.

Despite the loss of his friend and mentor, Tony was looking forward to proving himself further in training camp. The Chargers held their camp in La Jolla, just minutes up the road from San Diego, and with the team's close proximity, it was easy for the families to attend either the morning or afternoon practices. But, contact with the players during training camp was extremely limited making the weeks the guys lived on campus in the dorm apartments difficult on them and us. During camp, I volunteered to work the education department's evening shifts at SeaWorld, which kept me at the park until after 10:00 p.m. Having something other than football or training camp to focus on seemed to be the key to coping with the stress and loneliness so many of the families experienced during those first weeks of the season.

While Tony may have been stressed at camp, I don't think he had time to be lonely. His day began at 6:30 a.m. when the team met for breakfast. Following breakfast, he saw the trainers to have his ankles taped. Most of the players took the time to have their ankles or wrists wrapped with athletic tape, which provided additional support and helped protect against injuries. It was then off to the morning practice followed by lunch, meetings, a 30-minute break when the guys would catch a quick nap, taping again, practice again, dinner, meetings, snack time and finally bedtime at 9:30 p.m.

With such a structured daily schedule, it was difficult to see Tony at all. But, I took advantage of my flexible schedule at SeaWorld and tried to attend at least two practices a week for moral support. For thirty minutes between when the guys finished practice and when they had to report to meals, Tony and I would have the chance to talk face to face. Immediately following practice, we'd take Tony's golf cart to the facility at the top of the hill where he'd change out of his practice gear and shower. I'd wait outside and then Tony would give me a ride to my car where we'd make a laundry exchange and say goodbye.

Sometimes the days I saw him were more difficult than the days I didn't. No matter how much time we had together, it was never enough and I always felt lonelier after I left. The team did permit the families to join the players for dinner at their facility three times during camp. Many of the players spent the time with their kids. Tony and I used the time to just enjoy each others company and talk about things other than football. I understood the intention of training camp was to remove the players from any distractions and focus solely on the game. But, understanding the reasons for it never made the process any easier.

As for the Chargers families, we were more fortunate than other NFL wives because some of the teams traveled to adjoining cities, counties or states for training camp. With such limited access to the players, I'm sure those families found it nearly impossible to see their loves ones at all during the weeks of camp.

Two weeks into the 1996 training camp, the pre-season opener took the team to the American Bowl in Tokyo, Japan for an exhibition game with the Pittsburgh Steelers. As is usually the case, the wives weren't invited. Tony wasn't looking forward to the brief overseas trip but after a few days in Tokyo, he found the Japanese lifestyle strangely intriguing. The people of Tokyo walked the crowded streets dressed in wool suits, cigarettes in hand, and were seemingly unaffected by the hot and extremely humid climate, which was causing Tony to drop pounds every day.

He was also astonished by the population's small stature and the city's accommodating architecture. Walkways and doorways were tight and even the hotel beds were small. Only as wide as Tony's shoulders and placed traditionally low to the floor, the bed forced Tony to wake up to roll over and each morning's ascent wreaked havoc on his knees.

On the flip side, the Japanese seemed genuinely intrigued by the behemoth American ball players. The sheer size of Tony and his fellow lineman compelled a few of the confounded people on the street to actually reach out and touch them. It made Tony uncomfortable. But he cracked up when a passing man, engaged in a conversation Tony couldn't understand, suddenly looked up at him and said, "Rambo." He realized he must have appeared just as out of sorts to them as they did to him.

The team traveled a long way to play a football game and Tony was hoping for a chance to see more of Japan than the New Otani Hotel, the inner-city, grass-covered sand lot where they practiced daily and the stadium. But, immediately following their 20-to-10 victory, the team boarded their chartered plane and returned to training camp in La Jolla.

Over the next few weeks, the offensive line was decimated by knee injuries to center Courtney Hall, tackle Troy Sienkiewicz, and guards Ike Davis and Eric Moten. Tony, having proven he was capable of playing left tackle by starting in three of the pre-season games, now began practicing at left guard to fill in for the injured. He excelled there as well. As a matter of fact, he was so adaptable, during the final pre-season game against the St. Louis Rams, he saw playing time at left guard, left tackle and right tackle. He didn't care about the position musical chairs. He was just pleased he'd secured a position as a starter and been given the opportunity to play at not one position but three. Being versatile always increased an athlete's stock.

Tony emerged from his second training camp feeling confident and ready to make his first professional start of the regular season.

His ability to secure a starting position proved his sudden drop to the sixth round of the draft was a fluke. He had the talent. Stan Brock's retirement and Harry Swayne's high salary and injured knee opened the door for Tony to become a starter. And when Eric Moten was injured, Tony really had the opportunity to show what he could do on the field. That was luck and because of it the publicity machine went into overdrive.

Tony was a golden goose. After all, he was a diamond in the rough; just another Bobby Beathard late-round draft pick, who turned into a shining star. That skewed fact made the organization and its management appear to be in-the-know all along and played right into the politics of the game. Whenever a player made the coaches or owners look good, they gained favor. Never mind Tony was initially projected to be one of the top linemen in the draft. The bottom line of NFL politics is if the coaches and management staff like you, you get to play. Tony had everyone's accolades going into the first game of the season and he was in the right place at the right time. All the pieces had come together perfectly.

On September 1, 1996, Tony stepped onto the field as the starting left guard when he replaced injured Eric Moten. His first assignment would be Seattle Seahawks' All-Pro defensive tackle Cortez Kennedy. Kennedy was considered by some to be the game's best defensive tackle and the San Diego paper had a field day profiling the match-up for days leading up to the game. Tony was nervous about starting but not the match-up with Cortez. He didn't buy into the hype or let himself get psyched out.

During the warm ups, Tony scanned the crowd in the family section and upon spotting me, nonchalantly raised his helmet while wiping his forehead on his sleeve to let me know he knew where I was sitting. I loved the idea that amid the chaos of the game day preparations, he'd acknowledge me in such an inconspicuous way.

When the game was over, the Chargers won at home 29-to-7 and the newspaper was asking "Cortez Who?" Tony's impressive performance earned him his first coveted game ball—an award presented by the team for outstanding play. In game four at Oakland, Tony moved to the starting right tackle position and claimed it as his own. He was amazing and I was so proud of his accomplishment.

Three games later, Oakland came to San Diego for a Monday night game. Monday night games hold a special significance because they are played during prime time to a national television audience. That game marked an epiphany for Tony. The Monday Night Football theme song, sung by Hank Williams Jr., echoed through the stands of Jack Murphy Stadium. The scoreboard flashed electronic fireworks and the thunderous roar of 62,000 fans reverberated off the playing field. Tony was standing in the backfield ready for the kick-off return when he suddenly got tunnel vision and the rumble of the crowd left his ears. The realization that he was actually living his NFL dream completely blew him away. He snapped out of it seconds after the ball was kicked. After that game, he never looked back. Starting 14 of the season's 16 games, he had become an integral force on the Chargers offensive line and felt redeemed professionally. The media loved him and he looked to be anchoring the offensive line for a long time. However, the team didn't fare so well. They went eight and eight in 1996 and it looked as though Head Coach Bobby Ross might be out of a job.

While the Chargers disappointing season created turmoil amidst the coaching staff and front office, 1996 shaped up to be a great year for me as well. Tony and I were looking forward to our upcoming wedding and plans were in full swing. I experienced a unique NFL opportunity during the season after a local radio station asked the Chargers public relations department about their DJs interviewing one of the wives the morning after a game. I had a good rapport with Robyn Walters and she referred me. After the initial interview, the morning DJs asked me to do it on a weekly basis. Thereafter, every Monday morning during the season they called me at 6:00 a.m. to discuss the previous weekend's game and to predict the score of the next week's game. I always picked the Chargers to win and my guessed scores were never even close. But, being interviewed on the radio every Monday morning was quite a unique experience. During the season, I also accepted a position as the Traffic Production Coordinator in SeaWorld's Marketing Services

Department where I was responsible for tracking virtually everything printed featuring the SeaWorld California logo from inception to completion. Despite tracking up to 300 jobs at any given time, the small department offered me flexible hours and I was able to tailor my schedule to Tony's.

Tony wrapped up his second year once again eager for season three. His contract would conclude at the end of February 1997 and he would become an exclusive rights (restricted) free-agent meaning the Chargers would have the exclusive opportunity to negotiate a new contract with him unless they chose to put him on the waiver wire. That scenario didn't seem likely since he'd endeared himself to the team and Bobby Beathard with his solid play in 1996. They'd gotten Tony cheap for the previous two seasons and it would have been silly for them to offer him to another team at that point.

With everyone high on Tony, it seemed as though we would be in the driver's seat when it came time for negotiations sometime in the next few months and we were concerned about Tony's agent, Brad Blank. In our opinion, he'd put Tony on the back burner after he dropped significantly in the draft. The two years represented in Tony's first contract were cut and dry with minimum salaries set by the League and few bells and whistles. Tony didn't even need Brad for that first deal because there had been little to negotiate.

During the first year of the contract, we rarely heard from him. But, during the past season, Brad would call me immediately following Tony's games and ask how Tony had done. Then, he'd call Tony the following day and basically repeat to him what I'd said regarding the game. We got the feeling Tony wasn't exactly a priority over the past two years and the upcoming contract had the potential to bring in a boat-load of money. Tony was no longer comfortable with Brad representing him and there was no reason Brad should continue to benefit from Tony's hard work. It was a good time to make a change.

Tony placed a call to agent Neil Schwartz, our second choice prior to the draft, and informed him he'd like representation. I think Neil was as ecstatic as we were about the new union. He was a go-getter. He was honest and up-front, tough and aggressive with the teams and fantastic with the players and their families and that's what we wanted.

As required by the NFL, we sent a certified letter of termination to Brad and forwarded a copy to the League's main office. To our surprise, Brad's office wouldn't accept the letter or sign for it. Tony tried to call him several times but Brad wouldn't take the call. We didn't know if that was common place when firing an agent, but we thought it showed a lack of professionalism and only proved that making a change was a good idea. Regardless, Brad's resistance didn't stop Tony from notifying the League he had retained Neil for representation as of December 23rd, 1996.

Chapter VI

First Team Wives' Club

Recalling my first home game experience after moving to San Diego in October of 1995, I remember Tony picked me up at 10:00 a.m., during his game-day break, and took me to Jack Murphy Stadium with him. He had to arrive approximately three hours prior to kick-off and I hoped the time would afford me the opportunity to mix and mingle with some of the wives in the players' parking lot. I had every intention of walking right up to what I hoped would be a friendly group and introducing myself. Having never been to a professional game as a significant other, I wasn't sure what to expect. The players' families and girlfriends at CU had always been warm and friendly to each other and while I also came to that scene late in Tony's college career, they were cordial to me right from the start. They had pre-game tailgate parties, yelled and screamed together in the stands and socialized when the game was done. For the most part, they all knew each other and together they reveled in the players' personal and team successes. I assumed the pros would be no different with the wives tailgating and getting riled up for the game. I was eager to get into the spirit.

However, as we made our way past security into the players' lot, I could see the area was devoid of people. Half the parking spaces were still empty. I think Tony was as surprised as I was but he didn't have time to talk about it. He headed to the locker room and with no one for me to meet, I ventured into the stadium alone in search of my seat. I thought perhaps I would find some of the wives already in the family section. Tony informed me my seats were in a section designated for the families and he had arranged with the ticket office for me to sit next to someone's wife. But for the life of me, I can't remember who it was. I don't really remember much about that day except Tony standing on the sidelines in a Chargers golf shirt and jeans because the coaches hadn't named him one of the 47 active players for the game. No one initiated contact with me and I didn't meet anyone in the stands that day. I do know that in the parking lot after the game, some of the players and their wives began to congregate around Stan Brock's SUV where he had a cooler of ice-cold beer. I knew who he was because I'd met him briefly during one of my previous trips to San Diego. As I stood off to the side waiting for Tony to shower and emerge from the tunnel, I watched the majority of wives immediately disperse into small groups throughout the parking lot. I was surprised when few of the wives made any effort to mingle after the game. That was my first indication the atmosphere surrounding the pros would be different than that of CU.

One by one, the players entered the lot. I was struck by the number of them hobbling up the ramp with their knees, shoulders, arms, hands or feet wrapped in ice. There was a small contingent of autograph seekers within the lot and I wondered how they'd gotten past the security. Some of the players stopped to oblige autographs and some didn't. Some were nice about the refusal and some weren't. Most of the players headed straight for their Mercedes', BMWs or Lexus'. At the very least, I assumed the players would stick around after the game. But for every player stopping to grab a beer from Stan, five were already high tailing it out of the lot. I quickly realized that, in the pros, just because they were a team on the field, didn't mean they hung out after the whistle blew.

Nevertheless, that night, Tony introduced me to Stan's wife, Lori. She was playing hostess on their tailgate and had set-up a spread of smoked salmon, crackers and other munchies. I also met punter Darren Bennett's wife, Rosemary, tight end Deems May's wife, Susan and offensive lineman Greg Engel's girlfriend, Melissa. They were friendly and we chit-chatted while the guys rehashed the plays of the game. The group quickly dispersed after most of the traffic cleared the stadium.

I knew my weekly commuting between San Diego and Denver would limit my ability to get to know the wives or get involved with the team's activities and the amount of time I was actually working in Colorado hardly seemed worth the cost of my salary and expenses. But, the company seemed pleased with my effort and afforded me the luxury of keeping my job in Denver and living in San Diego with Tony. I liked the arrangement but I wanted to feel like I belonged in San Diego so the awkwardness I felt sitting alone in the stands at that first game would disappear. Tony was having such a wonderful experience and I wanted to feel good about it too! Over the next few weeks, I tried to make the most out of the time in the parking lot immediately following the games and on Monday nights when the players routinely went out. Tony was really good about introducing me to the players and their wives or girlfriends. But when I wasn't traveling, I was either getting ready to go or getting settled from just being gone. Tony and I quickly discovered our own time together was at a premium.

Because Tony was always sequestered at the Town and Country Hotel the night before a home game, I scheduled my return flights from Denver late on Saturday nights. This return schedule allowed me to work in Denver for half a day on Wednesday after catching the 5:30 a.m. flight from San Diego, full days on Thursdays and Fridays and another half-day on Saturday before returning to California.

I spent Sunday mornings catching up on much-needed sleep before taking up the routine of game day. Kick-off was usually scheduled for 1:00 p.m. and I needed to be on my way to the stadium no later than 11:00 a.m. or there was a good chance I would be unable to get through the stadium traffic and into the players' parking lot. After making my way into the inner parking ring, I'd head straight to the family seating section to wait out the remaining hours until game time.

After sitting in the family section for a few games, it didn't take long for me to discover, within the team, there were all kinds of cliques and inner circles. Some of the friendships were based on the commonality of playing position while others were based on religious dedication, ethnic origin and salary level. In other words, the players and the wives hung out with the people in which they had the most in common. Which explains why Tony was befriending mostly offensive linemen and I was finding friendship among the ladies who didn't care I didn't drive a Mercedes or BMW, wear Versace or Gucci or shop exclusively at Nordstrom or Neiman Marcus. Those wives were open and friendly, which was a good thing because some of the other wives didn't like anything about me and they were bitches from the beginning.

Early in the season, I tried to introduce myself to one of the ladies sitting directly behind me in the family section. But, she brushed me off, looked past me as if I was blocking her view and acted as though she couldn't be bothered. I made up my mind right then to never buy into the pretentious wife bullshit. Then, I learned from a friendlier wife, the girl wasn't yet married to the player; she was only his girlfriend. She was a secretary or something when she met him and I thought how ridiculous for her to act as though she were all that. Then, one evening at a dinner gathering for a birthday, I overheard her ostentatiously declaring to quarterback Stan Humphries' wife, Connie, she only shopped at Nordstrom and only drank Cristal Champagne. I wondered if she realized how absolutely ridiculous she sounded or if she really thought the crap spewing from her lips sounded intelligent and refined. Her boyfriend, another offensive lineman, was really down to earth and Tony and I liked him. He eventually married the obnoxious cow, but I never figured out his attraction to such a nasty personality and I never attempted to be friendly with her again.

Instead, I preferred the ladies who were all about having fun and enjoying the unique lifestyle rather than judging people for it. Susan May and I bonded first. She had the sweetest southern drawl and she was funny, easy going and quite the character with her trademark pants featuring the wildest of prints. She sold real estate back home in North Carolina and occasionally traveled back and forth to close a deal. Her and Deems had met in college and he'd been in the League since 1992.

Rosemary and Darren Bennett came to America from Australia in 1994, and Darren was quickly becoming an established punter in the League. Rosemary was one of the most down to earth people I'd ever met despite the fact that, back in Australia, Darren was as popular in Australian Rules football as John Elway was in the American game. We quickly became friends and she was great at playing hostess. She got lots of practice as half of Australia, it seemed, elected to pay them a visit during the season.

Greg Engel and his girlfriend, Melissa, became good friends with both Tony and me. He'd joined the organization in 1994, and was somewhat of the team clown. His mounds of useless information earned him the nickname "Cliff Claven," the quirky mailman on the television show "Cheers." Melissa was light-hearted and, obviously, had a terrific sense of humor.

Stan Brock's mentoring relationship with Tony perpetuated my friendship with Lori Brock and she probably was the closest representation of what I initially imagined the wives in the NFL to be like. She made a point of making me feel welcome from the moment I met her. She and Stan had known each other since second grade and after 15 years in the NFL, she wasn't interested in any social hierarchy. They had four daughters and they weren't wrapped up in the spectacle of the NFL. Their children went to school and participated in activities which kept them grounded and made them a part of the San Diego community despite the fact they lived in Oregon during the off-season. The Brocks had been around and they'd seen it all. Lori knew all the wives and they all knew her. She was friendly and likeable and she was good at making the NFL fun with her occasional pre-game tailgate parties and regular post-game cooler of beer and tailgate buffet. Stan was the team captain of sorts and everyone looked up to him. Fifteen years in the League earned him everyone's respect and he and Lori made a point of getting the younger guys together. They hosted the offensive line for Thanksgiving dinner when lots of us had no family in town and no where to go. They planned a Christmas party at a local restaurant and even hired a band when the Chargers organization failed to plan any festivities to celebrate the season. At the party, Stan stole the show when he sang Bob Segar's song "Turn The Page." Darren Bennett played the Digerydo, a long wooden instrument of sorts from Australia, and after a few drinks, I even got up there and gave the tambourine a try. Those were the kinds of events which brought the team together and created chemistry. I think Stan thought Tony was the heir-apparent and he wanted to set an example of how things could, and should, be done. I wish we would have known Stan was retiring when he and Lori took us in tow and we crashed their friend's invite-only New Year's Eve party following the last game of the 1995 season. It was the last time we went out with them and we never really had a chance to thank them for introducing us to the fun side of the NFL.

During the remaining months of the 1995 season, Lori, Melissa, Susan and Rosemary became my chosen circle of NFL wives. Along the way, I met more of the other wives. But they were hot and cold. Sometimes, they would be very friendly and other times they wouldn't give me the time of day. In addition to having a whole lot of attitude, I got the impression they weren't receptive to me because Tony and I weren't married. It was easy to ascertain that, among some of the wives, being a wife in the NFL carried a whole lot more weight than being a girlfriend. I was aware some of the players changed girlfriends as often as days of the week. But, Tony and I had been together for almost two years and I didn't think they needed to ostracize me just because I didn't have a ring on my finger. Their snubs hurt a little and made me hope Tony was actually closer to taking the next step in our relationship than he purported to be. But, then again, the majority of those ladies prided themselves on being pretentious snobs and the one thing they all had in common was they met their husbands after the guys were professional athletes. With or without a ring, I never intended on being like them.

Toward the end of the 1995 season, I was disappointed when Susan announced her return to Carolina for the off-season and Rosemary planned on departing for Australia following the Super

Bowl in Phoenix. Before joining Tony in San Diego, it never dawned on me the majority of players and their families might actually live in other states during the off-season and only return to southern California during football. But, many of the wives and their children left San Diego before the season even ended in order to celebrate the holidays at home. Others planned to leave immediately following the last game and not return to California until training camp was over the following August. I was even more surprised to learn some of the players' families never moved to the city at all during the season and only flew in for occasional visits during home games, which explained why I occasionally met someone's wife or children and then never saw them again. It was no wonder all the families seemed estranged at the beginning of the season; they were.

With few friends in San Diego outside the realm of football and the Mays, Bennetts, and Brocks all departing for their out-of-state, off-season homes, Tony and I realized the importance of expanding our circle of friends during the off-season to include people who weren't part of the League. Neither one of us wanted to be friendless at the end of each football season.

Everyone's sudden departure at the end of Tony's rookie season was disappointing. But, it didn't compare to the let down we felt when Stan Brock announced his retirement only a few months into 1996. After sixteen years in the League, Stan and Lori called it quits. We regretted not having the chance to say formal goodbyes or thank them for assisting us in our awkward transition into the League.

Stan left his imprint on Tony and the game and I believed the guys would miss his presence. But, Lori's absence would be equally noticed. Whether the wives liked her or not, they respected her and she controlled much of the group's dynamics. There was simply no one of equal caliber to fill her shoes as den mother and social director the following season and, through the spring, I wondered if anyone would even try.

During training camp in 1996, Rosemary, Susan and I began discussing ways to facilitate family introductions and improve communication between the wives and the organization. We agreed the Chargers were terrible at welcoming new people to the team and my own experience led me to want to improve the situation for others. Susan and Rosemary believed creating chemistry among the wives and players early in the season could help win games. Their thoughts were influenced by their experience as part of the 1994 Chargers team, which went to the Super Bowl. They felt the '94 winning season might have been chalked up to the chemistry created when the wives were allowed to purchase travel packages to accompany the team to the American Bowl in Berlin, Germany. During the ten-day trip, the wives got to know one another and forge friendships before the season. The positive experience built chemistry on and off the field for both the players and their wives and the players returned to training camp feeling positive about the team. The chemistry carried over into the regular season. Susan and Rosemary believed the trip laid the foundation for a positive support system both on and off the field. While I'm not sure about the correlation between the wives being included by the organization on such a trip and the team's winning season, the Chargers did advance to the Super Bowl for the first time in franchise history.

With San Diego set to play in the American Bowl in Japan in 1996, Rosemary and Susan were understandably disappointed the organization made no attempt to include the wives in the trip. And, when the Chargers made room for the cheerleaders to accompany the team, the snub pissed off a few of the veteran ladies including a prominent quarterback's wife. I don't know if I would have opted to go so far in such a short amount of time but I agreed it would have been nice to have been given the opportunity.

Late in August, a few of the wives attended a meeting organized at the urging of Coach Ross's wife, Alice. Attitudes toward the team were negatively-charged and Alice Ross wanted to address the wives' perceived communication problems. She hoped the meeting would result in the wives becoming more involved in the organization and improve their feelings about the team.

At the meeting, we discovered many of the wives were uninformed of public relations events and the occasional team social opportunity because the Chargers organization simply put memos into the players' boxes at work and relied on them to pass the information along. The guys rarely sorted through the boxes of autograph requests, solicitations and junk mail, so the memos were never read much less taken home.

In response, Rosemary, Susan and I suggested doing a monthly newsletter, which would provide helpful hints for newcomers, information on activities, events and promotions pertaining to the players, coaches, staff, and families as well as recognizing special events in the players' lives like births, birthdays, engagements and marriages. Since the newsletter was our suggestion, we were elected to pursue the project.

We named ourselves the Chargers Women's Association because we wanted to facilitate better communication between the players' significant others, whether girlfriend or wife, and the Chargers organization. Because of my background in marketing, advertising, and graphic design, I was given the responsibility of designing each month's newsletter.

After having the content approved by the public relations department and the controller, the first issue was sent directly to the players' homes early in September of 1996. It was extremely well received and Rosemary, Susan and I began immediately receiving feedback from the majority of addressees. They were all concerned with how the Chargers treated the families and how they felt the organization could improve.

The newsletter opened a can of worms and since we were the only responsive sounding board, we heard a lot of bitching about everything from having to sit in the bleachers with all the other fans during training camp to the lack of security in the players' parking lot to the cheerleaders going to Japan. After wading through all the muck, we did find some viable suggestions from the families. There were a number of requests for a designated meeting area, other than the parking lot, to meet the players after the games. That was part of the security issue. Some of the wives were finding it difficult to get in and out of the players' lot while some of the hoochies and autograph hounds were not. One wife claimed there were prostitutes in the lot after a game in 1995. While there were occasionally scantily-clad women mingling in the players' lot after games, I wasn't sure they were ladies of the night. But, Coach Ross responded by announcing a post-game gathering room in Jack Murphy Stadium where players and family members could get together immediately following the games to relax and hopefully celebrate.

The team had never set aside a formal post-game gathering place before. We usually just sat in the players' parking lot, F1, after the games waiting for the traffic to die down. Continuing Stan Brock's post-game tradition, Tony set out a large cooler of beer and water on the tailgate of his truck after each game. But, the room idea sounded great to everyone and, to our surprise after the next home game, the new meeting area offered light refreshments and complimentary beverages. Many more players and their wives stayed after the game than usual and they commented on the organization's positive change of policy. It was a nice perk and very well received.

Another request asked for information on how to contact the team if a husband was hurt while playing in an away game. I'd never thought about it before but I didn't know how to get a hold of anyone should Tony get hurt in another city. I knew I would feel absolutely beside myself if I saw Tony get hurt on TV and had no way of finding out his condition. It was an excellent inquiry and after some prodding, the public relations department put together a phone list for each of the season's away games providing a contact should a player get injured while on the road.

Dr. Bucky, the team psychologist, became extremely interested in the wives' group and convinced the organization it would be a positive thing to offer a monthly ladies luncheon. He suggested featuring special presentations by guest speakers on a wide variety of issues including dealing with the media, curbing anger and frustration, understanding communication skills, prioritizing family relationships and expectations, and improving family life in the NFL.

The luncheons gave the wives an opportunity to meet in an organized setting and discuss how being married to or dating a professional athlete affected us and the people around us. We discussed the emotional ups and downs of winning and losing, handling media criticism, the myths and realities of our lives in the NFL and compared the Chargers organization's treatment of families to that of other teams. We also came up with ways the organization could involve the wives in charity events.

The Payless Shoe Drive, my favorite event financially supported by the Chargers, was the first to openly welcome the wives participation. Each fall, social service agencies throughout San Diego compiled a list of school-age children in need of assistance. One thousand kids were chosen to be bussed, about fifty at a time, to several Payless ShoeSource store locations where the Chargers players assisted them in picking out any pair of shoes they wanted. While the boys loved the players' attention, the little girls were sometimes intimidated and didn't always want the tennis shoes the guys often steered them toward. So, in 1996, the wives stepped in to help the girls and the boys sometimes too. The one-on-one interaction with the kids was extremely rewarding and their gratitude alone heightened the wives' interest in participating in other events.

Promoting the organization's activities through the monthly newsletter and formally inviting the wives to participate opened the lines of communication and reduced the feelings of isolation many of them experienced in years past. After the first public relations tie-in, the ladies started talking and took the initiative to get better acquainted. Soon, a few wives were getting together regularly on Saturday nights before Sunday away games to play Pokeno; a card game similar to bingo. Each week, we went to a different home large enough to accommodate the growing number of game participants. Everyone brought a wrapped gift and game winners could either select a gift from the pile or steal one from a previous winner. Sometimes I went home with two or three items and sometimes nothing at all. Regardless of winning or losing, the interaction broke the ice and, soon, the group of ten to twelve wives including quarterback Stan Humphries' wife, Connie, defensive tackle John Parrella's wife, Leigh, Glen Young's wife, Gina,

David Binn's girlfriend, Tamar, Rosemary Bennett, Susan May, and Melissa Engel eagerly looked forward to the game nights. The friendly events were quite a change from the year before.

In October of 1996, the wives group decided they wanted to get involved with the Polinsky Children's Center (PCC). The Center was an emergency shelter for children in San Diego and each month took in more than 500 children, aged birth to seventeen, because of neglect, or physical, sexual or emotional abuse. With the group finally coming together, we felt we had something viable to offer the community and we wanted to formally reach out. When contacted, the volunteer coordinator for PCC invited us to a luncheon in conjunction with a tour of the facility. Eight wives accepted and expressed interest in directly volunteering as baby rockers, story readers, or arts and crafts activity leaders.

At the luncheon, the participating wives showed up with bags of clothing, totes, shoes, crayons, and sporting equipment; all of which appeared on PCC's donation wish list. The positive energy behind the collective contribution felt good and I hoped the Association might find ways to tie-in with the PCC on a regular basis.

However, while on the tour, I quickly realized the volunteer coordinator wasn't as interested in us volunteering our time as she was in us making a large financial donation. She kept mentioning the cottages, where the children were grouped by age, could be sponsored for a mere $600,000. While I would certainly have liked to help them, we weren't, even collectively, in a position to put up that kind of money. Unfortunately, several of the wives felt uncomfortable about the solicitation and never pursued volunteering at the PCC any further.

Susan and I, however, still wanted to do something with the facility. So, we worked with the coordinator to schedule a makeover day for the teenage girls at the facility. We contacted one of the make-up counters at Nordstrom and they graciously volunteered to send over three artists for the session. The teenage girls at the shelter were eager for the attention and, I think, very much enjoyed the ninety minutes of instruction and product sampling. After,

Susan and I sat down for an open discussion with the girls and the questions they asked told us a lot about their lives prior to taking up residence at the Polinsky Children's Center.

The first thing they wanted to know was if we were rich. Then, they wanted to know our age. And, then, from the back row, a very pregnant 13-year-old girl asked if we had any kids. When both Susan and I replied we didn't, the girls were noticeably surprised. They couldn't get past the idea we were in our twenties, Susan was married and I was engaged and yet we still had no children. And, they wanted to know why. After we explained we just weren't ready, they wanted to know if we graduated from high school. Susan and I simultaneously explained we'd both graduated from college. But then, they went right back to asking questions regarding children. When I left the Center that day, I was acutely aware of how fortunate I was to have had a supportive home life and promised myself I'd try to do more for the kids living there.

In November, the Chargers held their Eighteenth Annual "World's Largest Blood Drive" at the Town and Country Hotel. The all-day event featured player autograph sessions, information kiosks, sports radio giveaways and interactive booths where participants could throw a football or try on a set of shoulder pads. All the activities were meant to entertain the thousands of people waiting sometimes five and six hours to donate blood. While the wives weren't included in any of the daytime activities, the Charger Women's Association did provide models for the evening's fashion show featuring some of the Chargers brass, the players and their wives walking the runway.

I, of course, nagged Tony to death until he agreed to appear in the fashion show. Those kinds of events were completely against Tony's grain. But, he relented, when so many of the other players were also coerced into making a fashion statement. My first runway set featured a pant suit courtesy of Nordstrom and I walked the runway with Susie Spanos, wife of Chargers owner Dean Spanos. Tony, dressed in a beautiful suit from a small boutique, followed in a set with Darren Bennett. Tony and I then changed into formal wear, a black tuxedo and an aqua-marine sequined gown, and walked our second set together. More than a dozen players and their families volunteered to participate and after the show, the guys threw small footballs into the crowd and then jumped into the audience to thank everyone for donating blood. Continuing another Stan Brock tradition, we formed a train of sorts and walked through the entire convention hall and even into the blood room where participants, who were in the middle of actually giving blood, hadn't been able to see the show. We stopped in the middle of all the beds and started clapping. The people seemed genuinely surprised we were acknowledging them. But they were really the ones putting out an effort to make the blood drive successful.

On December 1st, the Chargers held their fifth annual holiday toy drive to benefit the Child Abuse Prevention Foundation (CAPF), an affiliate of the Polinsky Children's Center, at Jack Murphy Stadium prior to the game versus the New England Patriots. The Chargers hoped to collect 10,000 toys and it was the first time the wives were asked to participate in the event. We were to staff the collection barrels located at the gates around the stadium and simply thank the fans for their donations as they dropped off toys to awaiting CAPF volunteers.

An extraordinarily high number of wives turned out to participate in the event. I think it was because the toy drive gave the wives their first opportunity to directly interact with the fans as associates of our husbands. Though, standing there in our significant other's spare jersey, I don't think most people realized we were the players' wives and girlfriends. Disappointingly, most people entering the stadium were without toys. Many said they were unaware of the drive or they would have brought one, which was little compensation when, at the start of the game, the trucks came around to pick up the bins and many were virtually empty. We certainly didn't collect more than a few thousand toys that day and, nearing the end of the season, I never heard another thing about it from the organization.

Tony faired very well his second year, starting 14 of 16 games, and as the 1996 season came to a close, I felt the Charger Women's Association (CWA) had established a foundation and opened a reasonable line of communication between the families and the organization; an outlet, if you will, for information, questions and concerns. Through the year, the wives remained upbeat despite the mediocre 8-and-8 season and the media's severe end-of-season criticism of the coaches and some of the players. CWA seemed to provide a much needed support system and I was eager to expand the wives' group in 1997.

Chapter VII
Celebrity-ism

When Tony was in college, the CU Buff players enjoyed a certain amount of celebrity based on their team's success. They were well known on campus, kids hung around after games to get their autographs and when we'd go out to a bar or club, there was always a fan or alumni offering to buy a drink or two. But, it was all pretty low-key. We were aware that by stepping up to the NFL, Tony's celebrity status would grow. But, as an offensive lineman, we knew he would never see the kind of notoriety showered on those who throw the ball or those who catch it, which was fine with me. I liked the perks of complimentary dinners, never waiting in lines and VIP invitations. But, I didn't like the idea of security issues, privacy concerns and relentless autograph hounds. The limelight wasn't always pleasant and there was something to be said for having a little fame but a lot of anonymity.

Truth be told, Tony probably felt like less of a celebrity his first year in the pros than he did his senior year in college. In the NFL, everyone was a professional athlete. But, not everyone was created equal. While it still holds true people treat you differently when they think you're someone important, there were players who were obviously thought of as more important than others. I called that phenomenon the social hierarchy. Tony never bought into my social hierarchy theory, but there was something to be said for the varying degrees of NFL star power.

The Terrell Davis' and John Elways' of the football world top the social hierarchy. They are the guys with lots of talent, big names, big paychecks and their own charitable foundations; the ones who stand up and stand out. You see them on television in commercials and cameo appearances, on the front of cereal boxes, and packaged as action figures in the toy aisle. Everyone in the country recognizes their name, fans idolize their jersey numbers and kids want to be like them. They have maximum star power and they are the persona of the professional athlete. Nothing is out of their reach.

The down side of that notoriety, however, is everyone wants a piece of them and they can't go anywhere without being recognized or mobbed by fans. For example, when former Denver Broncos running back Terrell Davis was at the height of his career, he couldn't even go to the movies because people would continually approach him during the movie to get an autograph. He either had to wait for movies to come out on video so he could watch them in the privacy of his own home or rent out the entire movie theater for himself. And, I once saw John Elway and his kids at a Colorado Rockies baseball game. He spent so much time signing autographs he couldn't enjoy a single pitch until a security guard was stationed near his seat. His kids didn't see the star, just the people interrupting their outing while they were trying to watch the game. Within two innings, they'd vacated their seats. Unfortunately, there is always a price for fame and fortune.

Many people believe *all* professional athletes lead supercharged lifestyles at the top of the social hierarchy. And, by all means, some of them do. But I know plenty who don't. Every player's experience in the NFL is unique and different and while some of the guys do live the extreme lifestyle conjured up in people's imaginations, I believe that lifestyle is reserved for only a select few and they're the ones who make the persona larger than life.

Below the high-brow crowd of well known names and faces, lies the middle of the social hierarchy. This is where the majority of ball players find themselves. They get there by being middle to high round draft picks and riding the wave of their potential, even though they have yet to prove themselves in the NFL. Or, they're veteran players who have been with the same team long enough for every football fan in the city to know their name. But, while their names are recognizable, perhaps their faces are not. They have contracts for more than the League minimum, lend their names to local charities and events and, maybe, draw a middle-sized crowd of autograph seekers following a game. They'll never see a ten-million-dollar signing bonus, but they consistently get the job done on the field and receive a comfortable amount of perks while still remaining anonymous enough to go to the grocery store without causing a scene.

In 1995, Tony was kind of at the bottom of the NFL social order, which is naturally where you find the lower round draft picks and free-agents with short contracts for the League minimum. Those guys don't see much in the way of playing time or perks because they are always overshadowed by bigger names and contracts. They're at risk for being cut, without fanfare, before they ever play a down in a professional game or set foot on the field when the stands are full because they're unproven and potentially expendable. The funny thing is every team in the NFL has guys like that and they're really the work horses at practice and in the locker room because they have to get noticed to stick around.

Tony, unconcerned with fanfare and focused only on playing, would have been happy at the bottom of the social hierarchy with little or no celebrity status. But in 1996, he began gaining celebrity ground. The more he played and the more his name was mentioned, the more perks we received. By mid-season, we started getting invitations to attend and even host charity events where we mingled with other VIPs. We suddenly found ourselves sharing a photo opportunity with Hulk Hogan or hanging out in the player parking lot with celebrity Charger fans like professional golfer Phil Mickelson or actor Mario Lopez from the television shows "Saved by the Bell" and "The Other Half." While Tony enjoyed participating in the events and meeting new people, he never bought into the celebrity bit. I, on the other hand, liked wheeling a little importance even though the status had not one thing to do with me.

In 1997, when I wanted to come up with a really unique wedding gift for Tony, I thought it might be fun to arrange a meeting between him and one of his favorite characters in NHRA auto racing, John Force. Top-fuel drag racing was the only sport Tony ever watched on television and, for reasons unknown to me, he was a devout John Force fan. Through the Chargers public relations department, I contacted John's marketing people and asked what I could do to facilitate an introduction between John and Tony. I was willing to pay John's expenses to come to a game or surprise Tony with a trip to meet him at a destination of John's choice. Imagine my surprise when I learned John Force's racing facility was located in Yorba Linda, California, about 90 minutes from San Diego. After explaining Tony's fondness for John Force and auto racing, we were invited to spend some time with John and tour his facility.

It was an awesome experience and Tony was knocked out by the unique surprise. We spent over four hours hanging out with John talking about racing, his car collection and football. John gave Tony all kinds of racing memorabilia and invited us to the Grand Nationals in Pomona. He also asked Tony to send him an autographed poster for his sports memorabilia room. In exchange for his invitation and generosity, we offered for John and his crew to come to San Diego and attend a Chargers game as our guests. We picked a game and set it up. Tony even got approval from General Manager Bobby Beathard for John to park his enormous tour bus in the player parking lot so he and his crew could have a pre-game tailgate party.

Unfortunately, the day of the game, the weather was terrible and it was pouring down rain. Half of John's crew was stranded in Phoenix and couldn't catch a flight out. At the last minute, John cancelled the trip. Tony was disappointed they couldn't make it. Fortunately, the Chargers ticket office agreed not to charge us for the ten tickets we requested since they weren't picked up at will-call. We never did make it to Pomona and I don't recall why. But, we did see John again when we were his guests at the Mile High Nationals in Denver.

I liked the races okay and John was a really interesting guy. But, one of the coolest perks we experienced was at a Matchbox 20 concert. In 1998, Tony and I were both big fans of the band and he approached the Chargers public relations office about possibly securing tickets for the show. In the past, the staff had access to a limited number of prized tickets to various events in the city and occasionally offered them to the players. However, in that instance, Tony was told to approach first round draft pick Ryan Leaf for assistance. His agent had connections in the music industry and he was the one to get it done. Ryan was a rookie quarterback so Tony had no problem asking him for a favor.

As the second overall selection in the draft, Ryan was big money and he was riding the wave of his potential. When he met us at the concert venue, we got the royal treatment. We had our own security detail because he was so high profile and we were ushered past the waiting lines, the front gates, and immediately escorted onto a private patio to await the band. Presented with all-access passes, we had unfettered access to complimentary food and drinks.

When Matchbox 20 arrived, introductions were made and a photo opportunity was organized. We spent the next hour having publicity shots taken with the band. Guitarist Adam Gaynor was the sports fan in the group and, even though he wasn't at all familiar with the Chargers or Tony's career, he took the most interest in us. He was very cordial and we spent the majority of our time talking about music and sports. He even introduced us to his dad and the warm reception made me like the band that much more.

Minutes before the concert started, we made our way toward our seats. But, the second Ryan was visible to the crowd, heads turned, people yelled, applauded and pointed. Realizing we weren't going to be able to blend into the crowd with Ryan in tow, we instead used our passes to access the stage. Five feet from the band, to stage right, we made make-shift seats out of empty equipment boxes. Dancing behind the stage curtain, we sang along to every song. Adam kept looking over at us and laughing. He was entertaining us and apparently we were entertaining him. When the show was over, we followed the band out to the buses. Lead singer Rob Thomas talked with us a while and then thanked us for coming. We thanked him for the great time and, of course, Ryan too. Without him, we would never have had such a run of the place.

The next morning, the radio DJs were talking about how terrific the concert was and a listener called in to report the Ryan Leaf sighting. He was big news in San Diego and supposed to be the answer to the Chargers elusive success. The DJs asked all about seeing him and who he was with. The caller told them Ryan appeared to be alone, no girl in tow that is, but the guys he was with had their girlfriends with them. I thought it was funny the girl recognized Ryan, who hadn't yet played a game for San Diego, but not Tony who had been the starting right tackle the previous two seasons. It was odd to hear them talking about our evening on the radio. Mildly amused, I called Tony to tell him about it and offer up the Matchbox 20 experience as proof of my NFL social hierarchy theory.

Sales people were an interesting study of the phenomenon as well. When Tony and I decided to buy a new car in San Diego, we drove his big pick-up to the Lexus dealership. Wandering through the models on the lot, we could see the salesmen standing on the showroom floor watching us through the glass but not one of them came out of the building to ask if we needed any assistance. Twenty minutes later, one of the salesman slowly sauntered out. As he walked toward us, I kidded Tony the guy must have chosen the smallest straw. Everything in his demeanor told us he wasn't happy about having to come out and talk to a pair of looky-loos. After some brief small talk, he flat out asked us what Tony did for a living. I thought it was a rather rude approach to qualifying us as buyers. But, he quickly changed his tune and immediately starting kissing our ass when Tony said he played for the Chargers. Suddenly, there wasn't anything he couldn't do for us. So, when we asked to take delivery of the car in Nevada to avoid paying California's luxury tax, he volunteered to drive it out himself. And he did. Right to our front door! After the notary signed the paperwork at the airport, the salesman boarded a plane back to San Diego. It was the damnedest thing. I guess there was something to be said for star power or at least fifteen minutes of fame.

I wasn't partial to the 180 the salesman pulled when he ascertained what Tony did for a living. But the response wasn't uncommon and we encountered it often. When we met people outside the realm of football, they acted normal until they learned Tony played ball. Then, they'd suddenly act intimidated and jealous or smothering and clingy. The obvious change always annoyed us and we would immediately distance ourselves. Occasionally, it was difficult to tell the difference between someone who really liked us and someone who just wanted to be friends because of football. Unfortunately, we learned that lesson the hard way.

I met one of the dolphin trainers at SeaWorld and we really hit it off. He had one of the greatest jobs in the world and his own form of notoriety. At first, he was a great friend to Tony and me; always the life of the party and a lot of fun. He knew everyone in San Diego and was consistently introducing us to people. He became our third wheel accompanying us everywhere. But, while he had hundred of acquaintances, I thought it strange he rarely brought other friends around. And, while Tony tried to remain low-key when we went out, this guy always made sure everyone around us knew Tony played for the Chargers. It was bothersome but he was such a likeable guy we didn't really notice his friendship had an agenda. It took a while for us to determine he was a social climber using us to "move up."

After introducing him to quarterback Ryan Leaf at the Matchbox 20 concert, he stopped calling us. Then, within a brief period of time, I spotted him in the players' parking lot with Ryan Leaf's little brother after a game. It wasn't long after that encounter we heard he was living in Ryan's house, driving his cars, going to the games on Ryan's tickets and living the lifestyle on Ryan's nickel. We were angry with ourselves for being so gullible and trusting. But, it made us realize we had to be careful about the people we met. Tony started telling people he was a garbage man when they asked what he did for a living. He figured if they still stuck around to talk to us, they were worth talking to.

The funny thing about the whole Ryan Leaf situation is that Ryan amounted to little in the League. The Chargers paid him something like $7 or $10 million in signing bonus alone and he never made much of a contribution to the professional game of football. He had tons of talent but just as much bad attitude. I will never understand how an outstanding college athlete, with the organization, team owners, and media already in his corner following a successful draft and lucrative contract offer, comes to the NFL and amounts to little. Guys spend their entire careers trying to reach the NFL apex and Ryan had it handed to him and even after he continued to disrespect his teammates, coaches, and even the team owners, they still gave him ample opportunity to take the helm. But, he just plummeted down the depth chart until he went away.

 I realize teams feel the need to save face with their fans, critics and peers when their signings don't pan out, but I've always been surprised by just what some of these players can get away with on and off the field before a team actually makes a move to cut their losses. In Ryan's case, the Chargers waited through several subsequent drafts before letting him go. But, not before he alienated everyone on the team and his antics off the field made an ass out of him and the organization. I don't think the fans forgot about the enormous amount of money he cost the team or what a terrible draft choice he turned out to be. But, after a few seasons, no one seemed to notice his quiet departure and the only reminder of his time spent with the Chargers was his name listed alphabetically in the team's media guide under the All-Time Roster list.

 What bothers me most about him and others like him is that during their reign, they still get paid, give good players dedicated to the game a bad name and get opportunity after opportunity in the NFL. Ironically, the minute the Chargers cut Ryan loose from his multi-million dollar contract, the Tampa Bay Buccaneers were chomping at the bit to sign him. The guy made $15 million dollars for three or four years worth of bad attitude and limited team contribution in San Diego and you'd think other teams would take that into account when considering adding him to their roster. But, they didn't. And when the Bucs let him go after one or two unproductive seasons, he got yet another chance with the Dallas

Cowboys. He never received another big pay day and his celebrity status was forever lost in San Diego but he had millions of dollars already in his pocket. Proof that equity equals opportunity in the National Football League.

Chapter VIII
Groupies, Cheerleaders and Infidelity

During Tony's senior year in college, we were at a Boulder bar one night after a game and the place was packed. I walked in, sandwiched between my bookends, 6'6" Tony and 6' 8" Derek West. As they made their way to the bar for drinks, I was pushed out of the way by some of the patrons trying to reach them to offer congratulations on the game. Another time, in San Diego, we were at a country bar called In-Cahoots with two other Charger players and three of my girlfriends from SeaWorld. Initially, we were talking with the guys. But, we started talking amongst ourselves when the guys' conversation turned to football. During the brief exchange, a female patron approached the boys and before we knew it, she and her two friends were standing between us and them. We found ourselves staring at the girls' backs as they attempted to carry on a flirtatious conversation with Tony and the guys. My girlfriend, Jennifer, commented on how quickly they'd swooped in. It was a given people would try to get close to the ball players because of who they were and what they did. Sometimes it was an over the top sports fan who wanted to ask a hundred questions but, usually, it was someone of the female persuasion.

While the Chargers didn't exactly have groupies per se, there was no shortage of ladies biding for the players' attention and the players had little trouble attracting women or getting them into bed. One player often had an entourage of scantily-clad women in tow, which once awaited him in a limo in the player parking lot following a game. The girls weren't shy about flaunting their stuff from the open limousine sun roof or loudly commenting on other players' physiques. Their unabashed behavior irritated at least one of the player's wives who contended the four or five girls were hookers and, for all I know, maybe they were. Despite the lack of any obvious regulars, the players were always moving targets. Girls fell all over themselves trying to meet them. Obviously, having a little celebrity could do funny things to a woman's perception. Tony and I called it the ugly factor.

The ugly factor was consistently proven true by a Chargers player who was, by far, one of most gross and disgusting men I've ever met. He, once, invited Tony and me to drop by his apartment, which was located a few miles from ours. We were stunned by his squalid living conditions. There were weeks-old dirty dishes in the sink, moldy food and empty pizza boxes on the floor, his white bed sheets were soiled gray and I won't even go into the condition of his bathroom. During the season, his mother flew into San Diego for a visit and spent the entire time doing his laundry and cleaning his apartment. I couldn't believe, with two professional football seasons under his belt, he'd actually choose to live that way.

And not only was his apartment deplorable, but the guy himself was grimy. He boasted about wearing the same shorts, without underwear, and beat-up deck shoes, without socks, nearly every single day of the season. If his t-shirt was dirty on the front, he'd turn it inside out for another day. For away games, he fulfilled the required dress code by wearing a pair of wrinkled dress pants, a dirty dress shirt and mismatched sport coat. He once boarded the team plane for a two-day road trip with nothing but a toothbrush.

But worst of all, the guy was a sexist pig and treated women like garbage. His comments were derogatory and demeaning and he didn't even draw the line at making raunchy comments about other players' wives or girlfriends. I usually refrained from saying anything to him directly about his lack of respect, but I once got so pissed off when he publicly degraded Greg Engel's girlfriend, Melissa, after she jokingly warned a friend at a bar about his lack of hygiene, I reacted by telling him to shut the fuck up. The words just tumbled out before I could stop them and I was stunned by my own lack of censorship. He didn't say anything; just walked away. After the altercation, he never spoke to me again but whenever I was around him, he always had a weird smirk on his face as if he was privy to something I wasn't. He was just plain creepy.

Stinky, as I preferred to call him, was an abomination and yet he bagged more hot chicks than I could count. He was screwing a cheerleader, which was a no-no, dating a doctor who was extremely attractive and he never left a bar without a nice looking girl drooling all over him. Of course, he wasn't shy about letting it be known he was a Chargers player. But, nevertheless, all of us, players and wives alike, wondered what those girls could possibly be thinking. Was the power of being a professional athlete so strong it could facilitate attraction over the guy's obvious delinquency?

Tony once asked him what the girls thought when he took them home to his dirty apartment. He said he didn't know but thought they liked it because it made them feel dirty and the sex was better. The guy was warped. The mere fact he was able to date any women at all, much less very attractive ones, became known as the ugly factor. Simply put, any player with such negative attributes would serve himself well to get married while he was playing ball because when it was over, he would never be able to date the kind of women he could while he was playing.

I mentioned Stinky even bagged a cheerleader. Contractually, cheerleaders agree not to fraternize with the ball players. But, it happens. Like models and rock stars, cheerleaders and ball players go hand in hand. Personally, I wasn't bothered by the cheerleaders in general. I figured they were out there entertaining the crowd and most of them were more interested in furthering their modeling careers or prolonging their high school cheerleading days than landing a ball player. And, really, I didn't even care if they dated the single players. But, what I didn't like was when one of them would set their sights on one of the guys who should have been considered off limits.

While out of town at an autograph signing for another player opening a car dealership, an engaged ball player hooked up with one of the cheerleaders. Obviously, I blame the ball player for the entanglement. But, the cheerleader should have had more respect for herself than to encourage the situation. By Tuesday morning, the entire team was talking about the incident. Rightfully so, the guys gave the cheat a lot of heat in the locker room for everything from the act itself to the forced confession to his fiancé regarding the indiscretion. When several of the wives rallied around the girlfriend and openly bad-mouthed the cheerleaders, the girlfriend was embarrassed further. As public fodder, everyone had an opinion on what should become of the relationship. Fortunately, despite the public interference, they worked it out privately after a brief break-up.

I heard other stories pertaining to particular cheerleaders and married players but I wasn't privy to anything first hand. However, there were a couple wives who expressed much animosity for the girls and never missed the opportunity to flash them a dirty look or crack a joke at their expense. Their behavior, perhaps, lent credence to some of those rumors.

I would be lying if I said infidelity wasn't an issue in the NFL. There was always gossip and rumors quietly circulating about players who discreetly fooled around. But, occasionally, a ball player was brazen and just put it right out there. I remember, at a player function, one of the guys brought a "friend" with him. Before I realized he wasn't alone, I asked him about his wife and he replied she was home with the kids. Later, I saw him getting real cozy with his guest. Another incident involved a player who was having an affair and the girlfriend became pregnant. His wife lived on the East Coast with their kids in the city where they used to reside when he was with another team. The situation turned ugly when one of the Chargers wives, who new his wife from the previous team, threatened to call her on the East Coast and disclose what was going on in San Diego. I don't know what became of the threat but he told his wife of the affair during his girlfriend's second trimester of pregnancy. He divorced the wife and married the girlfriend but she was never welcomed into the wives' social circle.

The most incredible infidelity story I ever heard occurred the year before Tony was drafted by the Chargers. At the end of the

1994 season, one of the players actually put his wife and girlfriend on the same flight and booked them at the same hotel for a playoff game. I don't know the logistics of the scenario but Head Coach Bobby Ross was forced to address the issue in a team meeting and tell the guys if they were going to be so brazen with their relationships then they should be smarter than to make decisions which could so negatively affect the entire team and its morale. The necessity for the speech became a running a joke and people still talked about it whenever the issue of fidelity came up.

Chapter IX

Starting on the Wrong Foot

1997

Following the less-than-stellar 1995 and 1996 football seasons, Head Coach Bobby Ross resigned from the San Diego Chargers on January 3rd, 1997, amidst intense media scrutiny and mounting pressure from the team's owners. Tony's offensive line coach, Jack Henry, and the rest of Ross's coaching staff were forced to resign or be fired. Two weeks later, General Manager Bobby Beathard named former Jacksonville Jaguars Offensive Coordinator Kevin Gilbride the San Diego Chargers' new head coach. The change was exciting because the team had little spark during Coach Ross' final season and we thought the younger Gilbride would elevate the level of play and bring a new energy and chemistry to the team.

Full of positive expectations, we began the 1997 off-season the same as in year's past. Tony took a break from daily conditioning during the months of January and February to give his body a chance to recuperate from the rigors of the season and, with no time constraints or demanding football schedule to follow, we began another off-season travel odyssey with a February camping and jet-skiing trip to Lake Havasu with several of our friends from SeaWorld. The next month, we joined Ken Ready on his annual players' trip and sailed the western Caribbean aboard the ship *Carnival Destiny*. Chargers defensive tackle John Parrella and his wife Leigh made the trip with us. Despite John's affiliation with the University of

Nebraska, the University of Colorado's (Tony's alma mater) arch rival, he and Tony became stead-fast friends in San Diego. Conditioned at CU to think of the Nebraska Cornhuskers as the greatest nemesis of all time, I was surprised Tony allowed himself to get so close to John. Back in the day, the rivalry ran so deep, Tony hated me to wear anything reminiscent of Nebraska red, even fingernail polish, and there he was befriending the devil himself.

At the beginning of April, we traveled to my parent's new home in Livermore, California, for a weekend visit and to assist my mom and sister, Audra, as they worked on the centerpieces and place cards for our wedding. Because Tony wanted a cowboy wedding and I wanted something more formal, we comprised, which made finding coordinating décor difficult. But, with my mom's and sister's help, we made most of the themed pieces. Even Tony had a hand in making the centerpieces after we discovered converting oil lamps to accommodate candles required a strong hand and several pairs of tin snips.

In the middle of April, Tony eagerly attended his first mini-camp with new Head Coach Kevin Gilbride and there he met George DeLeone, his third offensive line coach in as many seasons. Unfortunately, after only five days of practices, Tony developed an aversion to Gilbride's brash style of singling out players and verbally humiliating them in front of the whole team. Tony didn't respond well to that kind of criticism and he knew that type of coaching would never create the team chemistry so lacking the past two seasons. But, determined to remain focused, he brushed it off and concentrated on learning Gilbride's chaotic system of plays and calls.

At the end of April, we took a weekend trip to Colorado to finalize the arrangements for our upcoming wedding and look for property to potentially build an off-season home. We spent the first few days coordinating with caterers and other vendors and the next few days driving up and down the Front Range from Fort Collins, my home town, south to Denver looking for a suitable piece of property to build the ranch-style home we envisioned with plenty of room for kids and toys. We still hadn't found the ideal location, when on our last scheduled day of searching, it snowed. After spending two football seasons in San Diego's mild climate, snow at the end of April wasn't very appealing to either of us and we suddenly weren't certain about making Colorado our off-season home. We returned to San Diego and elected to wait for Tony's impending contract negotiations before pursuing the issue further.

With support from my SeaWorld office mates, Jennifer and Corrine, I took the entire month of May off to complete final preparations for the wedding. Tony and I made only two trips to Colorado during the entire planning process. So, while he continued to intently focus on working out and preparing for the start of the 1997 football season, I was finalizing many of the wedding details over the phone.

The Chargers hadn't yet tendered Tony a new contract offer, but we tried not to let their procrastination detract from either of our tasks. He was, after all, a restricted free agent and didn't have the luxury of going to another team at free will. The Chargers owned his rights and they could negotiate in their own time. Neil told us not to worry about the contract issue and instead focus on our wedding, which was a good idea because our plans were going awry.

When our wedding RSVP cards began arriving, we were taken aback by the number of people accepting each invitation because, in some instances, the number accepting actually exceeded the number invited. To our surprise, some of our guests invited guests of their own. Apparently, since Tony was somewhat of a celebrity, they were feeling compelled to invite their adult children, sisters, aunts, brothers, friends and anyone else who was a fan to the celebration. Aware of the facility's maximum capacity of 125 and intending on having a small ceremony with close friends and family only, Tony and I agreed we needed to stick to our guns regarding the guest list. Telling people they could bring only guests specified on the invitation was an uncomfortable task and neither of us wanted to do it. But, we had to.

To reduce the feather-ruffling, we agreed I would call Tony's invitees and he would call mine. We hoped the approach would make the daunting task a little less uncomfortable and difficult. After ascertaining some of the uninvited guests had been intentionally left off the guest list and others were complete strangers, we felt more comfortable with the process and politely explained seating was limited and we were unable to accommodate any guests not specifically named on an invitation. We were disappointed when a few of the offending guests chose not to attend the wedding at all. As a matter of fact, a few of them never spoke to us again.

Nevertheless, Leigh and John Parrella and John's parents, Joe and Shirley Parrella, made the wedding as did fellow San Diego teammates Darren and Rosemary Bennett. Jennifer Wright, my close friend and co-worker from SeaWorld, made the trek to Colorado with her beau Vinni Zoni, and Neil Schwartz proved Tony was a priority by making the occasion all the way from New York.

Our wedding was country formal. I wore a form-fitting sequined and lace gown with a five-foot train. Tony wore a traditional black tuxedo with western tie, three-button vest and cowboy boots. My sister, Audra, served as my maid of honor and my bridesmaids wore long, western-inspired burgundy dresses and lace-up boots. Chris Byrd, Tony's best friend from high school, served as his best man. Simple floral arrangements of white and Fire and Ice roses (white with red tips), greenery, wheat stalks and western rope adorned the posts of the outdoor patio and decorative hay bales marking the altar. The beautiful pine trees and incredible views of the snow-capped mountains provided a breath-taking backdrop. I was calm all day. But, as my dad walked me down the isle, the emotion of all those important people in my life sharing the incredible moment suddenly got to me. I didn't stop crying until the Chargers team chaplain, Shawn Mitchell, got to the part about the guests forever holding their peace. That's when all the male members of my extended family, in a pre-arranged moment I thought would be light-hearted, stood up revealing hidden children's cap guns and pretended to take a stand against anyone about to speak their mind from Tony's side of the gallery. The joke went off without a hitch and, after a moment of gasps, everyone including me started laughing hysterically. The best part of the joke was watching my Aunt Sonja, unaware of the secret plan, trying to physically force my 6'6" tall uncle, Eddie, to sit down as he stood up to implement the joke. Even Chaplain Mitchell, hesitant at the initial proposal, enjoyed the silly hi-jinx. Once everyone calmed down, Tony and I concluded the 19-minute, non-denominational ceremony by exchanging serious vows while overlooking the gorgeous Continental Divide. I felt very lucky and blessed to have him in my life.

In a caravan of sorts, we took several days to make the drive from Colorado back to San Diego. My parents, Dwight and Joy, and my grand parents, Bill and Carmen, followed us in my parent's RV and some family friends, Cassie and Brad, who lived in the San Diego area, followed in their van. While stopped in Vegas for a day, Tony and I took note of the dry climate, warm weather, close proximity of Lake Mead, incredibly reasonable housing prices and Nevada's no state income tax policy making it a haven for professional athletes and celebrities alike. Only a five-hour drive from San Diego, Las Vegas seemed like a great place to visit. After finding Colorado not as appealing as we initially thought for our off-season residence, we kicked around the possibility of purchasing a vacation home in Vegas. We promised to revisit the idea once Tony re-signed with the Chargers.

In no hurry to get home, we took the scenic route to San Diego via Laughlin, Nevada. We weren't concerned about the lack of cellular service until we came within range of a tower and Tony's phone displayed three messages from Neil. The Chargers had finally tendered Tony an offer and Neil was trying desperately to reach him to discuss the details of the three-year deal. After a short briefing, Tony agreed to sign the contract in San Diego the next morning, May 29th, 1997, at the stadium trailers.

The terms provided for a bonus of $150,000, payable upon signing of the contract. In addition to the signing bonus, Tony's salary for the 1997 season would be $200,000. His salary for the 1998 season would jump significantly to one million dollars and his 1999 salary would be $1.4 million. Three additional incentives for each year—Pro-Bowl selection, first team All-NFL or first team All-AFC—could earn an additional $70,000 per season.

To be honest, we hoped for more money up front. Signing bonuses were guaranteed cash in hand. But, salaries, no matter how big on paper, were always subject to a player making and staying with the team. If a team no longer wanted to keep a player or pay his salary, management could rid themselves of him and his salary via cuts or the waiver wire. Players, on the other hand, were locked into the contractual terms unless they forced renegotiations by holding out or refusing to be part of the team until the organization committed to more money or better terms. Only a player with viable leverage is usually able to successfully force a renegotiation of an existing NFL contract, which is one of the few contracts in the world where the parties actually agree the employee (the player) is bound but the employer (the team) is not.

In a world where multi-million dollar signing bonuses are a common occurrence, Tony's $150,000 signing bonus was small change. So, in exchange for agreeing to the terms, Neil stipulated Tony's 1998 one-million-dollar salary had to be guaranteed. Guaranteed contracts are almost unheard of in the NFL because they take away the team's ability to rid themselves, at no cost, of a player they feel is overpaid, under producing, or injured. We happily accepted the signing bonus knowing the back-loaded deal ensured Tony, at the very minimum, would make $1.2 million over the next two seasons. That night, Tony and I popped open a bottle of Dom Perignon to celebrate and we raised our glasses in a toast to his success in the National Football League. He'd worked hard over the previous two years in the NFL and he was finally being financially rewarded.

The next morning, May 29th, 1997, Tony and I arrived at the stadium trailers temporarily housing the Chargers staff until their new practice facility and administrative building on Murphy Canyon Drive was complete. Tony signed the deal and was immediately handed his $150,000 signing check. The following day, the *San Diego Union-Tribune* ran the sports headline, "Berti aims to anchor line for a long time." It was a flattering article kicking off the newspaper's coverage of the Chargers second spring mini-camp, which began on the following Monday. In addition, Pacific Trading Cards, Inc. released another of Tony's trading cards featuring him as a "best kept secret" and wearing Chargers number 75. Feeling confident in his future with the Chargers, Tony went into the second camp upbeat, positive and eager to master Gilbride's extensive play book.

But, after only a few practices, Tony felt George DeLeone, the new offensive line coach, was ineffectual. He was pleasant, enthusiastic, and appeared to know a lot about football but, as a first year coach, he was also contradictory, frenzied and completely unfamiliar with the nuances of coaching an NFL offensive line. Even the addition of veteran center/guard Raleigh McKenzie with thirteen seasons under his belt made no difference. When the mini-camp broke, Tony held little hope George could solidify the struggling offensive line before the team's training camp in July.

In June, Tony put the trying sessions behind him when we departed for our last vacation of the year on a week-long Alaskan cruise my parents gave us for our honeymoon. We'd done an enormous amount of traveling during the 1997 off-season but Alaska was by far the most impressive. The trip offered incredible scenery, spectacular wildlife and a chance to relax before the busy football season began again in less than a month. On the trip, Tony put the frustrations of the spring mini-camps behind him and returned to San Diego recharged.

The next weekend, we drove to Vegas to meet with a real estate agent referred by Ken Ready. The guaranteed salary clause in Tony's contract made us comfortable in making our first real estate investment and, after looking at only two communities, we purchased a newly-built vacation home eight miles from Lake Mead. The gated community provided security and the homeowner's association handled all the yard maintenance. It was an ideal situation and, by purchasing the three-bedroom town home in

Nevada, we could establish residency there and our investments wouldn't be subject to California's incredibly high state tax. The savings would nearly cover the cost of the purchase. In addition, the transaction helped me escape the capital gains taxes from the sale of my home in Colorado in 1995. While Tony and I wouldn't be able to utilize the house until the following off-season, it felt good to have a place to call home.

Tony reported to training camp on July 17, 1997. The very first practice was representative of what Kevin Gilbride had in store for the team throughout training camp. In addition to the long, full contact practices in complete pads, he belittled and degraded the players with pointed personal attacks and incredulous and derogatory screaming. No longer did the players wonder why Head Coach Buddy Ryan punched him in the face during a game when he was an assistant coach with the Houston Oilers. After only two weeks and with no change of pace in sight, seasoned veteran players began commenting Gilbride's training camp was one of the most difficult they'd ever been through. Even the act of tying the rookie assistant strength coach, Mike Schleelein, to the goal posts with athletic tape and leaving him there after practice didn't lighten the mood of the players for very long. Tensions were high and players were fighting amongst themselves, verbally and physically, pushing the team's confidence to an all-time low. Gilbride continued to beat them into the ground physically and mentally and, day after day, the injuries started piling up. An incredible fifteen starters found their way onto the Injured Reserve list before the season even started. By the time training camp broke on August 14th, the team was exhausted and the talent pool was in a shambles. Gilbride was touted as an offensive guru and he turned out to be just plain offensive.

To make matters worse, Jack Murphy Stadium was renamed Qualcomm Stadium after an agreement with the City of San Diego led to extensive renovations to increase its capacity, entice future Super Bowl opportunities and keep the Chargers in San Diego until the year 2020. But, during the remodel, no one involved remembered to preserve or set aside a designated section of seats for the families. At least that's what we were told. Traditionally, NFL teams provide each player with two complimentary tickets per game, which I think is a reasonable policy across the board. If a player needs additional tickets, a limited number, which varies by team, are available in the family section for purchase at face value. The Chargers allowed players to purchase up to ten additional tickets. In a stadium retrofitted to a capacity of 70,000, I found it incredulous the Chargers made little effort to provide a reasonable family section. The notion the organization forgot, in several years of planning, to designate a family section was either a lame excuse for taking away the then more expensive seats in order to sell them or a very good indication the organization didn't give a rat's ass about the families.

The wives were not pleased to discover their seats were moved from sections 41 through 43, on the home side between the 35 and 40-yard-line to Loge 17 through 19. The new sections were behind the goal posts, on the visitor's side and in the furthest corner of the stadium on the second level. The players' wives and kids had been relegated to the cheap seats because our former seats, exactly the same but now billed as being in the Gold Club, were fetching $125 each, an increase of nearly $60 from the year before. Of course, the organization gave us every opportunity to buy our former seats at the new price. We could all afford to buy the better seats. Hell, Junior Seau had a box at a cost of around $80,000, or something like that. But that wasn't the point. Our husbands were integral members of the Chargers team and the families were, once again, made to feel totally unimportant and disregarded by the organization.

Rosemary Bennett and I felt so slighted by the seating issue, we sent out NFL family life questionnaires to twenty-seven wives we collectively knew on other teams to see where their team's had them sitting. While we were at it, we inquired about parking, game-day leisure rooms, after-game meeting areas, private player/family organized team activities, community team activities, communication, away games, special perks and the level of family support offered by their organizations. We received responses from wives with the Arizona Cardinals, Jacksonville Jaguars, Seattle Seahawks, Denver Broncos, New England Patriots, Oakland Raiders, St. Louis Rams, and Pittsburgh Steelers. We discovered some clubs offered private rooms for the families both during and after the games, babysitting, complimentary food and beverages, designated family parking areas, BBQs, picnics, Christmas parties and various other events and perks to make their families feel good about being part of the team. In regard to the seating issue, we substantiated what we already knew. About half the teams put their families in some of the best seats in the house between the 35- and 45-yardline on their team's home side, of course. The remaining teams didn't offer seats quite as good but none were as bad as the Chargers new designated family section. So, the seating became a hot button for the wives and when the wives were bitching, you better believe their husbands were hearing about it.

Going into the regular season, we were informed the previous season's after-game meeting room would no longer be available and we were relegated back to the players' parking lot. We were also told the seating situation would be remedied. However, no changes were made and when the coaches' family section turned out to be on the lower level in the Gold Club seats, several of the wives got verbal regarding their level of frustration. Adding fuel to the fire was the rumor one of the office interns, who was required to be on the field during the games, was receiving and selling two complimentary Gold Club tickets each week and pocketing the money. Whether or not that's true, I don't know. But, the grumbling over the seats quickly made its way up the grapevine to the heads of the organization. The rebuttal, returned in true Chargers style, stated our husbands all made more than enough money to buy the better seats. The sentiment from the organization was always the same and trickled down directly from the top. It was no secret how owner Dean Spanos treated the families. I experienced it first hand one night after a home game. I was talking to Christine Beathard, wife of General Manager Bobby Beathard, in the players' lot and Dean walked up to talk to her. He rudely interrupted our conversation and when Christine attempted to introduce me, he turned and walked away before the sentence was fully out of her mouth. If he, as the owner, was that disinterested in getting to know us, the organization would never improve their approach to the families.

By game six, the team was poised to implode and the chatter among the players was they absolutely despised Gilbride and had no respect for him as a coach. It was becoming painfully obvious the team's inability to succeed on the field and Gilbride's abusive behavior were having a cyclical affect. During the bye-week in October, when the Chargers weren't scheduled to play a game, Tony was desperate to escape San Diego and the constant media analysis of the team's woes being played out daily in the paper and on the television and radio.

Back in 1995, when Stan Brock's oldest daughter Sarah used to tell me she hated going to school on Mondays after a loss because the kids were so cruel, I hadn't put much stock into the stories. But, two seasons later, I understood exactly what she was talking about. When I walked into SeaWorld on Mondays, all the somebodies and nobodies felt compelled to tell me just how much we sucked. I had to hear every armchair quarterback's critique of the players, the game and the calls. They wanted to know what happened, why we lost, why a certain player was put in or taken out, why a play was called or wasn't! At first, I engaged them in the conversation and gave my opinions. But, after weeks of losing and answering the same stupid questions, I got sick of it. I was not a player, nor was I privy to what transpired on the field. People outside my immediate office thought no negative comment was off limits or too personal. They didn't think twice about saying Tony had a bad game, missed a block or even sucked. I knew when he played a bad game because I watched it happen just like everyone else. The hardest part about losing was being aware of my husband's bad day at work and knowing the whole world was going to feel obliged to comment on it the next day. I know that's part of the reason athletes make big money but it didn't make the harsh criticism any easier to take.

And, as far as having the inside track on the intricacies of the game, I had no idea what was going to happen on the field. I understood the general format but I didn't play. I was just a spectator like everyone else. I didn't have any secret knowledge or information which would suddenly explain why the team was winning or losing. There were far too many variables that determined how the team played, all of which had nothing to do with me sitting in the stands. I was just a face in the crowd.

Tony and I withdrew to the sanctity of our new house in Las Vegas for the bye-week's two-day reprieve. Many of the players took advantage of the rare time off to escape the city and break away from the intense football scrutiny consuming San Diego. But, the brief time away didn't improve the team's attitude. The following week in game seven, the Kansas City Chiefs whooped the team 31-to-3. Even the win against Indianapolis (35-to-19) in game eight of the season, which brought the team's record to 4-and-4, didn't improve the overall negativity of the team. Tony won his second coveted game ball that day for outstanding performance but he was struggling mentally. The team was in a pressure cooker and each time Gilbride worked them over verbally, the pressure intensified. Tony could no longer shrug off the intense criticism and he began to question his own abilities. Instead of playing confidently, he was over-analyzing the plays and worrying about the guys on the other side of the line beating him on every single play. Instead of focusing on the game and getting the job done, all he could think about was sitting through another Gilbride tirade if he didn't play well. The pressure was reaching a boiling point with everyone. The offense blamed the defense, the defense blamed the offense, the coaches blamed the players and the players blamed the coaches. Everyone was pointing fingers and placing blame.

Gilbride had a thing for Tony personally and it was clear he felt Tony, along with the other offensive lineman, exhibited little talent. He publicly criticized them in the newspaper, on the field and in the locker room and privately blamed the line for much of the team's problems in several of the lost games. He also blamed the quarterbacks, the wide receivers, and then the corners. According to Gilbride, the Chargers didn't have anyone with an ounce of talent. Tony felt much of the team's trouble stemmed from Gilbride's incredibly difficult playbook and the simple fact Gilbride's players hated him. He had created a volatile situation and the real root of the team's problems began with him and his lack of chemistry with the players. Offensive line coach George DeLeone wielded little influence and the team simply fell apart, emotionally and physically. Including the fifteen starters on Injured Reserve, the team posted twenty-seven major surgeries throughout the year making it the team with the most casualties.

The Chargers nose-dived into oblivion losing eight straight games in a row. Tony's confidence tumbled as he lost more games in 1997 than in all his college years put together. Working under two head coaches and three offensive line coaches in three seasons, all with different approaches, styles and preferences, only served to thwart any chances the team had of success. Tony said as a pro, he should have been able to play better through the bad coaching. But, they'd gotten into his head and his mental game was affecting him physically. One of our friends trying to console Tony during the season mistakenly said, "You get paid either way. Losing is no big deal." Tony retorted, "Only losers get used to losing."

Tony couldn't shake the feelings of doom and gloom each day he had to go to practice. I'd never seen him so withdrawn and quiet. Tony, known in our inner circle as the Social Chairman because of his penchant for getting people together, planning events and being continually up-beat, suddenly didn't want to go out or talk about football at all. If I asked too many questions, he became agitated and told me so. He even stopped reading the newspaper because the sports section was filled with heated Gilbride quotes and team criticisms. Tony was always one of the guys who played for a sense of accomplishment and the love of the game. Suddenly, he, like everyone else, couldn't wait for the season to be over.

I had trouble of my own in 1997 with one of the Gilbrides. It started when, after being responsible for putting together the wives' newsletter for the past two seasons, I found myself in the soup with Kevin Gilbride's wife, Debbie. She was living on the East Coast until their son finished high school and, having never met her, I was surprised when she phoned my office at SeaWorld to inquire about the recent newsletter she received. She questioned why the newsletter article on the upcoming Chargers Women's Association luncheon featured the connotation children were not permitted to attend. I explained to her Dr. Bucky's monthly luncheons were educational meetings and we were joined by guest speakers from the community. In the past, there was a consensus children, primarily toddlers, were not permitted to attend because they tended to disrupt the formal presentation and subsequent discussion. Older children and attendance by babies was left up to the discretion of the mother. For the past two years, the policy was never an issue and the wives, even those with children, always approved. But, for whatever reason, Debbie Gilbride decided to make it an issue. She attacked my explanation and asked why I felt I was the one to make that decision. I explained I was only the messenger reiterating what had been acceptable policy. But, that wasn't good enough. Thereafter, she made the issue personal. She phoned the wives prior to each luncheon and asked them to bring their children. She even had the audacity to have her sister-in-law attend one of the meetings and bring her disruptive four-year-old who proceeded to crawl under the linens, dump out coffee cremes and bang on the table with the flatware while Kimberly Hunt, news anchor for San Diego's Channel 10 and wife of former Charger Billy Ray Smith, attempted to educate us on how best to deal with the media during a trying season. The display was disrespectful and embarrassing and set off a chain of events which turned into a real pissing contest.

Dr. Bucky, who was responsible for coordinating the meetings, tried to calm the waters but inform Mrs. Gilbride she was somewhat out of line. He also discussed the situation with Susie Spanos, wife of team owner Dean Spanos, and Christine Beathard, wife of General Manager Bobby Beathard. But Susie and Christine wielded little power to address the issue or squelch the turmoil. Their lack of assertiveness only served to complicate the issue when they did nothing. Melissa Engel, Rosemary Bennett, a few other wives and I, whom had been actively involved in the luncheons, tried to conceal our disdain but take a stand. It was quite clear Debbie Gilbride was no friend to the wives. She had not attended one single Chargers event or met any of us, but she was already changing and dictating how things should be done. Once again, the wives' concerns were disregarded by the organization. The Gilbrides were a nightmare for everyone involved with the team and I missed Alice Ross, wife of former Head Coach Bobby Ross, who worked diligently in 1996 to instigate the wives' group and convince her husband and the Chargers there was value in the wives feeling they were a positive component of the organization.

When Debbie finally flew in from her home on the East Coast to attend one of the monthly wives' luncheons, she immediately alienated very-pregnant Rosemary Bennett. Past her due date with son Thomas, Rosemary's doctor recommended she undergo induction within the next couple days and the process was scheduled for Thursday. When Debbie introduced herself to Rosemary at the Wednesday luncheon, she commented on the baby's impending arrival and Rosemary replied she was being induced the following day. Debbie Gilbride then said, "What, you couldn't get it scheduled on a Tuesday?" She was, of course, referring to the only day of the week the players had off. The insolent comment was in poor taste and if she was kidding, no one saw the humor.

Several of the wives expressed their displeasure with Debbie Gilbride by declining any Chargers requests for charitable participation in community activities. I chose to show my displeasure by declining any events in which she directly had a part. I simply liked participating in the charitable activities too much to let her drive me away completely. As a matter of fact, I pushed the wives to become more involved in some of the activities so we would maintain majority power within the wives' organization we worked so hard to create the previous year. But, it was wasted effort and the momentum of the Chargers Women's Association (CWA) came to a screeching halt. The infighting, dismal morale and horrible season put an end to our cause.

My final attempt to take back the CWA came by way of the

1997 annual holiday toy drive. I asked the Chargers public relations department to chair the event and they agreed. I used my influence with SeaWorld and their vendors to put together what I thought would be the very best toy drive the Chargers ever had. First, I asked SeaWorld to give anyone who brought a new, unwrapped toy to the Chargers vs. Kansas City Chiefs game on December14th, a free child's admission ticket to the park. They agreed and covered the cost of printing the coupons. Second, I contacted one of SeaWorld's graphic design firms, John Webster and Associates, and asked John if he would donate his time to design a logo, a four-color postcard and a poster to promote the event. He graciously agreed. I, then, contacted Commercial Press to see if they would print all the collateral promoting the event free of charge and they agreed.

To reach more prospective donors, Tony and I recorded a toy drive public service announcement and forwarded tapes and press releases to all the local radio stations for airplay. The radio station, which in 1996 tapped me for the five-minute interviews every Monday morning following a game, invited me to appear on one of their radio shows to promote the event. Rosemary Bennett and I visited several other radio stations in San Diego to talk about the toy drive with their morning DJs. In addition to the radio promotions, I appeared on every morning television news show in San Diego to create awareness of the upcoming event. We had a full-blown media blitz going on to reach the fans and The Child Abuse Prevention Foundation was ecstatic about the generous contributions and the increased effort to highlight the event.

The Chargers, as their sole contribution to the effort, were to send out the toy drive postcards to their season ticket holders and announce the drive over the public address system during the two home games prior to the event. However, the day before the postcards were scheduled to go out, I received a call from Robyn Walters in the PR department. She informed me I needed to come up with $2500 to cover the postage cost of mailing the postcards. I was absolutely floored. I could not believe the Chargers would not cover the cost of the mailing to promote their event to their very own season ticket holders. Disheartened, I phoned my contact with the Child Abuse Prevention Foundation (CAPF) to discuss my dismay. She told me even though the Chargers had approached CAPF years before about holding the annual toy drive, CAPF had always been responsible for the entire cost of promoting and executing the event. So while the Chargers organization slapped their name on it, they never put one penny or one toy into the bin. I was appalled again, but not surprised. I called a friend who owned a telecommunications company and, fortunately, he agreed to cover the last minute postage expense even though his company, Teldata, would receive little recognition for their contribution that late in the game.

Deems and Susan May left the team prior to the 1997 season for a contract with the Seattle Seahawks and so only Raylee Johnson's wife, Diann, Rosemary Bennett, Melissa Engel and Connie Humphries joined me in volunteering to man the bins of the toy drive. I, personally, bought two shopping carts of toys and we nearly filled a bin ourselves. But, despite my best efforts, the 4-and-10 Chargers made for a lousy draw. We didn't get anywhere near our goal of 10,000 toys and I was disappointed in the Chargers organization, which was always so quick to point out all their community good deeds. Publicly, the Chargers were very philanthropic. But, behind the scenes, they weren't as generous as their public relations propaganda would have you believe.

Chapter X

Travel Secrets

People are often surprised when I tell them I attended my first and only away game in September of 1997, when the Chargers played the New Orleans Saints. I'd never been to New Orleans and I thought the game was the perfect opportunity to visit the historical city. My mom mentioned she'd like to go as well and so we booked the weekend at the team's hotel. Typically, for Sunday away games, the team left San Diego on Saturday mornings. But, because New Orleans was three time zones from the West Coast, the team's chartered flight departed on Friday. And, because families were not permitted to travel with the team, my mom and I, leaving on Friday as well, flew on a commercial carrier.

I hoped the team's hotel would be within walking distance of the historical district but, after a significant drive in the hotel's shuttle, we found ourselves quite a clip from the sights of Bourbon Street, the Mississippi River and the Louisiana Superdome. Upon our arrival at the hotel lobby, I spoke briefly with Tony before my mom and I made our way via cab to the House of Blues for dinner. While waiting for a table, we bumped into some of the more cordial Chargers office staff and learned much of the administration had made the weekend trip to New Orleans. A few of the staffers joined us for dinner and, after a few robust cocktails, their idle chit-chat gave way to a juicy discussion regarding the limousine ride they shared with one of the married brass in the Chargers organization. Apparently, there was some extra-marital kissing and fondling going on and one of the office gals took a few photos of the scene. Upon their arrival at the hotel, the film was surreptitiously confiscated and destroyed by his security. Most certainly inebriated by the time my mom and I left the bar to take in Bourbon Street, I doubt they remembered openly discussing the debauchery. But, details of the limousine ride were still quietly circulating in the hotel the following morning when my mom and I departed to tour the city.

During our excursion to the river front, the French Quarter, the French Market and Café Du Monde, where they served the most incredible beignets, my mom stopped near the edge of an old cemetery to visit with a tarot card reader. The women predicted several generalizations about her future wealth and happiness and my mom encouraged me to have the cards read. But, since college, I was superstitious about psychics after one prophesized all kinds of good things were coming my way and, shortly after, my car broke down, I broke up with my then boyfriend and I got very ill with the flu. I decided then, there would be no fortune tellers in my future.

Following a delightful carriage ride through the city, my mom and I made our way to a local bar, recommended by Robyn Walters in PR, where the Chargers fan club was holding a rally for the team's traveling supporters. Several of the public relations people, intoxicated the previous evening at the House of Blues, were in attendance. But, the party was rather lame, so we didn't stay long.

The following day was game day Sunday and my mom and I took a cab to the Superdome at 10:30 a.m. for the noon kick-off. Tony had requested and purchased two game tickets for us through the Chargers office and while I'd been told home teams always provided visiting teams with really bad seats, I didn't know just how bad until my mom and I climbed to section 617 at the very top of the stadium. We could barely make out the ant-sized players through the view-blocking metal railings, which guided fans up the steep stairs. And, because we were able to see little of the action on the field, we spent most of the game making fun of our choice seats with the other Chargers fans around us. We were pleased when the Chargers defeated the Saints 20-to-6 and we were able to descend the steep, nose-bleed section.

My mom and I returned to the hotel, said goodbye to Tony and the team, retrieved our stored luggage and caught the next shuttle to the airport. Our commercial flight was scheduled to depart New Orleans 90 minutes before the players' charter flight and I was relieved it was on time. We flew into Los Angeles, where my mom boarded her connecting flight to Oakland, and I boarded mine to San Diego where Tony picked me up at the airport.

It was possible for Tony to pick me up at the airport because, even though he left Louisiana more than an hour after us, he wasn't subject to the usual travel hassles. My mom and I had to contend with airport security and make connections in Los Angeles. The team's buses, however, drove straight out onto the tarmac and delivered the players directly to their awaiting private plane, which left immediately, flew non-stop into San Diego, and arrived 90 minutes before my flight landed. While I very much enjoyed the experience in New Orleans, I wasn't overly eager to attend more road games.

Contrary to popular belief, with the exception of training camp, the guys spent little time away from home. When on the road, the team left San Diego the day before a game unless it was on the East Coast or crossed three time zones. Then, they left two days before. But, they always returned immediately following the game. They traveled in comfort in the back of the chartered plane and two players shared three seats, which gave them plenty of room and still left additional seats for coaches, management, radio, television and print media up front. Flight attendants served an abundance of food and not your ordinary airline fare either. There were candy bars and fruit for snacking and main dishes of shrimp and steak. To pass the time, the players were shown first-run, in-flight movies and they brought CD players, DVD players, and laptop computers on board. And, there was always a card game or two being played.

Immediately upon arrival at their destination, buses whisked them to the team hotel. Depending on their arrival time, they might have a practice, meetings or free-time. Per the Collective Bargaining Agreement (the union contract), players received a per-diem for any meals missed during the flight and airplane food didn't count as a meal. So, they received around $100 to cover the missed meals while in the air and, if time permitted, were allowed to go out for dinner. Tony always asked the Concierge at the hotel about the best steakhouses in town and was often directed to a Morten's of Chicago or Ruth's Chris Steakhouse. He was introduced to one of his favorites steakhouses, St. Elmo's, by Derek West when the Chargers played the Colts in Indianapolis.

Following dinner, the players were required to return to the hotel for meetings. After meetings, they received a snack of fruit or sandwiches prior to curfew, around 11:00 p.m. for an early game, before heading off to their rooms. To ensure everyone was where they were supposed to be, the assistant coaches or Dick Lewis, the head of Chargers security, actually went room to room for a bed check.

John Parrella was Tony's roommate when the Chargers were on the road and also in training camp where the Chargers put four guys together in a two-room dorm apartment. Other teams like Denver and Green Bay footed the bill for the guys to have their own rooms but the Chargers didn't. Tony didn't mind sharing close quarters with John on the road. The short trips didn't afford John the opportunity to clutter up the room like he did during the weeks in training camp when it was necessary for Tony to run a thick line of white, athletic tape down the center of the room to keep John's dirty clothes, CDs, empty cups and garbage from spilling over onto Tony's futon mattress on the floor and eventually taking over Tony's side of the room. Despite John's penchant for clutter, they liked rooming together and the habit provided Tony with good fodder for ribbing. They were good friends both on and off the field and neither of them snored, which was an important factor in getting a good night's sleep the night before a game.

The routine of away games was similar to that of playing at home. The guys got up early and ate breakfast. Then, boarded buses to the stadium where they were taped and dressed for the game. Warm-ups on the field lasted about twenty minutes before the players headed back into the locker room for last minute things like going to the bathroom, getting a drink, wiping down the sweat or readjusting tape or pads. Twenty minutes later the pregame pomp and circumstance began. Tony liked the routine of early games. He hated when the players sat around the hotel for hours waiting for the same routine to begin for a late game. It made him anxious and he would chew his fingernails to the nub.

Immediately following the game, the team boarded buses to the airport and flew home no matter the time of day or night. On the return flights, beer was available. Anything stronger was frowned upon, but the guys were at liberty to bring whatever they wanted on board. Tony would call me from the plane once they were airborne and, if they won, I could hardly hear him over the jubilant celebration. But, if they lost, the pitch was more subdued. Either way, the players were usually hyped up immediately following the game and it always took them a while to settle down.

There were plenty of away game nights when Tony walked in the door after 2:00 a.m. I wouldn't actually wait up for him but I rarely fell into a sound sleep until I knew he was home safe and relatively injury free. If the game went well, he might fall asleep shortly after arriving home. But, if things went bad on the road, it was far more difficult for him to unwind from the game and settle down. Sometimes, it took hours before he was able to sleep and early the next morning, the players were required to attend a brief practice and workout to relieve game-tired muscles as well as a presentation of the game film to evaluate mistakes. In 1997, Monday mornings came all too early when the Chargers lost six of their eight away games.

Chapter XI

Down But Not Out

The media was brutal to the team throughout the 1997 football season and not one player was above reproach. Head Coach Gilbride was in the hot seat too and his boorish style only seemed to fuel the media's criticism. When the 4-and-12 Chargers finally closed the dismal season, Tony and I couldn't wait to get the hell out of San Diego. Tony needed to blow off steam and escape the negativity that all but consumed him during the season. Realizing we would be spending a lot more of the off-season away from San Diego than in years past, I turned in my notice at SeaWorld. The company and my co-workers were so very supportive of me during my employment I was extremely sad to give up the position. Working there kept me grounded and gave me an identity outside the realm of football. One of my biggest fears in marrying Tony was I would lose myself to who he was and how the world perceived professional athletes and their families to be. I never wanted to be just "Tony Berti's wife" and it was important to me I maintain some degree of independence even though football dictated every facet of our life. But following the tumultuous season, I wanted Tony to know, above all else, he was my number one priority and I supported his need to get away from it all for however long necessary.

In January, we made our annual trek to Colorado where I went skiing and Tony went goose hunting. Even though Tony consistently reminded me of the necessity of hunting to keep flocks healthy and populations down, I had absolutely no interest in the activity. I'd been forever turned off after he returned from a day of hunting when we first started dating and kissed me hello with blood on his shirt and feathers stuck to his shoes. He always looked forward to the seasonal hunting trips and blowing the heads off those poor little creatures seemed to relieve much of his end-of-football season anxiety. I'm not sure if quietly sitting in a freezing cold goose blind allowed him the reflective time to relax or if the gun in his hand re-established a sense of control but, either way, he returned with the weight of the season less obvious.

Tony was lured during the Colorado trip to his former high school, Skyview, under the guise of speaking to the student body about motivation. He took to the podium and was shell-shocked after learning he was the guest of honor in a surprise ceremony to retire his #72 football jersey. With several school district administrators and former teachers looking on, Tony was speechless as they presented him with a plaque, bearing the details, which would be prominently displayed at the school. The surprise was the highlight of the trip and the novelty of the situation lifted his spirits.

The subsequent meeting with Ken and our accountant, to discuss finances, eliminated any remaining tension. During the 1996 and 1997 seasons, we paid off all our school loans and debts and managed to put away a substantial amount of Tony's six-figure salary. We liked being on the road to financial security and win or lose, the NFL did provide a comfortable living.

Following the Colorado trip in January, we returned to our apartment in San Diego to attend Super Bowl XXXII, or at least the parties leading up to it. With San Diego as the host city, the Chargers organization was heavily involved in the week's NFL events and fan fare and asked their players to participate. Tony and I volunteered for NFL Commissioner Paul Tagliabue's pet project, Christmas In April. We joined other volunteers in refurbishing a poverty-area home in need of repairs. Chargers snapper, David Binn, and quarterback, Craig "Wheels" Whelihan were on hand with several other players and we primarily painted the outside of the home while skilled volunteers tore out carpeting, replaced appliances and installed a heating system to replace the only existing source of heat, a wood stove in the kitchen.

Just like Phoenix in 1996, the city of San Diego was at a fevered pitch. Every bar and nightclub in the Gaslamp Quarter was overflowing with excited sports fans and all we had to do was show Tony's NFL Player's ID card and we could get in anywhere without cover or waiting in line. At the Sony Play Station NFL Players' Party downtown, we checked in at the VIP area. A booming voice over the loudspeaker then announced Tony's name and affiliation with the San Diego Chargers. It was surreal. Fans, several deep, lined the red carpet walkway and thrust hats, shirts, footballs and even bare arms and shoulders at Tony seeking his autograph. I'm quite certain half of them had no idea whom he was. But, it didn't seem to matter. He was part of the machine and they wanted a piece of him. The scene was invigorating and I couldn't help but get wrapped up in Tony's perceived importance. It was the biggest ego stroke I ever felt and I grabbed his hand as we strutted down the aisle as they announced the next player to arrive.

At the NFL Experience, we ducked in and out of exhibits meant to entertain football fans of all kinds. They could throw or kick a football like a professional, tour displays, play video games, get autographs and spend the whole day checking out booths designed to promote, educate and cater to the football enthusiast. The Chargers' display featured a huge mural of the entire team. Life-sized, cut-outs allowed children and adults alike to stand amidst the players and marvel at their size. I took a photo of Tony and Greg Engel standing next to their life-size, cardboard likenesses.

After days on the Super Bowl party circuit, we once again elected not to attend the game. Instead, we went to a Super Bowl party at the home of my friend who owned the telecommunications company, which so generously bailed us out on the Chargers toy drive. The next day we returned to Las Vegas.

Back at the town home we purchased just prior to the start of the 1997 season, we quickly realized how much we liked the busyness of the 24-hour city, the mild weather and the comfort of knowing we had a refuge from San Diego and the constant scrutiny associated with a losing team. Our intended two-month, off-season hiatus in Las Vegas was expanding indefinitely and we made no immediate plans to return to San Diego.

In February, we attended a Las Vegas boat show and going into it I knew we would probably leave with a boat. Tony spent much of his adolescence on small lakes in Colorado and he couldn't escape the desire to have his own boat. Lake Mead was one of the reasons we elected to buy in Nevada and he eagerly researched boats on the Internet in anticipation of getting one. At the show, one of the boats caught Tony's eye the minute we walked into the convention hall. The Sunesta 252 sport deck had all the bells and whistles. The canvas top was up, the blender plugged in and the table set. Tony was sold the minute we climbed on board. The salesman asked if we had any questions and Tony asked a number of them. The salesman was friendly but I could tell he didn't really expect to sell the beautiful 25-footer. Tony calmly asked the price and then we headed off to check out some of the other offerings.

But, Tony was already sold and I knew he was aching for me to buy into the idea. After a few minutes of him half-heartedly looking at another boat, I told him he earned the boat and if he wanted it, he should go for it! He smiled big and made a bee-line back to the Sunesta. On the way, he informed me I would be the "hammer" and handle the negotiations. We agreed on a spending limit and I approached the same salesman as before. I think he thought we were going to ask more questions about the boat, but the first words out of my mouth were, "Are you a Chargers fan?" He reluctantly said "Yes" and then I threw out the football card. It was another perfect opportunity to use Tony's celebrity to our advantage.

I explained Tony played for the Chargers and we wanted to purchase the boat. Obviously excited, the salesman haphazardly flipped through the stack of papers on his clipboard several times before getting flustered and stumbling over his words as he reiterated the sales price. He had no game face and I low-balled the quoted price by several thousand dollars and maintained the price was out the door with tax and licensing. He said he needed to call the owner of the dealership as he jumped down from the boat and literally ran off into the crowd. Tony began opening doors, lifting seat cushions and pushing buttons. When the salesman returned a few minutes later, he quoted us an out-the-door price not far from our original offer and Tony shook hands to seal the deal.

We named her the Water Buff and within days, a freshly painted cartoon buffalo, sipping a cocktail through a straw, adorned the stern. Tony came up with the name but I insisted if the boat's mascot was going to be reminiscent of Tony's days as a Colorado Buffalo, then the buffalo's shorts had to be green and gold to symbolize my alma mater of Colorado State. He relented because our collegiate rivalry ran deep only one day a year when the teams met up on the football field in the fall. That green and white boat, with a giant buffalo on its ass-end, hitched to Tony's big, green pick-up was a sight to behold parked in front of our tiny town home.

During the boat show weekend, my parents arrived in Las Vegas to spend a few days with us and were in awe of the incredible housing values in the Vegas valley. They extended their stay by several days and purchased a new home under construction. My dad's job required him to travel extensively and so he had the luxury of living anywhere and still maintaining his employment. Believe it or not, he determined taking a flight from Las Vegas to San Jose and then catching a cab into Silicon Valley would take less time than his regular 45-mile commute once a week into the office from their home in Livermore. I had not lived in the same city as my parents since they departed Colorado for California eight years earlier and I was excited to have them moving so close. And, the best part about their new house was the gated RV parking perfect for storing our new boat.

At the end of February, Tony and I once again indulged ourselves in off-season traveling by joining Ken Ready at his Second Annual Player's Travel Escape in Maui, Hawaii. The tropical trips were always first class all the way and we loved spending a week on the beach with other ball players from around the country. The planned activities often inspired the guys' competitive spirit as they vied for prizes in the beach Olympics or sand castle building contests.

But, mostly, it was a chance to have fun, visit with friends and relax with people who shared our intimate knowledge of the football profession.

We spent much of the week in the water including a wonderful evening whale-watching on a huge catamaran after one of the money managers on the trip footed the bill for the first thirty of us who signed up. Player Darryl Gardner got the photo opportunity of a lifetime when a humpback whale and her calf swam within inches of his feet as he dangled them off the back of the boat. It was on this trip, I coerced Tony into taking a Discover Scuba Diving course at the resort pool. I took a diving class in college for physical education credit but never completed my open water dives for full certification. Tony loved the water and was certainly game to give diving a try.

Upon completion of our class session in the pool, we dove our first open water dive from the beach shore adjacent to the hotel. We saw huge lobsters and sea turtles and could hear the sounds of whales bellowing in the distance. When we surfaced, Tony was hooked. He fell in love with the sport and a new passion was born. He had every intention of getting fully certified the minute we got back to San Diego.

In the mean time, we returned to Las Vegas and spent the entire month of March and most of April out on the Water Buff. Tony effectively put the 1997 season behind him and was prepared to return to San Diego for spring football practice at the end of the month.

Following those practices, Gilbride met with each of the players to discuss their standing with the team. Tony was told that based on his previous year's performance, he would have been cut except for his guaranteed contract. Gilbride revamped the offensive line by signing players John Jackson, an eleven-year veteran tackle from the Pittsburgh Steelers, Roman Fortin, an eight-year veteran center from the Atlanta Falcons and Aaron Taylor, a five-year veteran guard from the Green Bay Packers. Gilbride told Tony he would find himself in a backup role in 1998 and see little playing time as long as he was the coach. Tony was understandably pissed off and his feelings of dislike for Gilbride quickly turned to hatred. Tony was well aware he hadn't played exceptionally well in all the 1997 games, but he refused to take the sole blame for an ineffectual offensive line. Besides, the offensive line couldn't be the lone source of failure for the lousy 4-and-12 finish to the season. Tony tried to remain positive about his career with the Chargers but with an egotistical ass like Gilbride at the helm, it was difficult.

Water activities seemed to calm Tony's anxiety and so, in May, we gathered our friends, family and the Water Buff and headed south for the Berti's Second Annual Lake Havasu Adventure. Then, it was off to San Diego for much anticipated beginner and advanced scuba diving classes. Tony was determined to take it as far as he could go and wanted to dive twice a day. To keep up with him in the cold Pacific waters off southern California and the Coronado Islands, I took an additional class to become certified as a dry-suit diver. The new—found hobby certainly took Tony's mind off his football troubles and it was something different we enjoyed doing together.

But, by June, I was water logged and happy to be heading to Colorado for CU's Alumni Weekend where Supreme Court Justice Byron "Whizzer" White, Colorado's first football All-American, was to be the first inductee into CU's Athletic Hall of Fame. I was obviously unfamiliar with his football achievements from 1937, but, in a strange coincidence, I'd met him during a school-sponsored trip to Washington D.C. in ninth grade. One of the trip's chaperones got us into the Supreme Court Chambers and Justice White, eager to greet our group from his home state of Colorado, shook hands and talked about his experience sitting on the bench of the U.S. Supreme Court. In ninth grade, I didn't realize what an honor it was to meet someone so accomplished. However, at the CU ceremony, I commented on meeting him in the Capital years earlier and he shook my hand and laughed. The honor of meeting him was not lost on me again.

After the Colorado trip, Tony and I flew to the thriving metropolis of Grand Island, Nebraska; home of Chargers defensive tackle John Parrella. Every year, John sponsored a football camp to benefit his local YMCA. He gathered players from all over the country to teach skills and techniques to kids. Don Gregory, one of the Chargers scouts, and Tony were happy to support John's cause and participate in the event. We were close with the Parrella family and going into the 1998 season, the Parrella's and the Bennett's were the only remaining members of our original circle of friends still with the Chargers.

We returned to San Diego just prior to the start of the 1998 football season and spent our last free week diving and taking a medic first-aid class to further our scuba diving certifications. All the diving had honed Tony's cardio abilities and he was ready to handle the physical rigors of football season. But, mentally, he never before experienced a season like 1997 and the severe frustration of lousy coaching, his inconsistent play and the losing 4-and-12 record all taxed his confidence. He was worried about Gilbride's impending training camp and I think he took the first-aid class just to keep his mind off it. Gilbride had alienated the players on the field and his wife had certainly alienated their wives in the stands. I, too, was concerned about Gilbride's antagonistic attitude and wondered if Tony's previous run-in would supercede the fresh start. If Gilbride failed to evaluate the lost season, change his tactics and improve his own attitude, gaining the respect of his players would be extremely difficult and winning games virtually impossible.

Unfortunately, training camp in 1998 began the same way it had the year before. Despite the departure of George DeLeon and the addition of seasoned offensive line coach Joe Bugel, the fourth o-line coach in as many years, the players were immediately in full pads and going at full throttle. Tensions were high and the full contact practices only added to the strain. I attended several of the first week's practices and felt the tension extend right into the stands as the usually jovial training camp crowd murmured quietly, lowered their heads at various plays and showed no signs of being impressed by what they saw.

Near the end of the first week, Tony took a rough hit to the shoulder during the morning practice and was unable to lift his arm above his head. He called me on his way to having an MRI to determine the extent of the damage. I'd grown accustomed to his constant football-related aches and pains and he always assured me they were part of the game. But, the call shocked and scared me. He told me to calm down and not worry. Even if he needed surgery, the procedure was no big deal. But, I wasn't so sure. You never want to see someone you love hurt and while I'd been through ankle and knee sprains, broken fingers, cuts and intensive bruises; this was more serious.

The MRI revealed a minor tear to the rotator cuff caused by a bone spur from a previous shoulder surgery in high school. While painful, the injury was relatively minor. Tony was given the choice of having surgery to repair the damage and returning after four to six weeks of rehabilitation, sometime around the third game of the regular season, with approximately 80% strength or he could elect not to have surgery and undergo injections and rehabilitation for three to four weeks to reduce the swelling. Putting off the surgery would allow him to return to the field sooner. However, it would negatively impact his performance and further injury requiring more intensive surgery could result.

The doctors were fairly certain that, with surgery, Tony would be ready to play by the third regular season game with little risk of additional injury. At the doctors' and team trainers' urging, Tony agreed it was better to sit out a few weeks during pre-season than miss part of the crucial regular season and risk doing more severe damage. We discussed the procedure over the phone and he tried to calm my fears about the impending surgery. Injuries were always part of the game but I still worried about the whole process.

First thing the next morning, a trainer took Tony to the private orthopedic facility for surgery. By the time I arrived, I was a basket case. In the prep room, I began crying adding obvious anxiety to the already stressful situation. Tony told me I was freaking him out and if I couldn't get it together I should go home. By the time they wheeled him into the operating room, he was consoling me. I knew he was in good hands with qualified doctors and with one nurse for every patient I should have been more at ease with the situation. But, I wasn't and I left the facility to pull myself together.

When I returned early in the afternoon, Tony was already in recovery and his shoulder was rehabilitating on a passive movement machine. The machine was slowly moving his arm up and down to varying degrees and a cooler at his side continuously pumped ice-cold water into a pack wrapping his shoulder and arm. Coming out of the anesthetic he'd been combatant so they sedated him and he was pale and out of it.

As expected, the injury was minor. They fixed the tear and removed the bone spur, which initially caused the damage. Within twenty-three hours, he was released to recuperate at home.

Tony's rehabilitation, which began only hours after surgery, continued for the next four weeks. I think it was helped along by his intense desire to rejoin the team out of fear the injury would do further harm to his already threatened career. He was regaining strength at a rapid pace and the doctors enthusiastically expected him to be able to play by the first game of the season, if necessary. He wouldn't be at full strength but he'd be capable of playing. He was proud of himself for rehabbing so quickly and working through the pain.

On Monday, August 25[th,] 1998, Tony was cleared by the doctors for limited practice including warm-ups and non-contact drills. When he took to the field to stretch with the team for the first time in a month, Kevin Gilbride walked over to him and asked what he was doing on the field. He barked that Tony couldn't be there and needed to go see Bobby Beathard immediately.

To Tony's astonishment, Gilbride had placed him on the Injured Reserve list for the rest of the year which meant, despite Tony's return to health, he would not be permitted to play, practice, attend meetings or step foot on the playing field for the rest of the year. Before it even began, the season was effectively over for Tony and he was devastated. It was a personal shot and we knew it. Gilbride was intent on getting Tony off his roster no matter what and he'd done it.

Tony and I discussed the 1997 season to death and analyzed everything that happened during the previous 18 months from his level of play to my continuous conflict with Gilbride's wife,

Debbie. I worried my pissing contest somehow affected Gilbride's decision to put Tony on Injured Reserve. After much debate, we decided regardless of what prompted the decision, whether personal or professional, the deed was done and so was the season.

I was surprised General Manager Bobby Beathard allowed Gilbride to make such a ridiculous decision. The move was of no benefit to the team. Tony was ready and able to play and the organization had to pay him his million dollar salary whether he sat on IR or saw action on the field. It was a decision, which made no sense. The more I thought about it, the more I believed Gilbride took advantage of the Injured Reserve option and used it in a way never intended. It was just another decision detrimental to the team and, of course, Tony and his career.

Unfortunately, Tony wasn't the only player to have trouble with Gilbride. Back-up quarterback, Casey Weldon, a seven-year veteran in the League, had spent time with the Philadelphia Eagles and Tampa Bay Buccaneers before playing in San Diego. Rumor had it Casey came to practice and was overrun by media wanting to know what he thought about being cut from the team. It wasn't unusual for a player to learn he'd been cut from the media, but Casey hadn't heard a thing before showing up at practice. Once in the building, Gilbride called him into his office and reportedly belittled Casey by telling him he displayed the worst case of quarterbacking Gilbride had ever seen. After the extensive verbal beating, Casey left the facility questioning his longevity in the League and feeling smaller than small. Ironically, he signed with another team shortly thereafter.

Tony found being placed on the Injured Reserve list one of the most horrific experiences of his professional career. It's one thing to be place on IR if you're actually hurt and need the time to rehabilitate and recoup. But, it's something completely different if you're healthy and only being placed there in spite. The biggest problem with being healthy on IR was once the doctors cleared Tony to play, he no longer needed rehabilitation. So, it was no longer necessary for him to go to the facility to see the trainers and he wasn't permitted to interact with the team in a professional capacity in any way. I still don't understand the logic behind the segregation but I suppose IR could have provided a loop hole for teams to hide developing players. If the players were permitted to do everything with the team, they could learn the team's system without taking up one of the valuable 53 roster spots. Because there's no limit to the number of players a team can place on Injured Reserve, they could have feasibly kept additional players under contract by putting them on IR.

Tony's IR experience was defeating and his bonds with the other linemen slipped away because he was no longer privy to the locker room chatter, the required meetings or the daily practices and work outs. Gilbride didn't permit IR players to travel with the team to away games and Tony, still under contract with the team, felt like a non-entity isolated and in limbo. I don't know if Gilbride's IR was representative of other IR experiences around the League but, in San Diego, the IR players were invisible.

At first, Tony tried to stay involved with the team. We attended the next home game because Tony thought it would be fun to sit in the stands, eat a hotdog and have a beer. In all his years of playing football, he'd never before been to a professional game as a spectator. We arrived ninety minutes before kick-off and sat in the family section. I was surprised when no one asked why Tony was sitting in the stands. But, then again, Gilbride had shuffled the roster so much I barely knew any of the family members sitting around us. To be honest, I didn't want to talk to anyone anyway. I didn't have anything nice to say about the organization or the coaches. I finally understood the social dynamics, which so confounded me back in 1995.

Just prior to half time, Tony confided he couldn't hide his unhappiness with not being on the field. We left early and went home. The following week, we watched the game on television. The week after that, Tony went scuba diving during the game.

Each Sunday thereafter, he woke up in a bad mood. Unable to deal with the frustration of being forced out of the game, he began scuba diving every Sunday and all during the week. He left early in the morning and returned late in the afternoon. He needed something to hold onto and diving seemed to fill the time when he normally would be playing. He logged over sixty dives during the remaining months of football in '98. I was glad he had something to take his mind off the situation. But, I felt like I was walking on egg shells all the time. I'd quit my job at SeaWorld at the end of 1997 and I had nowhere to focus my energy. I liked diving but not that much and Tony was in his own world. The mere mention of football darkened his mood and so we simply didn't talk about it.

To cope with my own sense of isolation, I began volunteering at the Davis/Grossmont Family YMCA near our apartment in La Mesa. When I first called to inquire about opportunities, the receptionist asked if I was looking to fill court-ordered community service. I explained I was not but rather a Chargers wife seeking information. The girl took my name and number after explaining the extensive volunteering process necessary to work at the facility. But, I wasn't interested in going through the training or formal channels to volunteer for only a few months.

About ten minutes after I hung up the phone, the volunteer director called me back to invite me to the facility for a meeting. My status as a player's wife superceded their protocol and I found myself on the auction committee for their upcoming annual fundraiser. I spent the next month stuffing envelopes and approaching businesses for donations. My tenure was successful and they invited me to stay on as a volunteer. I was so happy to have something to fill my days.

Midway through the 1998 season, the Chargers fired Kevin Gilbride. The news spread amongst the players faster than any gossip ever had. Our phone rang off the hook with people wanting to know if we'd heard the great news. The team seemed to breathe a collective sigh of relief and Tony's burden disappeared. A small contingent of former and current players headed out to dinner in celebration of his firing. Several bottles of wine marked the special occasion and we laughed when we heard through the grape vine ballsy Casey Weldon had called Gilbride and left a fitting message on his answering machine. The message said something to the effect that his firing must have been the result of the worst case of coaching anyone had ever seen. I don't know if that's exactly what was said or if it's even true, but I've told that story a hundred times and each time I love it more. I hope it is true because I can't think of a better way to kiss Gilbride goodbye.

Quarterback coach June Jones was named interim head coach and with eight regular season games remaining, the Chargers started hinting Tony might be released and permitted to go to another team where he could feasibly play out the rest of the season. We were really excited by this news. It was a chance to play and Tony would be released from IR and the remaining year (1999) of his contract with the Chargers. We preferred to stay on the West Coast close to home but we were open to anything. At that point, there were no drawbacks to leaving San Diego behind. The bitter events earlier in the season guaranteed any loyalty we once felt toward the Chargers was long gone. We were willing to go anywhere the Chargers worked a deal as long as Tony received all of his guaranteed salary for 1998.

At first, the Chargers wanted Tony to simply injury settle. In exchange for an agreed upon amount of money, Tony would hold the Chargers harmless for his injury and they, in turn, would release him from his contract. But, we refused. Tony had a guaranteed contract and we were not going to take less than the full contracted amount from the Chargers. After everything we'd gone through, we felt they owed us. But, they kept dangling the carrot that if Tony would just take less, then he would have the chance to re-sign somewhere else and maybe make up the difference. But, maybe was the optimum word. We were not going to give up guaranteed money for a maybe. The turn Tony's career had taken might mean he would never have the opportunity to see that kind of money again.

But, the Chargers needed to unload Tony's salary to free up cap room and sign players to add depth to Gilbride's depleted ranks. So, they asked Tony if he would be willing to release them from the guarantee if they could find a team willing to pick up the remaining amount of the million dollar contract. It was the best case scenario. Tony would sign with another team, have the opportunity to play out the remaining games of the 1998 season and receive his full salary.

The Chargers shopped Tony around to NFC teams. But, that late in the season, it was difficult for any team to find salary room to accommodate the remaining $400,000 on Tony's contract. Seattle was very interested, but Bobby Beathard was hesitant to send Tony to an AFC team. It would look pretty bad if the Chargers released him and he came back with Seattle to kick their ass in the same season. They kept looking elsewhere to make the deal.

Unable to find a team in the NFC, the Chargers were desperate. In a financial bind, they allowed Tony's agent, Neil Schwartz, to attempt to coordinate a deal. Within 24 hours, Neil had Tony basically signed, sealed and delivered to the Seattle Seahawks. While Tony was diving to escape the stress of the situation, I personally assured Seattle Seahawk's General Manager, Randy Mueller, via a three-way call with Neil, Tony was 100% healthy and incredibly eager to see time on the field. I explained the whole absurd Injured Reserve situation and he was keen to have Tony join the team still competing for a play-off berth.

When Tony returned from his dive, he was elated to hear of the impending signing. Neil said Seattle was a done deal as far as he was concerned. It was November 5th, 1998, and Tony packed his bags as we waited for the phone call to confirm the deal was done. He'd be on the next flight out and he needed to be prepared to spend the next five to six weeks in Seattle.

But, two days passed and the deal still wasn't signed. Neil and Tony were in an uproar over the delay as the Chargers claimed Bobby Beathard couldn't be reached to finalize the deal. At 10:00 p.m. on the second night, the phone rang and we were informed Bobby had nixed the deal at the last minute. He didn't want Tony going to an AFC team the Chargers still had on the schedule in only a few weeks. Tony was angry, Neil was angry and certainly the Seahawks were angry. The Chargers started the ball rolling with Tony and then, once again, screwed him over. The whole ordeal was bogus and we were happy when the *San Diego Union-Tribune* picked up on the story and made the Chargers look like the chumps they were. The paper correctly laid out the scenario and painted a pretty good picture of the screw job Tony was getting.

Two weeks later, Bobby called Tony to inform him the Chargers wanted the Seattle deal done. Tony phoned Neil and Neil immediately phoned Bobby to read him and the Chargers the riot act about what went on the last time. Bobby promised the deal would go through. I cancelled our Thanksgiving plans with my family and phoned my good friend and former Chargers teammate Susan May to tell her of our impending arrival in Seattle. She graciously invited us for Thanksgiving and I was comforted in knowing we were going to a team where we knew several of the players and their wives. At 2:00 a.m. on Thanksgiving Day, we arrived in Seattle with two suitcases of personal items for the remaining weeks of the season. The team put us up at the Embassy Suites for a few days while we secured a furnished corporate apartment. For transportation, we rented a car.

Shortly after getting settled, someone from the organization's front office called to invite us to the team's annual Christmas party. The caller even inquired as to whether or not we had any children because the team was giving gifts based on the child's age. I was immediately impressed with the team. The Chargers had done so little for the families, Seattle's Christmas party was a welcomed change. We attended the affair and were in awe of the quality of the event and the attention to detail. The food was plentiful and there was an open bar. Each table was decorated in the Christmas theme and a band entertained the crowd. Santa Clause handed out gifts to a line of eager children next to a tiny buffet set-up specifically for the kids. We felt quite comfortable sitting at a table of ten and mingling with Seattle Seahawk players and former CU teammates Mike Pritchard and Christian Fauria and their wives Louisa and Rhonda. It was a new start in spite of the Chargers ridiculous run-around.

Unfortunately, over the next few weeks, Seattle didn't offer Tony the playing opportunities we hoped for. Why the management vied so hard to get Tony there was a mystery. After being told he would start on the offensive line as soon as possible, he never put on his #72 Seahawks' uniform. He remained inactive for the remainder of the season, only seeing time on the field during practice. Seattle's failure to incorporate Tony into the line didn't make sense. They were paying him a lot of money to stand on the sidelines and, once again, we were left to speculate about the situation. Perhaps part of the problem was Head Coach Dennis Erickson and his coaching staff already anticipated being fired at the end of the season. Maybe it was because the Chargers delay lasted long enough for the Seahawks to be knocked out of play-off contention and Tony's anticipated contribution was inconsequential. Maybe the coaches felt loyalty to the existing guys on the team. Maybe, three months off the field had affected Tony's level of play. At that point, it was hard to say. Players could drive themselves crazy trying to figure out why coaches did the things they did and still never determine concrete reason for their actions.

While we were disappointed in the outcome with the Seahawks, one huge benefit came from our brief time spent in Seattle. By signing with them for the remainder of the 1998 season, Tony's final contract year with the Chargers (1999) was null and void. Seattle owned him only until mid-February when Tony would become an unrestricted free-agent able to negotiate a deal with whomever he wished. We rode out the remaining games in Seattle, collected our paychecks and flew home to Las Vegas with another football season behind us.

Chapter XII

Fumble

1999

No longer linked to the Chargers or needing a residence in San Diego, we terminated our month-to-month apartment lease and moved all the contents to storage in Las Vegas before making our annual January trek to Colorado to visit Tony's family and meet with Ken to go over budgets and financial strategies for the coming year. Neil felt strongly Tony would be courted by several teams once free-agency began in February and we looked forward to choosing our new team.

The Seahawks tendered Tony a one-year contract to stay in Seattle and Neil also spoke with the Detroit Lions, Pittsburgh Steelers (Kevin Gilbride went to Pittsburgh as the Offensive Coordinator) and Denver Broncos. When Neil mentioned Denver, Tony and I got very excited at the prospect of playing back home where we had lots of friends and knew the city well. We both wanted Tony to sign with the Broncos and we never gave another thought to any of the other teams.

Initially, the Broncos offered Tony a long-term contract but the financial terms of the deal weren't acceptable to us. Should Tony end up starting as the Broncos projected, he would be locked into the four-year deal, which paid not much more than the League's minimum salary per season. Signing the deal seemed unwise and we countered with a two-year deal for the same sum of money. The Broncos then countered with a one-year contract for the League minimum and a small signing bonus. We should have reconsidered the other interested teams at that point. But, we were so wrapped up in the idea of playing in Denver for the back-to-back Super Bowl champions we failed to look at the big picture. We signed the one-year deal for $400,000, which included the four-year veteran minimum salary of $375,000 and a $25,000 signing bonus. Agreeing to the minimum salary was risky but the contract included up to $900,000 in playing time incentives. If Tony participated in just 1% of the offensive plays he would receive an additional $150,000. Then the scale graduated until, if he participated in 95% of the offensive plays, he would receive an additional $900,000, bringing his total salary to over $1.4 million for the year; the exactly amount Tony would have received by playing out his final contract year with the Chargers.

We were elated to return to Colorado and we believed the Broncos when they said Tony had an excellent shot at securing a starting position on their offensive line. The up shot, Tony would be replacing right tackle Harry Swayne, who left the Broncos after the two Super Bowl wins to sign a mega contract with the Baltimore Ravens. He was the same Harry Swayne Tony, as a younger player, replaced in San Diego.

Four days after signing with the Broncos in Denver, we departed for Ken's third annual travel escape. The 1999 cruise took us to Barbados, St. Lucia, St. Thomas, St. Kitts and St. Maarten where we intended on diving. Ken's players could extend the travel invitation to anyone they wished and it wasn't unusual for the ball players to bring their kids, parents, brothers, or friends on the getaway. Tony and I always had such a great time on Ken's annual trips we invited my parents, my sister, Audra, and her friend Terry, Tony's sister, Lori, and his aunt Mary to join us.

I think everyone thoroughly enjoyed themselves. Though, I have very few photos taken by the ship's staff to prove it. Every time we went to check out the on-board photo kiosk of photos for sale, there were never any photos of the ball players on display. Like the other passengers, the ship's photographers were taking our pictures as we disembarked to go into a port, or at the formal

Captain's Dinner or even just poolside. Because, I'm the photography buff in the family and typically behind the camera, I counted on the ship's photographer to provide my keepsake photos proving I was actually there. Several trips to the kiosk failed to yield any photos and many people in our group were wondering what was becoming of our pictures. After the ship's photographer gathered the entire group of ball players on the grand staircase for a photo, the ship couldn't print the pictures fast enough to satisfy demand. Ken discovered the other passengers were removing the photos from the display board and buying them as souvenirs before we had the chance. Ken was furious the cruise line didn't have a policy to discourage the practice and ordered the ship to stop openly selling the players' photos immediately. From then on, our photos were kept behind the kiosk desk and we simply asked for them in order to make a purchase. The whole idea of strangers buying our vacation photos before we ever even saw them struck me as absurd and very funny.

Tony and I planned on diving in Key West and visiting my Aunt Sonja, Uncle Eddie and other extended family members in Sarasota, Florida, once the ship returned to port. Unfortunately, the airline lost our dive bag somewhere between Puerto Rico and Miami and the entire first day was shot as we waited for them to locate our gear. Tony's size required custom equipment so we didn't have the luxury of heading to the local dive shop and renting what we needed.

The next day, our gear finally arrived at the hotel and Tony got to dive a wreck called the Eagle Ray with my cousins, who drove down from Sarasota to meet us. But, the following morning, Tony woke up with a severe eye infection. We had to drive 45 minutes north to Marathon to find an ophthalmologist. She put an end to our diving plans by recommending Tony wear dark sunglasses and stay in the hotel room with all the blinds closed because the steroid drops prescribed would make him light sensitive. It was during that time in the darkness we began seriously considering the idea of starting a family.

Early in our relationship, we discussed wanting two children, preferably boys. Growing up, I was more tomboy than girly-girl and dealing with dolls, little frilly dresses, and puberty made me nervous. Tony liked the idea of boys because he grew up with a sister and two stepsisters all very close in age. Once, when they were young, the girls got upset with him, tied him up with the phone cord and whacked him in the head with the telephone receiver. He never forgot the incident and never wanted to be outnumbered again. He may have had a rough time in the house full of girls, but the experience taught him more about women's issues than even I care to know.

But seriously, while we preferred to raise sons, we knew we'd be just as happy with daughters. Tony and I even discussed the name Kaitlyn Frances should we ever have a girl. We both liked Kaitlyn and Frances honored my dear paternal grandmother who passed away when I was thirteen. Boys' names, however, were more difficult to choose because Tony associated every potential name with a face from his years of playing football. There was no one name we both liked and a long way from actually having a baby, the name game seemed silly any way. But, we did decide having been together for five years and married for two, March would be a good time of year to get pregnant because the pregnancy would coincide with football and the baby would be born at the end of the season leaving Tony plenty of free-time with the baby and me. Tony jokingly boasted of his potent manliness but was truly convinced I'd get pregnant right away. Based on some of my friends' experiences, I thought it would take some time.

When we returned from the Florida trip, the Broncos strongly suggested Tony move to Denver during the off-season and participate in the team's workouts at their facility. But, we weren't going to uproot the family and move to Colorado year-round based on a one-year deal. We liked living in Las Vegas and compromised, instead, by renting a corporate apartment for five weeks during March and April, which allowed Tony to participate in the off-season program and be seen at the facility on a regular basis.

Tony worked-out several hours a day at the Broncos facility and while he was gone, I visited with friends, worked-out at a local gym and watched television to occupy my time. Watching television sticks in my mind because I was watching the day of the Columbine High School shootings. Tony called me on his way home and I told him the show I'd been watching was interrupted because of something going on at Columbine. When I think about that apartment, I remember watching in disbelief at the magnitude of the situation. Only when we left Denver to visit the Parrella's in Nebraska during the break in spring camp was I able to turn off the repetitive news coverage.

In anticipation of spending a potentially snowy football season in Denver, we planned the Grand Island trip with the intention of buying a four-wheel drive Ford Explorer from John's car dealership. We spent four days with John, Leigh and their boys and the trip wore me out because when we returned to Denver, I couldn't get enough sleep. Tony attributed every one of my aches, twinges, headaches and naps to being pregnant and I was only a day late when he excitedly suggested we go to the drug store and buy a home pregnancy test. I told him not to get his hopes up because we would have had to of gotten pregnant within a single week of discontinuing birth control and I thought that highly unlikely.

But, we went to the store and I humored him by taking the test as soon as we returned home. I left the tester in the bathroom for the three-minute wait but after about 30 seconds, Tony anxiously dragged me into the bathroom to watch the developing results. After another minute, there was no doubt I was pregnant. I smiled and shook my head confirming he was going to be a dad. We hugged and laughed; giddy with excitement. Still in disbelief, I convinced Tony we should wait to tell anyone until I at least saw a doctor.

The next day, I called the Broncos' player personnel assistant, Jill, to ask about an OB/GYN referral. She recommended a doctors group which had handled many Bronco pregnancies and deliveries. Unfortunately, they weren't able to take me until the end of April, which made keeping the secret that much more difficult. I really wanted to tell my mom and Tony and I agreed since we were heading back to Vegas just days after the scheduled appointment,

I could tell her first face to face. He teased me about giving up the secret but he was the one having a hard time hiding his excitement. He didn't tell anyone but came home with a Broncos newborn outfit from the Denver Bronco store at the facility. When I asked if the outfit was for a girl or boy, he just laughed. Finally, at the end of the month, the doctor confirmed my pregnancy and end-of-football-season due date of December 15, 1999. It was perfect timing and I'd even be able to go to the Super Bowl should the Broncos actually make it three in a row.

The day before leaving Colorado, my best friend since high school, Bunny Reid, met me for lunch at Applebee's. She took one look at my untouched plate of food and pale green face and asked if I was pregnant. Shocked by her skills of observation, my face gave it away. The first to know, she jumped up screaming and rushed around the table to give me a huge hug.

With the spring mini-camps complete, we returned to Las Vegas. After being home only a few minutes, I told Tony I couldn't keep the secret from my parents any longer and when they arrived at the house to welcome us home, I handed my mom the newborn Bronco outfit with a neatly attached ultrasound photo. Her and my dad started to cry. It was a wonderful moment and there were hugs and congratulations all around. Tony then called his parents and sister to tell them the wonderful news. We spent the rest of the day on the phone calling everyone close to us to tell them about the baby.

Within days, Tony was back in the swing of his rigid off-season work-out schedule. He hadn't much cared for the program the Broncos strength and conditioning coach ran in Denver. He got into a better rhythm and experienced better workouts when he was home and able to go to the gym four hours a day, four times per week. But, the Broncos weren't happy about him returning to Vegas. They wanted him at the Denver facility for all of their "voluntary" work-outs. To appease them, he immediately arranged to fly to Denver every Monday during the month of May to participate in the Bronco's 45-minute workouts on Tuesdays and Thursdays. He stayed with his sister, Lori, during the week and returned home to Vegas every Friday. Tony was eager to prove his dedication to the Broncos and get back on the football field but I thought it was absurd the Broncos expected him to move to Denver or travel there weekly for 90 minutes worth of workout time.

At the end of May, we planned our third and final three-day Lake Havasu Adventure. In my first trimester of pregnancy, the trip wasn't nearly as fun as in the past. Sleeping in a tent in 100-degree heat exceeded my threshold for discomfort and I turned green each time they lit up the camp stove or we took a ride in the boat. Tony realized his boating days were numbered for a while and made the best of the trip knowing he'd be winterizing the Water Buff when we got back to Vegas.

Tony resumed his off-season workouts in June and once again began flying back and forth to Denver weekly. I was surprised when he phoned one Wednesday to tell me the Broncos invited him to their Super Bowl XXXIII Championship Ring Celebration the following Sunday and Monday at the Broadmoor Hotel in Colorado Springs. He was very excited because the event was a big deal and his offensive line coach, Alex Gibbs, made a point of telling him to get me out there and attend the party. The June 6th and 7th event was all-expenses paid courtesy of Denver Broncos owner Pat Bowlen and included complimentary spa and golf privileges. I, of course, wasn't going to say no and quickly made arrangements to make the trip.

When we arrived at the impressive, world-class resort, there was a complimentary bottle of wine in our suite, from Mr. Bowlen, welcoming us to the event. Tony was the first free-agent signed by the Broncos in 1999 and his inclusion in the special celebration recognizing the players responsible for winning the Super Bowl the previous year, gave Tony a sense of belonging. It also reinforced our belief that Tony was going to be the starting right tackle.

That evening, the ring presentation was held in one of the ballrooms and it was a full-blown affair with dinner, entertainment and dancing. Tony introduced me to many of the offensive line players and their wives including Dave and Audra Diaz-Infante and Dan and Amy Neil. I also met Matt Lepsis, a former University of Colorado player and Tony's primary competition for the starting right tackle position. Lepsis signed with the Broncos in April of 1997, but was inactive for that entire season. Then, in the spring of 1998, the Broncos sent him to NFL Europe to hone his skills with the Barcelona Dragons. He made Denver's active roster in 1998, but had never started an NFL game. Tony was confident his experience, 30 NFL game starts, gave him the advantage in securing the starting job.

As we mingled at the Ring Celebration dinner, I realized while Tony already knew many of the Broncos players from his collegiate career at CU and previous years in the League, I also recognized a few familiar faces. Broncos' Punter Tom Rouen lived in the same dormitory as I did at Colorado State University. We were friends before he transferred to the University of Colorado and became an All-American. We lost touch until I ran into him several years later at a Denver bar when he first signed with the Broncos and his roommate was then-rookie kicker, Jason Elam. We ran in the same circles for a while but eventually lost touch again. The celebration provided a friendly reunion.

In addition to knowing Tom and Jason, I also had two unique links to former Broncos General Manager, John Beake. His son, Chip, was the quarterback at my high school in Ft. Collins, Colorado, and appeared as a guest on a cable television show I produced as a senior project. The show's subject matter explored how best to deal with stress and expectations in high school. Much of the show's discussion revolved around the potential pressures Chip felt to pursue football because of his father's position in the NFL. He was a junior in high school during the taping and with the conclusion of the project and my graduation, we didn't stay in contact. But, John Beake's brother worked for Kraft Foods in Denver and I dealt with him on a regular basis when planning promotions and advertising for the restaurants and nightclubs. He kept me up to date on Chip as he pursued coaching opportunities overseas with NFL Europe.

We also ran into running back and Super Bowl XXXIII Most Valuable Player, Terrell Davis. Ken Ready handled both Tony and

Terrell's financial matters and Neil Schwartz represented each of them. The connection facilitated a friendship and Tony, as a San Diego Charger, agreed to assist the San Diego chapter of Davis's foundation "TD For Kids" by purchasing 25 game tickets for local San Diego children to attend the Broncos/Chargers game. The irony of Tony's participation in the charitable event was that while he paid for all the tickets, the kids showed up to cheer on Terrell and the Broncos.

Tony's existing relationship with so many of his new teammates had us feeling right at home in the suddenly small world of professional football. At dinner, we sat across the table from the Diaz-Infantes and spent the evening talking like we'd always been a part of the team. The only person quiet at our table was a young player seated to my right without a date. I didn't recognize him but I caught part of a brief table conversation which mentioned the time his father spent playing in the NFL. I didn't learn until after dinner, the quiet guy sitting next to me was Quarterback John Elway's heir apparent, Brian Griese. With Elway's retirement, the weight of the Broncos' bid for a third consecutive Super Bowl championship rested with him and he seemed awfully reserved to fill those big shoes.

Following dinner we moved to the hotel's nightclub where I discovered while dancing with a large circle of ladies I wasn't the only one pregnant. As many as twelve Bronco wives were expecting. Apparently, some celebrating of a different kind took place directly following the Broncos second Super Bowl win. Tony and I left Colorado Springs the following afternoon feeling absolutely high on the Broncos and Tony's opportunity to become part of such a fantastic organization.

We stayed at Tony's sister's house in Denver for a few days before heading to Grand Island, Nebraska, to once again attend John Parrella's annual football camp benefiting his local YMCA. While waiting to board our flight, we ran into Stan Brock. He and Tony bear hugged and jeered at the unexpected reunion. Stan was coaching one of the Arena League football teams and was on a flight layover. There wasn't much time to get reacquainted but it was a pleasant surprise and we promised to stay better in touch. Following the Grand Island trip, we attended a friend's wedding in San Diego and then returned to Las Vegas in anticipation of gearing up for the move to Denver.

An ultrasound early in July confirmed we were having a boy and with the news of a son, Tony not only gloated about his fertility prowess of impregnating me within a week but also his ability to make a man. He jumped on the machismo bandwagon and began quoting a saying John Parrella or Darren Bennett used to say, "It takes a man to make a man." Between John and Darren they had five boys so I guess they were somewhat of authorities on being proud baby boy papas and Tony was eager to join their club.

Once we knew the sex of the baby, I was determined to get the nursery set up before we left for football season. Our son would be with us when we returned and I wanted everything ready to go. We converted what would have been Tony's sports room, if we had ever taken the time to finish it, into a child's nursery. Tony painted the two-tone decor, baby blue on the bottom and pale yellow on the top, while I watched. He put the crib together while I watched and he and my brother, Marc, moved in the furniture while I watched. There just wasn't much I could do at five months pregnant. But, when everything big and heavy was finally in place, I went to work setting up the room for our return sometime in January or February, if we actually made it to the Super Bowl. My mom and dad gave us a cradle when they first learned I was pregnant and we planned to take it with us to Denver. The baby, due to arrive in mid-December, could utilize the cradle until we returned home to the convenience of the full nursery.

With the start of training camp just around the corner, I wanted to be settled into our Denver apartment before Tony reported. I couldn't imagine being pregnant and trying to unpack and get organized with Tony away at camp. Again, we turned to the Broncos' player personnel contact, Jill, for a recommendation. We liked the furnished corporate apartment she recommended and we rented during the spring. But, we wanted something unfurnished and a little less expensive for the season. She referred us to a large apartment complex where several of the Bronco players were living and also provided contact numbers for a moving company to assist with our furnishing and a transport company to move our car. Her help streamlined the moving process and we liked the idea she prided herself on handling player requests for everything from moving services to dinner reservations. It was nice to have a knowledgeable contact person within the organization whose job it was to offer assistance and her help and contacts certainly allowed us to get situated quickly.

Greeley, Colorado, a small city an hour north of Denver, hosted the Broncos training camp. Tony reported in excellent condition and was stronger than he had been in quite some time at a lean and muscular 285 pounds. I think part of his physical strength came from regained mental confidence and the belief he would be the Broncos starting right tackle. As always, he called me every night before he went to bed. During the first week, he was tired but decidedly upbeat. But as the week passed, the sullen tone of his voice indicated things might not be going as well as he hoped. Tony signed with the Broncos because they told us he would be vying for the starting right tackle position. But, he was getting few repetitions in camp and little opportunity to demonstrate his capabilities. If the Broncos were truly looking at him to fill the right tackle position, he should have been seeing most of the reps at practice. But, instead, Matt Lepsis and another player named Trey Teague were spending the majority of practice time at right tackle. Once again, it was impossible to know exactly what the coaches had in mind and I told Tony to stay positive and play his best whenever he got the chance. Perhaps they were temporarily focusing on Lepsis to gage his improvement over the previous year or considering moving Tony to another spot on the line. He was, after all, fully capable of playing tackle and guard on both the right and left side.

But, after only a few more practices, Tony felt certain the Broncos were decidedly set on Lepsis to fill the right tackle position. The Broncos spring rhetoric had us feeling so confident in Tony's future with the team the developments during camp completely blindsided us. Only a month earlier, we pegged Tony as the starting right tackle and now we were worried whether or not he'd even make the team. I wanted to kick myself for buying into the hype again. Neil assured Tony if he played well in the pre-season, got good game film and the Broncos still cut him, he would find himself on another team. But, I hated the thought of it because if Tony were cut and signed elsewhere, he would jet away immediately leaving me solely responsible for orchestrating the move to another city. Six months into my pregnancy, it was a nightmare I hoped would never come to fruition.

Before the first preseason game, Tony and I discussed his Broncos future or potential lack there of. It was looking more and more like he might soon be out of a job and it was the first time I ever heard him mention the word retirement. He always said he hoped to play in the League for ten years and leave on his own terms, but I could tell the feelings of self-doubt were creeping back into his psyche. I tried to remain positive but I knew Tony's career could be in grave danger.

If Tony was relegated to a back up role on Denver's offensive line, he might never step foot on the field during the regular season. Not an ideal situation for an eager veteran trying to reestablish himself. The only hope for Tony to increase his stock as a back-up would be for Lepsis to get hurt or play lousy. Lepsis had never actually started an NFL game before and there was always a chance he'd buckle, lose focus and make game mistakes under the pressure. Tony might then be given the opportunity to step in and shore up the position. But, there were no guarantees and Lepsis appeared solid. If Tony spent the entire season on the sidelines, even his successful play during the pre-season might not convince teams he was starting material and his high minimum salary would preclude them from signing him as a back-up. Back-ups were typically younger guys with less experience and smaller salaries.

Tony had fallen into a very gray area. He was really too expensive to keep as a backup and the Broncos weren't considering him as a starter, which led us to believe Lepsis was probably always their guy. The Broncos were playing a game and we were the pawns.

Tony was signed strictly as an insurance policy in the event Lepsis couldn't handle the starting tackle position. Obviously, in the spring, they weren't absolutely convinced he was ready. But, by training camp, they'd made their choice. He was a younger veteran and cost less money than Tony. He also had a history with the Broncos, who signed him as an undrafted free-agent from Colorado in 1997. He'd already spent two seasons learning the team's system and they were eager to give him the opportunity even though Tony had more experience. The Broncos were loyal to their existing players and that was fortunate for Lepsis. If the San Diego Chargers had been guided by the same philosophy in 1998, Tony may have still been playing there.

Tony claimed the 1999 Broncos' camp was the most difficult training camp he'd ever been too; even more difficult than Gilbride's notorious injury fest in 1997. Every time I spoke with him on the phone, he told me how even the Bronco veterans were complaining about the difficulty of the camp. Veteran players said past camps featured far fewer full-contact drills in full pads. The demands were extremely physical and the pace was exhausting. Tony thought maybe Head Coach Mike Shanahan was busting their asses to prove he was the reason for the Broncos' past successes and not the newly retired John Elway.

At the practices, Lepsis was getting all kinds of accolades and very little criticism. Tony was consistently the odd man out and realized, as the new guy trying to break into the established team, he was never going to catch a break as long as Lepsis showed an inkling of talent. No matter how hard he worked, the offensive line coach, Alex Gibbs, wasn't impressed. But, Tony's play must have been solid because despite the lack of repetitions (practicing of the plays) in camp, he was on the field for much of the pre-season games, which helped him maintain his confidence even with the lack of coaching interest he felt in practice.

Ironically, one of the Broncos pre-season games took Tony, eager to play against his former team, to Australia to play the Chargers in the American Bowl. I don't think the Broncos gave the wives the opportunity to go but at almost seven months pregnant, the thought didn't even cross my mind. I knew what those overseas exhibition schedules were like and I knew Tony would have a difficult enough time without having to worry about me and the baby.

The travel time required, coupled with the extreme time change, made the week-long trip very strenuous. During the 18-hour trip, the team "lost" a day. The players were given sleeping pills ten hours before landing so they could get some sleep and head straight to practice when they touched down. Tony hated those overseas exhibition games because the players never saw anything of the country they were visiting except the hotel, the practice field and the stadium. The trips reeked havoc on them physically and the reason for the games was solely financial. Team owners were paid by the television networks to air the game and the NFL got to promote itself in an overseas market.

In a rare opportunity to break away from the monotonous schedule, Tony appeared on "The Footy Show," a nationally televised Australian sports show, from Sydney, predominantly focusing on Aussie Rules football, which is a cross between rugby and soccer. Tony's appearance was coordinated by Australian-born Darren Bennett, the Chargers punter and former Aussie Rules player. The Footy Show's popularity in Australia was greater than that of The Tonight Show with Jay Leno in the United States and the appearance was the highlight of Tony's trip after the host asked Tony what he liked best about Australia. Having experienced nothing in the country, Tony was caught off guard by the simple question. Instead of mentioning his penchant for diving and the diver's dream of the Great Barrier Reef, he commented on the terrific high-flow showers in the hotel. The host, puzzled for a moment, began to laugh. Over the remaining days in Australia, Tony was approached several times on the street by Sydneysiders inquiring about the lure of the hotel showers. Tony reluctantly explained in his home state of Nevada, water conservation was a key issue and we didn't have the luxury of showerheads raining water like the ones at the hotel. The shower comment was a great conversation-starter with the locals but it was a good thing few of the other players caught the airing of the show or Tony would have found the ribbing over the shower comment extensive.

In addition to seeing Darren Bennett at the show taping, Tony also had the opportunity to hook up with former teammate John Parrella and his parents, Joe and Shirley, for dinner. When we were with the Chargers, I occasionally sat next to Joe on game days as he watched John on the field. He never took his eyes off him and he was just bursting with pride. Joe and Shirley often traveled from Nebraska to San Diego to attend the Chargers games and they also traveled to many of the away game cities to watch John play. Tony thought "Big Joe" exemplified the role of a strong and supportive father and when Tony and John developed a close friendship, Joe treated Tony as if he were another of his sons. I wasn't surprised to learn Joe and Shirley traveled all the way to Australia for the game, but I found it funny Tony was spending what little free time he had with his former teammate.

Immediately following the game, the team boarded the plane to return to the States. I can't remember who actually won but it didn't matter because pre-season games never counted in the record books. What mattered most was Tony saw playing time and secured game film to get him his next job.

Back in Denver, the guys were given two days off from training camp and Tony spent most of it trying to readjust to the significant time change. Then, he once again returned to training camp in Greeley. There were still several weeks of camp remaining when Tony noticed a tinge in his right shoulder similar to the one he'd felt in his left shoulder during the 1998 pre-season in San Diego. Concerned about the soreness, he informed the trainers of his discomfort. They felt it was simply muscle fatigue and encouraged him to ice it and continue practicing. I voiced my concerns but Tony believed what the trainers were telling him despite the increasing soreness. I didn't bug him about it because he was always telling me aches and pains were part of the job and you just had to suck it up. He was pushing himself hard and he didn't want a little muscle fatigue to impact his chances of making the team. He was determined to see action in all five pre-season games and he did.

The night of the final pre-season game, we concluded the evening by having dinner with Dave and Audra Diaz-Infante and several other players. Tony felt his pre-season play had been solid and warranted a spot on the Broncos roster, even if it were as a backup. Dave, also an offensive lineman, had been with the Broncos for several seasons and assured Tony he, too, thought Tony would make the roster. Dave told Tony to stop worrying and Tony seemed to respond to Dave's vote of confidence.

The next morning, September 5th, Tony went to work out as usual at the Broncos' complex. The final cuts were made that morning and when no one called the apartment or approached him as he went into the locker room, he finally felt assured he made the roster. He changed into his workout clothes and, feeling relieved of the burden of uncertainty, began thinking about his chances of again becoming a starter. But, after beginning his weight training regiment, he was pulled aside and told to take his playbook and go see Neal Dahlen, the Broncos' General Manager. Tony's gut hurt as he waited fifteen minutes to collect himself before walking the hall to the office. Neal informed Tony he'd been released and needed to see his offensive line coach, Alex Gibbs.

Alex claimed Tony was being released because the team planned to carry only eight offensive linemen instead of the usual ten. It was risky for a team to carry so few linemen with shoulder and knee injuries prevalent at those positions. But, Alex said the Broncos needed to carry additional wide receivers and the available roster slots had to come from somewhere. After meeting with Alex, Tony was sent to the Broncos head trainer for a medical release.

In the NFL, the team you're signed with is responsible for any injuries you may suffer while under contract with them, so they won't allow you to pursue any other teams until they're released of liability. Teams know time is of the essence when it comes to players finding roster spots elsewhere and so they push the players to sign the waivers fast. The head trainer reminded Tony no team would pick him up if he claimed injury. Wanting to get the hell out of there, Tony signed the medical waiver stating he had no injuries and released the Broncos from any liability despite the soreness in his shoulder. Taking nothing from his locker, that morning was only slightly less bitter than the absolute horror of draft day. He phoned me from the parking lot in disbelief; his voice quivered and shook as he told me the news. I absolutely couldn't believe it. We'd talked about the possibility of him being cut, but I don't think we really thought it was going to happen. After calling me, he called his agent, Neil, and told him to find him another team fast.

We believed the Broncos' stroking and promises and that naiveté cost us in many ways. Before signing the standard seven-month lease (July through January) on the unfurnished apartment in Denver, we inquired about adding a change of employment clause to the lease as a precaution in the event something happened. But, we were assured by the complex manager that they worked with the Broncos players all the time and while they weren't at liberty to change their standard contract, we'd have no problem in the event Tony was cut or traded. The sparsely-furnished, month-to-month corporate apartment we rented in the spring cost $2500 a month and we couldn't justify the expense of staying there for the whole season when renting a regular apartment and completely furnishing it with items in storage from the apartment in San Diego cost half that. Choosing the best financial option, we moved enough items from Vegas to Denver to fully furnish the two-bedroom apartment for the term of the lease thinking we'd be there all season. Financially, it was a big mistake. But, the move was also costly emotionally. The news of Tony being cut from the team was a shock because not only did we move unnecessarily but all our arrangements with local doctors and the hospital where I intended on delivering our son were for naught.

The first thing Tony and I discussed when he arrived back at the apartment was our mistake in electing to sign with the Broncos. As back-to-back Super Bowl champions, they were more interested in tweaking their team than making major changes. We should have kept the emotion of returning to Denver out of the equation when we evaluated their offer. They acquired only four players other than their drafted rookies, which should have indicated to us they were confident in the players they had. In addition, during the off-season, they re-signed linebacker Bill Romanowski, wide receiver Ed McCaffrey and center Tom Nalen to long-term deals worth millions of dollars, which quickly filled up their salary cap. We should have considered all that before we got so excited about returning to Denver. Signing with Denver rather than a team in the midst of rebuilding was a big mistake.

In the midst of the uncertainty, I felt compelled to ask Tony a really difficult question in order to comprehend the magnitude of what transpired. I thought he played well during the pre-season but I needed to know if he thought he played well. He said he had to be honest with himself and his answer surprised me. He felt Alex Gibbs cut him because his play hadn't been stellar and he hadn't mastered the Broncos plays and system as quickly as Alex would have liked. I was stunned by his admission. I wasn't sure if his confidence was so eroded he simply concluded he wasn't good enough to play any more or if the previous shoulder surgery and year away from the game really diminished his abilities. Tony needed my emotional support and at every opportunity I bad-mouthed the Broncos and Alex Gibbs. I couldn't let Tony believe he wasn't good enough to play or he wouldn't be. He needed to turn his angst into animosity. If success is the best revenge, then animosity is the fuel of the fire.

Tony and I phoned our families and a few close friends to let them know about the situation before they read it in the paper the next day. We'd talked up Denver so much in the spring the calls were hard on both of us. Announcing Tony had been fired from his job wasn't easy and the clichés people offered in consoling us didn't make us feel any better. Situations are not always meant to be and things that don't kill you don't always make you stronger. God may close doors and open windows but finding Tony a job elsewhere was going to be difficult. The final cut of training camp was the worst time to be cut. Like the Broncos, all the teams made their final roster cuts that day and selected their final 53-man rosters. If a team wanted to pick Tony up, they would have to let someone else go. That late in the game, most teams weren't willing to take a chance on an unproven player unfamiliar with their system. In addition, if, as a vested veteran, a player with four or more accrued seasons in the League signed with a team after the final rosters were announced, the team could not cut him loose later without paying him his full salary. Younger players with less than four accrued seasons cost less money and teams could cut them during the season without the penalty. Tony was a vested veteran and he was a risky acquisition considering his 1998 surgery and twelve-month absence from regular season play. With tight salary caps, teams were reluctant to sign vested veterans when they could sign younger players for less and cut them without penalty if necessary. We were not in a good situation.

But, two days later we thought we caught a break when Tony flew to Detroit for a physical at the behest of the Lions Head Coach Bobby Ross; former head coach of the Chargers. Tony flew out first class and Coach Ross told him the Lions needed to make a roster move to bring him in. It would take a few days and he suggested Tony be ready to play the following Sunday.

Tony returned to Denver that evening and the next morning, we started making plans to move to Detroit. Once Tony signed the Lions' contract, he would leave on the first available flight and I would be left to handle the moving arrangements. The first thing we did was give our apartment complex 30-days notice as required on the lease. However, despite our Bronco connection, we quickly discovered they weren't going to let us out of the lease as we had been told. Only 45 days into it, we attempted to negotiate with the on-site manager. But, she couldn't remember the verbal agreement we had regarding the out clause should Tony get released or traded and she wasn't interested in making a deal. After the 30-days lapsed, they would do their best to re-rent the apartment but we would be responsible for the entire lease until that happened. I knew we were going to get screwed. The complex was huge and I wanted to know what would keep them from renting every other vacant apartment prior to ours knowing we were financially responsible until they filled the vacancy. Surprisingly, the manager said they had a good relationship with the Broncos and would do their best. There was no doubt in my mind we would have to foot the bill for the entire seven-month lease. To our detriment, we'd foregone the employment clause in writing and, once again, put far too much trust into someone's word. Two other players living in the complex were also cut and received the same load of garbage. I was fuming, but fortunately we had the money to ride out the lease. The other guys were first year players and I'm sure without their NFL paychecks they weren't in financial positions to cover the entire lease term.

After I politely finished telling the manager what I thought of her lease, we phoned the very same moving and auto transport companies, which moved us to Denver only six weeks earlier and got quotes on moving the furniture and Explorer to Detroit. We cancelled the renter's insurance policy, which went into effect 14 days earlier and began making calls to the Detroit area to get information on housing options. Then, I unregistered at the hospital, informed my doctor I was leaving the area and requested copies of my maternity medical records. Within hours, Tony and I were repacking the boxes we stored in the garage. I kept busy because I was afraid if I stopped, I would completely break down and I didn't want Tony to see the true extent of my skyrocketing anxiety. He would only worry about me and the baby and the added pressure would affect his focus in Detroit. After making list upon list of things needing to be done, I called my mom and dad and, as usual, they lent their gracious support by offering to fly out during my planned baby shower weekend in October and lend a hand with the task of moving.

While we waited to hear from Detroit, Denver made another surprising roster move by cutting offensive lineman Dave Diaz-Infante. I'm certain Dave and his wife Audra never expected the Broncos to carry five starters and only two back-ups. The absurd decision was risky and meant the Broncos were either overly confident in their offensive line or completely strapped for roster spots. Their lack of depth on the offensive line could decimate them during the season and I, of course, hoped it would.

Two days passed and we heard nothing from the Detroit Lions.

Sunday came and went and then another couple of days and still nothing. Neil couldn't get a straight answer about the impending signing from the Detroit staff and Tony tried to personally call Coach Ross but his call wasn't returned. Neil shopped him to other teams without luck and we spent the next two weeks in agonizing limbo. Detroit did fly him home coach following his physical and with his shoulder still sore, Tony thought maybe he flunked the Lion's required physical. Coach Ross had been so keen on bringing Tony in we could think of no other explanation for the sudden blow-off. The uncertainty of the situation was almost insurmountable and Tony and I were beside our selves second-guessing whether we should sit tight in Denver or move back to Las Vegas. But, after a few more days, Tony couldn't handle sitting idle in Denver waiting for the phone to ring so we made arrangements to return to Nevada. At least in Vegas, we were home and removed from the constant reminder of football season well underway in Denver.

Despite the continued soreness in his shoulder, Tony adhered to a vigorous work-out and conditioning schedule when we returned home. He wanted to be ready whenever he got the call. But, with each passing day, the likelihood of signing somewhere diminished. Neil kept us abreast of what was going on around the League and what teams were doing and saying but, even with 30 NFL game starts and limited success in Denver's pre-season games, interest in Tony was minimal.

Early in October, we returned to Denver to move our belongings and attend the baby shower my sister, Audra, and friend, Bunny, planned in Colorado. I considered canceling the festivities but everything had been planned since early August and my mom and sister purchased plane tickets to attend the party long before the Broncos cut us lose. They convinced me to go through with the celebration and at the last minute my dad flew in too. Following the shower, they helped us pack the moving truck and clean every inch of the apartment in the hopes of getting our security deposit returned. When we were loaded, my dad and sister flew home. But, I was eight months pregnant, huge and forbidden from traveling by air because our son's head was crammed up under my rib cage and his breach position made sitting upright for extended periods of time extremely uncomfortable. The only transportation home was by car so Tony drove the moving truck and my mom drove our Explorer while I laid out in the backseat with my feet propped up and out the window.

The image of two socked feet rolling down the highway for twelve hours is funny now, but, at the time, the stress, anxiety and costs involved in the Denver fiasco seemed overwhelming. Between the apartment lease and moving expenses, we wasted $25,000 setting up house in Denver for six weeks. The only thing worse would have been if we'd actually moved to the city permanently like the Broncos preferred.

By November, Tony gave up on the notion he was going to get picked up during the season and, with his shoulder still sore, reluctantly agreed to see an orthopedic surgeon about his increasing immobility. It was no surprise when the doctor found damage to Tony's right rotator cuff and recommended the same surgery on the right shoulder as he'd already undergone on the left in 1998. The prognosis solidified in Tony's mind he failed the physical in Detroit and reasoned that was why the Lions failed to sign him as promised. Tony firmly believed he sustained the injury in Denver's training camp and their trainers' insistence it was only muscle soreness coupled with his haste to pursue other teams had coerced him into signing the medical waiver despite the injury. He was a rock with incredibly high pain tolerance. But, when he consistently said something wasn't right with his shoulder, I should have realized he had a significant problem and pushed him to have it checked out before the window to file a grievance against the Broncos closed. Uncertain of exactly when the injury occurred, we had no alternative but to let our personal health insurance pick up the tab for the surgery and rehabilitation.

In mid-November, Tony was referred to an orthopedic surgeon in Las Vegas, one of the sports doctors used by athletes at the University of Nevada-Las Vegas (UNLV), and underwent shoulder surgery for the second time. Once again, I was a wreck. I tried to control my emotions but at nine months pregnant, I already cried at the drop of a hat. Tony reacted calmly and tried to convince me, like the first shoulder surgery, this one on the other shoulder was no big deal.

I accompanied him to the prep room and stayed until the nurse wheeled him off to surgery, which was scheduled to last just over an hour. But, I spent several hours in the hospital waiting room before the doctor finally emerged to talk to me. He showed me graphic pictures of the three metal anchors implanted in Tony's shoulder to assist in the healing process as he explained the damage was more extensive than he first thought. He was unable to determine if the severity of the injury stemmed from the initial tear or was aggravated by Tony's continued workouts but said the rehabilitation period would be substantial.

In recovery and coming out of the anesthesia, Tony, once again, became combatant. Three hundred pounds of flailing muscle was dangerous to him and the nursing staff, so they restrained his arms. The doctor spoke with him about the surgery but in his state, he was unable to comprehend the analysis. He thought the doctors were forced to open him up instead of simply making the three necessary one-inch incisions used in the scope process and he was panicky. He asked me over and over again why they opened him up. I responded each time by saying they hadn't.

When Tony finally shook the affects of the anesthesia and calmed down enough to have the restraints removed, the doctor once again explained what had transpired. Discovering an unexpected tear in the Labrum during surgery, he was forced to repair more damage than initially anticipated, which increased the time Tony spent on the operating table. The more intensive surgery was complex but successful just the same. However, unlike the previous surgery on Tony's left shoulder, the extent of the repair on the right side required his arm remain immobilized in a sling for a minimum of two weeks before beginning any rehabilitation.

Following Tony's emergence from the surgery free of complications, I felt a huge sense of relief. I could turn my attention solely to the matter of our baby's impending arrival, which finally took precedence over football and Tony's career. During the final months of my pregnancy, football had both Tony and I in a tailspin but the events were inconsequential compared to what was about to happen in our lives.

The week following Tony's surgery, I was scheduled for a version procedure to reposition our son. At 37 weeks and two days, he already weighed over 8 lbs. and my doctor was concerned I would have complications if I went full term with a breech baby. If the version failed to turn him around, I'd undergo a cesarean section that very day. Tony and I took a Lamaze class a few weeks earlier just in case but I knew all along a C-section was probable. Tony was big stock and at 6'6" and 300 lbs., his genetics were dictating the size of our baby. Starting at 29 weeks, I measured larger than I should have and subsequent ultrasounds assessing the baby's weight and size confirmed he'd outpaced the growth charts all along.

With the Thanksgiving holiday behind us and my family in town for the weekend, the timed delivery was perfect. But it was strange waddling to the car with suitcase in hand and knowing exactly when we'd meet our son. Even though I knew a C-section was likely, I envisioned the craziness of going into labor and the mad rush to the hospital. But, I wasn't having contractions and my water hadn't broken. As a matter of fact, I felt great; just incredibly nervous.

I told my parents, sister, brother and grandparents not to come to the hospital first thing in the morning because if the version went well and they induced delivery, it would take hours for anything to happen. In the same vein, if I ended up having a cesarean, I assumed it would take hours to get the surgery underway.

You can imagine our surprise when the version attempt failed and my doctor gave the order to assemble the surgical team within thirty minutes. Tony was with me through the grueling attempt to turn the baby but I quickly sent him off to call the family and get them to the hospital when the doctor gave the word. Dressed in scrubs, Tony ran down the hall to make the calls and collect the camera. I didn't want any pictures inside the delivery room but my doctor insisted Tony have the camera in his hands in the event I changed my mind once the baby was born.

The most difficult part of the prep process was the epidural. Usually inserted during a contraction, which I wasn't having, the needle hurt worse than anything I could have imagined. After two failed attempts at the procedure, Tony was grimacing and I was in tears. But, his encouragement got me through the process and after the third attempt was finally successful, they wheeled me into the surgical suite. When the C-section began, I couldn't see a thing but the surgical sheet partitioning me from the rest of my body and Tony sitting off to my right. I was calm until the doctors were finding it difficult to get the baby out and one of them suggested increasing the size of the incision. I started to panic but Tony calmly talked me through it. After nineteen minutes and an enormous amount of tugging and pulling, Brennan, a name Tony discovered in a baby name book, arrived in this world at 8 lbs., 2 oz. He was bruised and battered from the difficulty in getting him out and the nurses appropriately nicknamed him Bruiser. Tony kissed me with tears welling in his eyes and briefly introduced me to our new son before departing for the nursery with Brennan. Things went a little hazy after that.

As Tony joined our pediatrician in examining Brennan while still in the surgical suite, he turned around to check on me. The doctors were closing the incisions and all of my insides were on the outside. Not expecting the show, he nearly fainted. The big tough football player who played through flues and dehydration, compound-fractured fingers and severely sprained ankles and knees was humbled. In recovery, Tony jokingly said after what he just witnessed, he would never complain to me about football injuries again.

Tony, Brennan and I shared the same room at the hospital for five days and poor Tony was forced to sleep on a fold-out chair designed for fathers much smaller than him. Like the beds in Japan, he had to wake up to roll over and his shoulder, less than two weeks out of surgery, was aching from the arrangement. But he was a trooper. My lack of mobility and doses of heavy painkillers had him changing every diaper and bringing Brennan to me for every feeding.

When we returned home, Tony took on multiple roles. On day fourteen and in typical Tony fashion, he began aggressive rehabilitation sessions at the Keith Kleven Institute, a facility known for rehabbing professional baseball players with shoulder injuries, as well as the infamous Mike Tyson. He wanted to regain his strength and mobility as quickly as possible not only to play football again but also to handle his duties as a husband and new father.

While my C-section incision was still tender, he left me breakfast, bedside, every morning before leaving for rehab, so I didn't have to navigate the stairs in our home. He also took over laundry duties and cleaning because, even though my mom was at our home daily, he wanted to prove he could handle everything. He was dedicated to me and Brennan and determined to be the father he never had. Sometimes, early in the morning, I heard him having conversations with Brennan about what kind of father he was going to be and all the things they were going to do together. I realized very quickly Tony was working through some of the issues he had regarding his own father and making sure Brennan knew from the start he would always be there for him. Knowing Tony as I did, I never had any doubts family would always be his number one priority.

I was suddenly grateful Tony wasn't playing football. In the midst of the season, he would have received only one token day off for the birth of his first son and missed so much in those first few months. Instead, he was able to be home everyday by noon and forge a bond with his son most fathers can only dream of. And as for Tony and I, the whole experience brought us closer and made me love him even more than the day I married him.

Chapter XIII

A Season To Remember

2000

At the conclusion of the 1999 football season, Neil once again shopped Tony to prospective teams. But there was little interest in him as a vested veteran with a high minimum salary and two consecutive shoulder surgeries to his name. His marketability was questionable and Neil was convinced Tony needed to show the League he could still play before any teams would take a chance. When Neil suggested Tony play in NFL Europe, formerly known as the World League, we winced at the idea. It was the minor leagues of professional football and Tony was a proven NFL veteran. We had a new baby and Tony wouldn't be comfortable leaving us for the four-month European season. The whole notion seemed ridiculous.

But, as reluctant as we were to even consider the idea of playing in NFL Europe, we quickly realized we didn't have a lot of options. Tony needed to prove he could still play not only to the NFL teams but also to himself and if the only opportunity to get back in came by way of NFL Europe, then we had to consider it an option. Still uncertain of the value of playing overseas and looking for guidance, I suggested Tony call Bobby Beathard to get his thoughts on the potential benefits of playing in NFL Europe. Tony didn't want to call the general manager of the Chargers for advice but he reluctantly did. The secretary said Bobby was in but not immediately available to take the call. Tony left a message but the call was never returned.

Tony didn't want his experience with the Broncos to mark the end of his career, so after fully discussing the situation, we decided we'd do whatever it took to get Tony back in the game, even if it meant a season in NFL Europe. We made the decision to go but Tony still needed to clear the league's strict eligibility limits. At 27 and with multiple NFL seasons under his belt, he was considered too old and experienced to be eligible for the league as an independent player. The league was designed as a developmental league and testing ground for young talent, so to by-pass the restrictions, Tony needed to be allocated to Europe by one of the NFL teams, which traditionally sent their youngest players for the purposes of evaluating potential, gaining on-field experience or washing out bad attitude. By allocating players, NFL teams were able to size up a player they felt had potential but needed a little more work before assigning him a valuable roster spot during the regular football season. If the player didn't pan out in Europe, valuable time and money weren't tied up assessing his performance during the regular season. All NFL teams allocated players to Europe and kept close tabs on their players' progress. So, playing there provided Tony with his best shot at proving he was still a viable asset and deserving of a second chance. But first, he had to sign with an NFL team in order to be allocated.

Once we gave Neil the green light, he went to work finding a team which would agree to sign Tony, allocate him to NFL Europe to get him on a team, and then cut him lose. Whichever team agreed to sign Tony risked little. However, the risk to Tony was great because if the team failed to cut him after the allocation was made, they would own his rights for the next football season. He wouldn't be able to sign anywhere else and the team could use him for camp fodder. Camp fodder describes the players brought in by teams during training camp who don't really have a chance in hell of making the team. They get the crap beat out of them while the team uses them as tackle dummies to simply fill position holes. Tony was adamant about not going through another training camp simply as fodder. So, it was imperative Neil secure a team which would release Tony after he was allocated for the four-month season spanning mid-March to June.

When Neil began the process of finding Tony a team, it was a coincidence he was in Denver on unrelated business and we were there introducing Brennan to Tony's family for the first time and attending our annual end of the year financial meetings. We met up with Neil at Ken's office where he had been on the phone all day trying to get Tony's deal done. The process proved more difficult than Neil thought because teams were hesitant to do what Neil was asking. It wasn't against the rules to sign Tony, allocate him and then release him but it was definitely circumventing the system and its intended participants. The process made teams nervous and one team after another considered the idea and then declined.

Unfamiliar with the whole NFL Europe process, we were surprised to learn the European draft for independent players was within days. While allocated players were generally assigned to one of the six teams, independent players went into a draft. Tony would become an independent player eligible for the draft once he was allocated and released.

With only two days remaining before the draft and without another willing NFL team, Neil asked Tony if, as a last resort, he would consider signing with the Broncos in order to be allocated and eligible to play. Denver would do it as a favor to Neil. Tony reluctantly agreed and the Broncos signed him, allocated him to Europe and released him in less than 36 hours. At the signing, Denver Broncos Head Coach Mike Shanahan told Tony he was glad he could help. I felt no gratitude toward him or the Broncos but I wondered if we would ironically end up in Spain with the Barcelona Dragons where the Broncos' allocated players were sent. I'd never been to Spain before and the idea of spending three months seaside in Europe had a better ring than the other possible destinations with the Frankfurt Galaxy, the Rhein Fire, or Berlin Thunder teams all in Germany. I visited Germany, Italy and France during a family vacation in college and I hoped to have the opportunity to go somewhere new. If the Barcelona Dragons were out as my first choice, then the Scottish Claymores in Scotland or the Amsterdam Admirals in Holland tied for second because of their country's historical significance.

Immediately following the NFL Europe draft, Neil phoned Tony to tell us we'd be spending our spring in Berlin, Germany, playing for NFL Europe's Berlin Thunder. There was no beach but at least I could speak the language. I studied German for six years in school at the behest of my grandmother, Carmen, who immigrated to America from Hamburg, Germany. After being allocated and then released by the Broncos, the Thunder freely drafted Tony from the pool of independent talent. My mom, who urged us to take the opportunity to live overseas, offered assurances that taking a four-month-old baby wouldn't be as difficult as I thought. But, because I was a new mother and didn't have any idea what to expect from the team, the idea of moving to Europe for 14 weeks was daunting. When I became hesitant about going with Brennan, Tony insisted he wouldn't go without us. Convinced it was his only avenue back to the NFL, he looked at the opportunity as a challenging adventure. He'd never been to Europe before and even though he'd visited Japan and Australia in NFL pre-season games, he'd never really seen much outside the United States. He believed the experience was the chance of a lifetime.

When contacted by the head coach, the first thing Tony requested was information for families wishing to travel with the team. Most of the players going overseas were young and unmarried, so the league had no set guidelines or rules regarding the families. The coach said families traveled at their own expense and he didn't have any problem with our family going along. With that said, we began to make arrangements.

My brother, Marc, agreed to stay in our home and housesit. In exchange for free rent for four months, he'd check our mail, pay our bills with checks we left and keep us informed of household needs via e-mail. To pack for the extended stay, I sent Tony in search of the largest duffel bags available, which still fell within airline guidelines. He returned with two gigantic hockey equipment bags, the maximum size allowable on planes without paying additional charges. On the Internet, I checked out monthly temperatures in Berlin and began shopping for appropriate clothing for Brennan and a good German/English dictionary to brush up on my German language skills. Tony's friend, Derek West, played for the Rhein Fire early in his NFL career and had nothing but wonderful things to say about his experience in Germany. He also put us in touch with a couple from his team who took their 10-month-old child overseas for the season. Ironically, they lived in Las Vegas and I called them to inquire about what was available in Germany in the way of baby products. I was pleased to learn almost everything available in the U. S. was also available in Germany. I knew the Germans had babies too but, as a new mom, I was obviously concerned about the lengthy trip.

Prior to departing for Europe with their final roster of players, the six NFL Europe teams met in Orlando, Florida, for a two-week training camp of sorts. I made travel arrangements to depart for Florida two days after Tony reported to the camp and asked my mom to accompany Brennan and me on the trip from Vegas to ease the burden of traveling alone with the baby and luggage for three months abroad. After Tony secured information on the team's Florida to Europe flight, I booked Brennan and me on the same outbound plane. But, I had to guess the date and time of the team's return leg to the United States because their return would depend on whether or not they made it to the championship game. The cost of our two round-trip tickets was a whopping $2500 because the team had purchased all the flight's inexpensive seats. But, despite our concern about budget, I thought it best to travel with Tony and the team as we headed into the unknown.

Brennan, my mom and I arrived at the Colony Plaza Resort Hotel in Ocoee, Florida, an Orlando suburb, on March 20th, 2000. Our room was two floors above Tony's and while the hotel wasn't much to look at, its claim to fame was Walt Disney stayed there for ten months in 1965, while he was scouting land for Disney World. The close proximity to the team and unrestrictive team policies allowed us to join Tony at the team dinners and say goodnight each night before bed. It was a rare treat having such access to Tony during a training camp. It was also nice having my mom's company and help with Brennan while Tony was busy with practices, scrimmages and meetings. At four-months-old, Brennan wasn't yet mobile but that didn't stop him from being the "Go-Go Baby." While Tony was working, we spent three days in Sarasota visiting my cousins, aunts and uncles and during the remainder of the two week vacation, toured MGM Studios, swam in the pool daily and attended Tony's scrimmages.

At one of the scrimmages at the Citrus Bowl Stadium, I noticed Reggie McKenzie standing on the sidelines. His twin brother, Raleigh, joined the Chargers offensive line in 1997 and we'd been introduced to Reggie after one of the San Diego games. He was the Director of Player Personnel for the Green Bay Packers and was checking up on his allocated players. After the short scrimmage, Tony spoke with him briefly, which was the kind of exposure we were hoping NFL Europe would provide.

Ten days into the fun in the sun, my mom returned home to Las Vegas and five days later the Berlin Thunder made their final cuts and announced the team roster. There was little doubt Tony was the starting right tackle. Most of his competition had never stepped on the field during a professional game much less started. He made it look easy and when he became the big fish in the little pond his confidence began to re-emerge. The other players looked up to him and his stories of playing in the NFL only served to wet their appetites for the game.

After fifteen days in Florida, our April 5th trip to Berlin began with a five-hour bus ride from Orlando to Miami. Tony got permission from Head Coach Peter Vaas for Brennan and me to accompany the team all the way. But when we boarded the bus with Tony, I saw a lot of astonished faces. During our stay at the hotel, I met many of the players and even more had seen us around the pool. But, I don't think any of them expected us to be traveling to Europe with them.

At the airport, one of the coaches took our airline tickets and made sure they, along with our luggage, were processed with the team's paperwork ensuring we would be sitting with Tony. The flight was long and with Brennan sleeping most of the way in his car seat, I found myself in need of some relief. I was still breastfeeding and without Brennan eating, I needed to express milk. In the middle of 40 ball players, I turned toward the window and inconspicuously put my breast pump to work. The hum of the flight was just loud enough to drown out the sound and no one seemed to notice. At that moment, I realized the trip was indeed going to be an adventure for all of us.

When our flight finally landed in Berlin, we were required to pick up our luggage, two gigantic hockey bags, three large suitcases, one carry-on, one backpack, one diaper bag, and one stroller with car seat to enter customs. As Tony tried to push a cart and juggle the bags, I pushed Brennan in the car seat/stroller with one hand and pulled a suitcase behind with the other. We were our own three-ring circus. Once through customs, we turned the corner to a crowd of cheering Berlin Thunder fans complete with face make-up, pompoms, horns and whistles. As we went by with the baby, they turned up the noise to show their enthusiasm for our arrival.

We loaded our luggage and ourselves onto awaiting buses and were immediately whisked away on a tour of the city of Berlin. The tour was intended as a photo opportunity for the local media. But it was also meant to keep the players awake in an attempt to get them adjusted to the six-hour time change from the East Coast.

The bus tour took us passed Checkpoint Charlie, a famous crossing point of the Berlin Wall where World War II allied forces confronted Russian tanks, on route to the Brandenberg Gate, the former western gate of the city and monument to the division of East and West Germany, where the media was waiting. The team stepped off the bus into drizzling rain and posed for photographs in front of the historical site. With Brennan bundled in a front pack, I explored the gate's massive stone columns and ran my fingers over bullet hole pock marks. After the brief media introduction, we were dropped off near the Memorial Church. With the ruins of its spire still charred and broken from heavy bombing during the War, the once ornate church served as a reminder of the destruction. A modern day mall surrounded the site and we walked among the stores, cafes and street vendors getting our first real glimpse of the city, which was home to nearly four million people. One of the vendors gave Brennan a pair of child's sunglasses. I'm still not sure why but when I resisted, he insisted. I thanked him for his kindness and we made our way to Nike Town and McDonald's.

When we finally boarded the bus for our hotel, Tony and I were exhausted. Brennan had taken cat naps all the while and the time change didn't seem to faze him at all. But, Tony and I had been up for 32 hours and we were in need of some rest. Upon our arrival at the Courtyard Marriott in Teltow, a suburb of Berlin, we were pleased to confirm each player had indeed been assigned their own room. We were told that would be the case but past NFL experiences made us weary. We were also told the German Marriott used the outdated system of charging a fee for each adult occupant in the room and the cost for me to join Tony in his would be 25 Deutsch Marks (DM) daily. The basic room charge was covered by the NFL and we were prepared to absorb the additional expense of $12.00 per day.

In the newly-built hotel, our room was reasonably sized with a small refrigerator, king-sized bed and a nice view of the parking lot. Unfortunately, the hotel was located in formerly communist East Germany and the staff spoke mostly German and Russian and very little English. They didn't like Americans very much and we were told not to use the hotel's main entrance but rather the side entrance near the parking lot. We were to stay out of the lobby and breakfast and dinner would be served in a private banquet room downstairs or room service was available at an additional charge.

The team was housed on two floors of the hotel. The first morning, I woke up at 4:00 a.m. and, unable to sleep, went down to the lobby for a look around. From a chair near the elevator, I watched the staff setting up until 5:00 a.m. when the restaurant opened. I was hungry and the restaurant featured a big breakfast buffet. I grabbed a plate hoping to find pancakes, French toast or eggs but, upon closer inspection, the spread of cheeses, breads, pickled fish and other unfamiliar German breakfast foods turned me off. I poured a glass of apple juice and selected some bread and cheese before sitting at a table. When I finished, I looked around for a server to pay the bill. I didn't have any German currency yet so I hoped they'd accept a credit card. A restaurant employee finally approached and informed me, as a member of the football team, I wasn't supposed to utilize the restaurant but there would be no charge for the food because regular hotel guests received complimentary breakfast in conjunction with the cost of their room.

The next few mornings, I accompanied Tony to the team's private banquet room for breakfast. But, the menu was repetitive and their attempts at American-fare left much to be desired. The bread rolls were hockey pucks and the scrambled eggs runny. Their occasional foray into French toast was a little better but, other than that slight variation, the meal was always the same. I tried to make due by eating the ample breakfast cereals available, but I just couldn't choke down the ill-tasting German milk, which was served at room temperature and never required refrigeration. After a week, we were desperate to find breakfast alternatives.

Fortunately, within walking distance of the hotel, we located a grocery store, called *Real*, which stocked items more to our liking. We were relieved to find two kinds of milk available in Germany; one required refrigeration and the other did not. The cold one was much closer in taste to the milk found at home and, when mixed with Hershey's chocolate syrup we also found at the grocery, the difference in taste was minimal. We filled our room refrigerator with milk, fresh fruit and breakfast bars, which alleviated my need to go downstairs in the mornings.

Tony and his teammates received lunch at practice, so I found a bakery near the hotel offering loaves of soft bread, which I used to make sandwiches for lunch. The Germans loved meats and cheeses and had an enormous variety available. For dinner, we braved the team's meal for the first ten days or so. But, the dinners were just as bad as the breakfasts. Their attempts at American entrees, using German ingredients and spices, tasted just plain awful. Waterlogged spaghetti in meatless red sauce, flavorless boiled chicken, incredibly terrible cheese lasagna and pork schnitzel were the rotating featured dishes. The players were not happy with the food choices and with each meal, the grumbling got louder.

One night at dinner, one of the players got into a young buffet attendant's face and raged he "Wouldn't serve the shit to his dog."

The server was just a young kid and I thought for a minute the player might actually strike him. But, when the obviously scared kid left the station, the player threw his plate of food at the serving table and exited the room. The food was indeed horrible but I felt sorry for the hotel wait staff. They were doing their best to politely serve us and they were taking a lot of verbal abuse for the food. Some of the players were downright rude and definitely hostile and their behavior was certainly over the line. Coach Vaas addressed the food issue in a meeting the next day and said the team's strength and conditioning coach was trying to remedy the situation. But, the hotel kitchen was stymied by the NFL's food contract outlining exactly which menu items were to be served to the players.

I'm certain whoever put together that contract, never taste-tested one of the U.S.-inspired meals prepared by the German chefs. I don't know what happened to remedying the situation, but the food never got better. Instead, we suddenly had all the ice cream we could eat and soda we could drink. The banquet room was outfitted with a full Coke fountain system and a freezer chest consistently filled with ice cream. Not exactly the ideal diet for professional athletes and we were soon done with the team's dinner offerings.

Tony lost ten pounds and though it wasn't negatively affecting his playing ability, as an offensive lineman, he couldn't afford to lose any more precious weight. So, we began eating dinner out nightly at our own expense. With virtually everything in Europe within walking-distance or easily accessible by public transportation, we found it very easy to get around. Once we familiarized ourselves with the small enclave of Teltow, we discovered two restaurants a short distance from the hotel. An Italian restaurant run by true Italians, who spoke no English, served wonderful pasta dishes and some seafood featuring small shrimp. We also found an Argentinian Steakhouse, which served beef. Beef was hard to come by in Germany and if you ordered a hamburger or steak at a restaurant other than a steakhouse, you'd get a hamburger or steak made of pork. Until we discovered the steakhouse, we hadn't eaten any red meat in almost two weeks. Tony and I both needed a shot of iron and we were elated to stumble on the steakhouse. By German standards beef is expensive. But Tony and I found we could both enjoy a good, full steak dinner for between $25 and $40, which was certainly comparable to a decent steak dinner at home in Las Vegas.

Soon after arriving in Berlin, Tony hit it off with Tampa Bay Buccaneers' allocation and veteran NFL quarterback Scott Milanovich. Though they'd never met before, they were both trying to revive their careers and had endured similar experiences during their four seasons in the NFL. Scotty's wife, Jaime, arrived in Germany within days and was one of only two other wives intent on staying in Europe for the entire season.

Jaime and I became fast friends. She was very much like me and I was glad to have her company because the other player's wife was unfriendly and behaved strangely. She never left her husband's sight except to sequester herself in their hotel room while he was attending team meetings. She went to every practice with him, rarely spoke to Jaime and me and made no attempts to socialize. And, when her husband stared at the floor and refused to make eye contact with us when we passed him in the hotel hallway, even our husbands commented on the couple's freaky behavior.

Jaime and I spent our days playing with Brennan at the hotel or accompanying the guys into the city on the team buses. Occasionally, we watched the team's practices on the very same fields where Hitler once addressed his troops. But, more often than not, we took the bus into the city with the team and then ventured off to other parts of Berlin for shopping or sight-seeing. Traveling alone by train or bus in Germany was never intimidating and Jaime and I often discussed we probably wouldn't feel as comfortable or adventurous in America without our husbands by our side.

Finding ourselves extremely compatible, Jaime and I were eager to attend some of the team's away games. We asked the Thunder's organization if, given our credit card, they would make the necessary arrangements for us to travel with the players on their itinerary. We were disappointed when we learned policy prohibited them from assisting because in years past the team purchased tickets for players' family members and then had to eat the cost when the recipient failed to show or the player refused reimbursement. Even with pre-paid funds, the organization was not permitted to make travel arrangements for anyone other than the players.

Jaime and I were not deterred by the lack of assistance and decided to make the away game arrangements on our own. Via our laptop computer, I accessed the Internet with flight information provided by the team's GM Michael Lang and checked on seat availability of the team's flights to Barcelona, Spain, and Edinburgh, Scotland. But, because the team once again purchased all the economy class seats, only expensive business class seats were available. If Jaime and I were going to make the trips on a reasonable budget, we needed to book our flights on alternate airlines. We hoped by booking arriving and departing times similar to the team's, we could still utilize their transportation and, with the coach's permission, their hotel.

In order to closely match the team's travel times and secure the best fares, we needed professional assistance from a travel agency. We inquired about finding one at the front desk of our hotel and were told a short ten-minute walk would get us to the nearest agency. Pushing Brennan in the stroller, Jaime and I left the hotel. Navigating broken sidewalks and cobblestone streets, the ten-minute walk took closer to forty-five minutes. Once in the store, I spoke with the agent and learned that particular agency only dealt with cruises. The agent referred us to a *Reiseboro* (travel agency), which specialized in airline tickets and was just another "ten-minute walk" down the road. We navigated the bumpy streets for another thirty minutes and still no travel agency. We tried to ask a few people sweeping their walks for assistance but, even with my limited German language skills, they assumed we were Americans and turned away without offering any information. They weren't hostile or anything, just not particular interested in helping us. Their distaste for Americans wasn't lost on me but it was a new and frustrating experience.

We were still walking when a small group of young boys rode by on bicycles. I called to them to ask if they knew of the travel agency's location and they stopped briefly before shaking their heads no and riding away. Jamie and I calculated how far we thought we'd walked before turning around to return to the hotel. To our surprise, the boys on bicycles excitedly caught up with us and announced the travel agency was only two blocks further. They eagerly offered directions and happily chatted with us in a mix of native German and broken English.

I realized we should have been asking children for help all along. The adults of Teltow and other areas surrounding our hotel harbored negative feelings toward us because, as former citizens of East Germany, they were educated in German and Russian and taught the virtues of communism. Only after the Berlin Wall came down in 1989, effectively opening the borders between East and West Germany were the children educated in English and German and exposed to the ways of democracy. The kids lacked the contempt for Americans many of the adults were displaying and they were much more receptive to our inquiries. Their limited English coupled with my limited conversational German bridged the gap just enough for us to understand each other as they correctly guided us to the travel agency. Fortunately, one of the agents there spoke English very well and when we concluded our business, he called us a cab to return to the hotel.

Prior to our first game of the NFL Europe season, National Football League Commissioner Paul Tagliabue visited the Thunder at one of their practices and had lunch with the players. Tony said while some of the younger players were excited about his pep talk, Tagliabue didn't say much except he hoped to see the Thunder again in the end-of-season championship game known as the World Bowl.

The first game of the season pitted the Berlin Thunder against the Frankfurt Galaxy. I was reluctant to take Brennan to the April 15th night game because of the late 7:00 p.m. kickoff. The time was set to accommodate the mid-Saturday Fox Sports Network's coverage of the games for the television viewing audience back in the States and the game would run close to eleven o'clock. But, I really wanted to show my support for Tony and the team and after discussing Brennan's amiability, we boarded the bus with Tony just after 4:00 p.m. for our first trip to Friedrich-Ludwig-Jahn Stadium. It was overcast and cold and both Brennan and I were bundled in mittens, hats and multiple layers of clothing. Arriving two hours before game time, Jaime and I easily found our seats, located twenty rows from the field, in the empty stadium. Unfortunately, Brennan's carrier was too big to fit in his stadium chair so I shoved it under the empty seat and snuggled him in my lap as we waited for the game to start.

During the warm-ups, I spotted a familiar face on the field. When we played in San Diego, Werner Hippler, a native of Germany, spent much of one season trying unsuccessfully to catch on with the Chargers. But, he was signed and cut numerous times. One of those times, he was packed to return to Germany when the Chargers re-signed him. He put off his return and unpacked only to be cut again a few days later. He was a nice guy and, as an underdog, I always hoped for the best for him because he hung in there despite the NFL's perpetual roller coaster. But, things never panned out and he was back in Europe playing as a German national for the Frankfurt Galaxy. We greeted each other through the fence, exchanged pleasantries and talked briefly about his wife and child. I commented on how nice it was to see him again and wished him all the best as he trotted off toward the Galaxy's bench.

Each of the European NFL teams carried six or seven national players from across Europe on their roster and the teams were required to use them in a certain number of plays during the games. I'm sure the incorporation of national players helped garner media attention and lure European crowds to the foreign sport of American football. But, most of the guys saw minimal playing time during games and I don't think any of them ever played out a full NFL contract season in the United States.

Pumped for our first NFL Europe game day experience, Jaime and I bought beers and proposed a toast to commemorate the team's season opener. We wondered how many fans would actually attend the Thunder's first game because the stands encircling stadium were nearly empty even as we neared game time. But, by kickoff, 11,000 fans filled the stadium and their drums, whistles, air horns, and bells made them sound like a crowd of tens of thousands.

During the first quarter of the game, the Berlin Thunder scored their first touchdown, the crowd roared and Brennan screamed. The sudden outburst scared the daylights out of him and I couldn't get us out of the stands fast enough. During the second quarter, I tried to lessen the impact of the noise by standing above the lower bleacher sections and close to the main building. But the noise got louder, the cigarette smoke in the stadium got thicker and the wind got colder.

With half time approaching, I watched an ominous thunder storm marching its way toward the stadium. I motioned to Jaime I was taking Brennan inside the building to weather the storm. Once inside, a Berlin Thunder staffer escorted me to the team's media room where I watched the remaining minutes of the quarter on closed-circuit television with a group of German reporters. During halftime, the storm moved in and lightening lit up the field and thunder shook the walls. Half time ended but the lightening directly overhead forced a rain delay. We waited and waited and waited and wondered why they weren't calling an end to the game.

At 11:00 p.m., the lightening finally ceased and the players were ordered to take the field. I couldn't believe they were expected to still play after the ninety minute delay. But, despite the field's standing puddles of water and the players' cold muscles after sitting in the locker room all that time, Quarterback Eric Kresser, a Cincinatti Bengals allocation, and Tony, the starting right tackle, led the team out to finish the second half. We lost but no one remembers the final score of the game. All they remember is the incredible rain storm and boarding the team buses at 12:30 a.m. for Planet Hollywood where the team was scheduled to have their after-game meal. By the time we got to the restaurant, the venue had already converted into a nightclub, the music was blaring and the players' dinner buffet was tucked into the back corner of the bar. I was worried they wouldn't let Brennan in, so Tony and I were prepared to forego dinner and hail a cab for the forty-minute ride back to the hotel. But, we walked right in and no one blinked an eye at the exhausted infant sleeping in the carrier.

The players hadn't eaten since their pre-game meal at 2:00 p.m. and though the Planet Hollywood dinner consisted of an array of fried appetizers cooked hours earlier, the guys were so hungry they ate them anyway. After the meal, Tony, Brennan and I took the first bus back to the hotel. There were always two team buses scheduled at each location; one left early and one left late. The players could catch whichever one they chose but if they missed the late bus, they were on their own.

Coach Vaas gave the players the next day off and Tony and I spent the afternoon coercing Brennan into wearing the furry rabbit ears I brought from home in anticipation of sending an Easter holiday greeting from Germany. Perched under the German Easter egg tree in the hotel lobby, we captured the moment perfectly with another player's digital camera and sent the photo to all our friends and family via e-mail. Everyone promptly responded and the computer connection helped us feel not so far away from home.

Game two was scheduled for Easter weekend (April 24th) and took the team to Spain to play the Barcelona Dragons. With the football team buying up all the economy-class tickets, the travel agency, trying to work within our budget, booked Jaime and I on an alternate airline leaving the day before the team. I'd never been to Spain before and the agency suggested we spend our first night in the beach-side resort of Sitges, which was not far from Barcelona. We loved the idea and intended on flying into Barcelona, spending the day and night in Sitges and returning to the airport the following day to join the team upon their arrival. Meeting the team at the airport would allow us to conveniently meet up with our husbands and utilize the team's transportation to their hotel. Tony and Scott were roommates on the road, so Jaime and I booked a room at the team's hotel as well. Once there, we could split into couples and share the cost of only one room. Head Coach Vaas was aware of the musical rooms and surprisingly vigilant about ensuring our hotel accommodations on the road were secure. Also apprised of our difficulty in coordinating travel with the team, he offered for one of the assistant coaches to drop Jaime and me off at the airport the morning of our flight despite the rule, probably for insurance reasons, that coaches were not to transport players or anyone else in the Thunder's staff vehicles. We, of course, accepted his gracious offer and thanked him profusely for making our lives easier.

At the airport, I was mystified when the European gate agent refused to let me check in because I didn't have a ticket for Brennan. I kept trying to explain Brennan was sitting on my lap and she kept asking me for his ticket. Finally, she made it clear that when flying within Europe, even children sitting on a lap were required to hold airline tickets, which cost 10% of the adult's fare. I was totally unaware of the policy and furious the travel agency in Teltow failed to mention Brennan's need for a ticket. He was with us the entire time we were making the travel arrangements and the agent never said a word about it. By the time I understood what I needed to do, our flight was boarding. Leaving Brennan and our bags with Jaime, I ran in a full sprint ten concourse gates to find the necessary ticket counter and purchase the full-fare lap-child ticket at a cost of $62.00. We were the last ones to board the plane and I chalked up the experience as another NFL Europe adventure.

Other than the misunderstanding over Brennan's seat, leaving the day before the players worked out very well. We arrived in Sitges close to noon and strolled from the Gran Hotel Verdi spa resort through the narrow cobblestone streets down to the quaint shops and cafes along the nude beach. Early in the evening, we returned to the hotel to do a little swimming at their indoor pool. The next afternoon, we took a cab to the airport and met up with the team as planned. Jaime and I were very glad to have arrived in Barcelona the day before and visited the beach because the team's hotel was over an hour drive away from the airport in the complete opposite direction of the water. The guys didn't even get a glimpse of the beautiful beaches of Spain.

By the time the busses arrived at the team hotel, the players' standard menu was already being served in a private banquet room. The guys took one look at the mass produced entrees and decided we'd venture out in search of something more palatable. We found a quaint restaurant in an adjacent shopping area and made ourselves at home. Jaime and I bragged about our previous night's stay on the beach until the guys lost interest in our ribbing when a tray of fresh bread, tomatoes and olive oil arrived at our table. We weren't quite sure what to do with the appetizer so Tony asked the waitress. She cut a tomato and a loaf of bread in half and began rubbing and squeezing the juice of the tomato on the bread. Then she poured on a substantial amount of olive oil and finished with a sprinkle of salt. The unusual treat was delicious and we were so excited at the prospect of having a change in edible fare, we ordered every dish on the menu featuring calamari or prawns. We toasted the great food with glasses of sangria right up until the guys had to report to team meetings.

The next day, we boarded the team buses for the Barcelona Dragons' home stadium. Built for the 1984 Olympics, the stadium was located on the crest of a hill and the views from the top were spectacular. The entire city was visible and much of the mountains surrounding it. With hours to kill before the game, Jaime and I walked the gorgeous grounds before making our way down onto the field where Brennan played in the grass end zone with Barcelona quarterback Tony Graziani's little boy. With the beaches, temperate climate and food choices closer to our liking, I certainly preferred Barcelona over Berlin.

The game got under way, the Thunder won 28-to-21 and Tony played satisfactorily at right tackle. When it was over, we boarded the team bus and returned to the hotel for the evening. The next morning, Jaime, Brennan and I took the team bus to the airport where we kissed our husbands goodbye and boarded a separate flight back to Berlin. In the air, I had trouble equalizing the pressure in my right ear and it felt as though there might be water remaining from our swim several days earlier. When we landed, I tried to release the pressure by creating suction with the palm of my hand. But, the process was painful and a small droplet of watery blood appeared in my ear. Probably an ear infection, I hoped it would work itself out.

Brennan stopped sleeping through the night shortly after our arrival in Germany in early April and the constant sleep interruptions coupled with the team's terrible food and an aching ear contributed to my declining attitude. I was bitching and complaining a lot about our stay in Germany and Tony was too. He didn't play as well as he would have liked in the first two games and my unhappiness and bad attitude were rubbing off. Only the fear of taking on the long, overseas flight alone with Brennan and the thoughts of missing Tony kept me from heading for the comforts of home.

One afternoon, Tony and his offensive line coach Bob Bicknell, who was about the same age as Tony, were watching game film (taped plays for analysis) when Tony started to complain about something. Bicknell cut him short and told him if he stopped bitching about everything and started playing football, things would work out. Tony thought about it for a second and decided Bicknell was right. His attitude was negatively affecting his play and he had to knock it off and so did I. When he returned from watching the film, we talked about it and agreed to make a conscious effort to stay positive and make the best of every situation.

Game three (April 29th), against the Scottish Claymore, was at home and Tony spoke with the Thunder's staff about possibly getting Brennan and I somewhere to sit other than the stands. We were pleasantly surprised when the Thunder offered up the use of a two-person press box. The private box provided a wonderful view of the field and we were protected from the weather and the extreme noise of the cheering crowd. I had privacy to nurse and there was ample space to put Brennan's carrier either on the counter top desk or under it depending on whether or not he was sleeping. I included Jaime in the coup and we really appreciated the team's commitment to accommodating us. Without the use of that room, I don't think I would have brought Brennan into the stadium environment again.

At the end of the game, we took the team bus to kicker Axel Kruse's restaurant for the post-game meal. Axel was one of the German nationals on our team and a former professional soccer player for communist East Germany. His colorful and out-going personality made up for his lack of English skills. He was quite a character and his rendition of how he escaped East Germany prior to the fall of the Berlin Wall was always interesting and animated. Banned from the traveling soccer team for several years because he was considered a flight risk, he was eventually allowed to travel. When he and the team's armed guards stepped out of their hotel in Holland for a cigarette, the guards turned their backs to re-enter the lobby and he spontaneously ran for the open passenger door of an idling cab and simply drove off. He then flew from Holland into free West Germany. His story was amazing when you consider the risks involved. At the time, he certainly would have been shot if caught trying to escape. Once settled in West Germany, he returned to playing soccer and made a name and nice living for himself. The Berlin Thunder signed him as a kicker and his notoriety and participation drew fans and publicity. He almost never went to the team's practices, but he never missed a PAT (point after touchdown) or field-goal and the local newspaper called him "Mr. Perfect."

Every home game thereafter, we were bussed to Axel's restaurant/bar for the post-game meal. Regardless of whether the team won or lost, the crowd always cheered our arrival and the atmosphere was warm and friendly. We were escorted to a private seating area and served an American-style buffet featuring delicious salads, meat dishes and desserts and complimentary German beer and Coke. We liked the place because of the food. But, the bar was popular nightly because Axel was always accommodating with drinks and the place was thick with young girls hot for the ball players.

During the home stands, many of the younger players spent their free time partying from the minute practice and meetings were over until the wee hours. But, Tony and I and the Milanovich's preferred to spend our free time touring Berlin's many historical sights like the still-intact sections of the Berlin Wall, the Topography of Terror where Hitler's Gestapo and SS (Secret State Police) buildings once stood, Checkpoint Charlie and one of the city's famous outdoor beer gardens. The warming spring days were a welcome change from the previous weeks of cold and clouds. But, the higher temperatures facilitated our need to do laundry. After 21 days in Germany without a washing machine, we'd depleted our stockpile of clean winter and summer clothes. At five months old, Brennan began eating solid foods in addition to breastfeeding. He took to the German baby food right away, which eased my mind about the transition. But, the foods were all carrot or berry based and did a number on his clothing and mine alike. I'd been washing Brennan's bibs and other miscellaneous things in the bathtub with the Dreft detergent I'd brought from home. But, my hand scrubbing and foot stomping in the tub was doing little to remove the stains. I attempted to wash several pieces of my clothing and air dry them in the bathroom but the increasing humidity never allowed them to fully dry and after a few days of washing adult underwear in the tub, the laundry situation needed immediate attention.

But, the hotel offered no self-service laundry facilities and we were told there were only four Laundromats in the entire city of Berlin and not one was within a reasonable distance of the hotel. As one of the largest cities in Europe, Berlin boasted a population of over 3.5 million people and we just didn't get the lack of services. Kim Kuci, one of the German national players, explained there was little need for Laundromats because everyone had washing machines in their homes or apartments. The hotel offered the ball players "special rates" on the hotel's laundry service, but when we calculated the $80.00 cost of the hotel doing just one load of our laundry, we had no other choice but to find an alternative.

On the players' next day off, Scott elected to stay at the hotel but Tony, Brennan, Jaime and I went on a laundry adventure. Based on directions provided by the hotel staff at the front desk, we took a cab on a wild goose chase in search of a Laundromat, which didn't exist. We spent the better part of an hour driving around to no avail. We returned to the hotel where another of the national players claimed to know the exact location of the closest Laundromat. Based on his directions, we called another cab and continued to search out a place to wash our clothes.

First, we took a cab at a cost of $7.00 to the nearest train station, which was in the next city of Zehlendorf. Then, we took the train, at a cost of $2.00 per person, four stops to Rathaus Steglitz. There, we got off the train and walked three city blocks to the nearest *Wasch Center*. Our next challenge was figuring out the washing process. The machines were individually numbered and there was a central money box on the wall where we slid the required $3.50 per load into whichever numbered slot corresponded with the machine. Once the money was deposited, another machine on the wall dispensed a cup of detergent. Doing laundry had never been so complicated and we watched other patrons to figure out the protocol. When the washing cycle was complete, we had to move our sopping wet clothes into a separate spinning machine at a cost of $.50 before finally placing them in a dryer at a cost of $2.00 per hour. The process was ridiculously inefficient and when the cost of doing five loads of laundry totaled 75 Deutsch Marks ($35.00 U.S. dollars), we finally understood why the hotel charged so damn much for their laundry services.

The next time we needed to do laundry, we took a bus instead of a taxi to the train station, which reduced the cost a little. The time after that, we quietly left the hotel and stealthily walked a block down the road where one of the Berlin Thunder assistant coaches waited with a team car. Tony, Brennan, Jaime, me and the coach, who wished to remain nameless, quietly disappeared bimonthly to do laundry. While we didn't particularly like spending a valuable day off at the Laundromat, the necessary secret mission approach turned the outings into fun as the five of us made sport of sneaking off with bags of dirty laundry and mysteriously returning with coveted clean clothes.

A few of the players didn't do a single load of laundry the entire time we were overseas. They just kept recycling their dirty clothes. Some did their best to wash by hand in the bath tub. Long, white socks hung from open hotel windows and dangled in the breeze as evidence of their endeavor. The rest of the players persuaded girls from the swarm of German groupies to take their laundry home and do it for them. And when I say swarm, I mean it. The running joke among our group of friends was we were staying at the "HO-tel".

When the players left their rooms in the mornings to board the practice bus in the parking lot, there was always a simultaneous exodus of girls dressed in club wear from the night before. Many of the girls were repeat visitors but not necessarily to the same room each time. There was an endless stream of willing girls and the young, single guys were taking advantage of it every night. Unfortunately, even some of the guys with wives or girlfriends back home gave into temptation and dabbled in a little hanky panky. I dreaded the introductions when a very jubilant wife or girlfriend arrived in Berlin for a brief visit with an offending player. What bothered me most was the players' uncanny ability to completely play it off knowing everyone around them was aware of the situation. Our close group of friends often commented to each other on the blatant breaches of trust but I knew openly commenting on team infidelity issues would only cause problems for Tony in the locker room and on the field. When one married player was rumored to have slept with a 15-year-old girl and another philanderer was overheard yelling through his hotel door at his state-side wife as she questioned his fidelity, the best I could do was offer a cold shoulder to those involved and leave it alone.

With an away game next on the schedule and another flight planned, I finally admitted I needed medical attention. Since returning from Barcelona, increasing congestion in my right ear made hearing more difficult and the consistent ache was getting progressively worse. Tony asked the team to make arrangements for me to see a doctor and the front office set up an appointment with a local practitioner. Brennan and I rode with the team to the practice facility and then Jaime and Coach Vaas's wife and daughters, in town for a two week visit, graciously offered to watch Brennan while one of the staffers took me to the appointment. I thought the staff person would accompany me but she dropped me off curbside and told me to have the office call her cell phone when the exam was complete. I entered the office and the receptionist didn't speak a word of English. With a combination of charades and broken German, I finally got her to understand the Berlin Thunder made the appointment for me and I needed to be seen for an ear problem. I sat down amongst the fifteen people sitting in the lobby area and waited patiently. I was the last one to be called back.

The exam room was reminiscent of a B-movie torture chamber and as I sat in the "dentist's chair," the hooks, gadgets and hoses hanging from the ceiling above made me really nervous. I thought my worst fears about going to a foreign doctor had come true. However, when the doctor came in and realized I was an American, he began to speak English and I felt better about the care I was about to receive. His diagnosis, as expected, was a mild ear infection and he prescribed ear drops, which could be purchased at a pharmacy two doors down.

When I asked the receptionist about my bill, she couldn't get past the idea I didn't have some sort of ID card used as part of Germany's healthcare system and she excused herself to speak with the doctor. When she returned, I owed 125 Deutch Marks or about $62 U.S. dollars. My prescription was 16DM ($8.00) and I left the pharmacy feeling good about the cost of German health care.

During the previous week, I'd asked Head Coach Vaas about coordinating some sightseeing trips for the team and he wanted to know what I had in mind. Many of the players said they would be willing to pay a fee to rent a tour bus to visit Auschwitz in Poland. But, after researching the idea, the nine-hour drive ruled out the trip because we didn't have that kind of time on our hands. However, because there was enough interest in that kind of trip, I scoured the Internet and located a concentration camp called Sachsenhausen about an hour north of Berlin. When approached with the trip idea one night after dinner, Coach Vaas liked it so much he approved taking the team's large passenger van, used to shuttle injured players, and one of the coaches' cars, which eliminated the cost of transportation. Coach Vaas announced the opportunity at a team meeting and because of limited seating offered a sign-up sheet. I was surprised when very few players outside of our offensive line clique committed to the trip. I approached a couple of players to see if they wanted to go and they asked me why they should. My answer was simple. World War II was the ultimate in discrimination resulting in mass genocide. It was a dark period in the history of the world and the United States played a major role in ending the war. My love of history drove my enthusiasm but they shrugged their shoulders and remained disinterested.

I approached the hotel staff for directions to the camp and for the first time they were actually helpful. They knew exactly where the camp was located and gave us explicit directions to get there. Our usual group, accompanied by Coach Vaas's wife and daughters, made the trip to Sachsenhausen. The camp was built in 1936 based on drawings conceived by Nazi SS architects and was the architectural model from which all other concentration camps were based. The camp imprisoned 200,000 people between 1936 and 1945. It was evacuated and its prisoners sent on death marches just prior to its liberation by Russian and Polish troops of the Red Army.

We walked the grounds in silence as we toured preserved barracks where the prisoners were kept, execution trenches, the infirmary where medical experiments were done, the cellar of corpses where the bodies were kept and finally the remains of the ovens and crematorium. While completely educational and morbidly interesting, I couldn't shake the eerie feelings of dread and sadness. And while we all felt very somber when we departed the grounds, everyone agreed the trip was very worth while and gave them a new perspective on history. On the way back to the hotel, we discussed how the reality of the concentration camps differed from the images we imagined when we learned about it in school. I thought about trying to plan more historical excursions but the next two weeks featured back-to-back away games and the time just started slipping away.

The fourth game of the season (May 7th), took Jamie, Brennan and I to Edinburgh, Scotland. Our arrangements, including a ticket for Brennan, had us leaving a few hours before the team so we could beat them to Scotland but catch their bus when it left the airport for a rare, scheduled tour of Edinburgh Castle planned by Coach Vaas. To make our travel easier, Tony and Scott took all of our checked baggage with them leaving us to simply deal with Brennan, the stroller and the diaper bag. The first leg of our flight departed Berlin late because of some type of ground crew issue and we almost missed our connection in Paris. Jaime and I, with Brennan in tow, sprinted through the Charles de Gaulle airport to make the second leg. In Europe, there's no such thing as an organized line and our flight offered no pre-boarding opportunities. The boarding mass at the gate was a free-for-all and, even with Brennan in my arms, no one cut me any slack. Jaime and I learned to push and elbow our way through just like everyone else in order to get where we needed to go.

We landed in Edinburgh and made ourselves comfortable as we waited for the team's plane to arrive. We spotted one of the video crew members whom had flown in with equipment on an earlier flight and he sat down with us to await the team. It was 1:00 in the afternoon and the team was scheduled to arrive at 1:30. After a few minutes, the public address system paged the crew member sitting with us and he left in search of the information desk. He returned with bad news.

A ground crew strike in Germany, which began immediately after our flight took off, temporarily grounded the team and they were delayed. At first, the airline said until 4:00 p.m. Then, it was until 10:00 p.m. Jaime and I were floored and the airline reservationist could provide little information as to the team's whereabouts or impending arrival. We hadn't thought to write down the name of the team's hotel or where it was located. We didn't even know if the team would be coming at all. We were in a serious quandary of our own doing and we weren't exactly sure what to do. I wanted to kick myself for not keeping the cell phone number of the staffer from the Thunder's front office who had taken me to the ear doctor.

The videographer periodically received information through the Scottish Claymore's football office and, after two hours, we were told the team was definitely coming but they would arrive as late as 1:00 a.m. We were relieved to discover the videographer was privy to the name of the team's hotel and its location. He'd been directed to take a cab there and return to the airport when the team arrived. We hailed a cab and were shocked when we were told the hotel was in Glasgow, an hour away, and the fare would be around 65 pounds or $125.00. The videographer didn't have enough money because his per-diem had only been 25 pounds; far short of the cab fare. Jaime and I had the cash to make up the difference and we all chided about how lucky we were to have run into one another.

When we arrived at the team hotel in Glasgow, Jaime and I learned two rooms were reserved in our names. Tony, still stranded in Germany, had taken the initiative and asked the Thunder to make arrangements with the hotel in the hopes we'd find our way there. Already late in the afternoon and with the castle tour obviously cancelled, we left the hotel in search of something to eat. Glasgow was a college town and within one city block, we stumbled on a street lined with bars and restaurants. A lively establishment caught our eye and we settled into an open booth. But, before we could even open the menus, a waitress approached to inform us Brennan was not permitted inside.

Back on the street, we checked out several restaurants and pubs but none would permit us to enter with a minor. Having had little trouble taking Brennan into bars in Germany, I'd forgotten about the usual age restrictions. After three blocks of inquiries, we came to a restaurant called Shananigan's, which was very similar in décor and menu to an American TGI Friday's restaurant. Jaime and I were starving and while the service was slower than we'd have liked, the pasta and hamburger and fries we ordered were pretty good. I'd fed Brennan a bottle while we were in search of a place to eat and so he was content cradled in the carrier as we ate. After the meal, we returned to the hotel to await the arrival of the team.

As we settled in and I unpacked the diaper bag, I realized there was no refrigerator in the room to store Brennan's milk. All of our previous hotel rooms in Europe featured a refrigerator and I promptly called the front desk to request one be brought up. I was surprised when informed they had none but ice could be obtained from the bartender downstairs. With that, I made my first of many trips to the bar over the next three days as I kept bottled breast milk, in a bucket given to me by the bartender, on ice in the bathtub. It wasn't exactly orthodox but it got the job done.

During that initial day in Scotland, the Thunder's staff began trickling into the hotel a little after 5:00 p.m. and informed us the players and coaches were diverted onto three different flights because of the ground crew strike in Germany. The first plane out with available seating carried a few of the coaches and the starting offense and defense. That plane was expected to arrive in Scotland any time and Jaime and I were relieved to know both Tony and Scotty were most likely on board. What we didn't know was while our husbands had indeed been put on the first flight out, in the chaos of the last minute decision to split the team up, the players boarding the flight weren't actually the ones named on the tickets. When the guys arrived in Manchester, England, to make the connection to Edinburgh, the airline had no idea who they were or where they were supposed to be going. It took hours for the team and the airline to sort out the mess and the guys bided their time at the airport pub by eating fish and chips and throwing back more than a few beers. Tony and Scott were highly intoxicated when the first plane of players finally made it to the team's Glasgow hotel around 10:00 p.m. The rest of the team straggled in over the next several hours on two additional flights. To add insult to injury, all the team's checked baggage, including ours, was still sitting on the ground in Germany.

By morning, Brennan's diaper bag was down to one last diaper and I just wanted to get a hold of a tooth brush. At breakfast, everyone looked like hell. The team's luggage was still MIA and disheveled players trickled into the buffet area wearing the same clothes from the day before. They were tired due to their late arrivals and quite a few were hung over. The team's staff was frazzled and worn after enduring nearly 24 hours of coordination chaos and substantial amounts of bitching.

After breakfast, Tony, confident his position on the team afforded him a little leeway, told Coach Vaas he needed to leave the hotel to find some things for the family and it was possible he'd be late for the team meeting. In the NFL, Tony would never have asked much less received permission to miss even one minute of team activities. Hefty fines were levied for every 60 seconds an NFL player was late to a meeting or practice. But, in Europe, things were less strict and a little more laid back. Coach Vaas reluctantly agreed and after talking with the girl at the front desk, Tony sprinted out of the hotel in search of a nearby pharmacy. Within twenty minutes, he returned with diapers and other necessities to get us showered and through the day. Our luggage finally arrived that evening and I was pleased to change clothes for the first time in a day and a half.

The next day was game day and, as usual, we arrived at the stadium hours before game time. As we stepped off the bus, a lone bagpipe player, clad in traditional kilt attire, began playing his pipes and the powerful sound resonated through the tunnel and the empty stadium. Brennan, startled by the thunderous noise, began to cry but I found the dramatic tones particularly poignant and the moment gave me goose bumps. The bagpipes played on until we took seats in the stadium and then the soothing sounds disappeared.

Jaime and I watched the guys stretching and warming-up for the next hour. But, we had each been to more football games than we cared to count and we hated the idea of having come all the way to Scotland only to see the airport, hotel and stadium. We really wanted to see some of the sites and questioned one of the Scottish Claymore's staff about Edinburgh Castle. We were quite surprised when he informed us the landmark was only a short ride from the stadium and suggested we take the tour during the game. Given the choice, I knew Tony would much rather I take the opportunity to see something of the country than sit through another football game. Upon our request, the staffer summoned a stadium security officer who called us a cab, walked us out to the proper gate and issued us credentials so Jaime, Brennan and I would be able to bypass the regular gates and re-enter through the security gate upon our return.

The cab wound its way up the once volcanic hill-top to the Castle dating back to 1093. Throughout the Middle Ages, Edinburgh Castle was one of the prominent castles of the kingdom and played a major role in the story of Scotland. As an avid history buff, I had great appreciation for the Castle's place in history. The cab dropped us directly in front of the ticket kiosk selling one and two-day tour passes and Jaime and I quickly realized our limited time would force us to bypass much of what the Castle had to offer. But, we were intent on seeing as much as we could during our four-hour window.

Two large, bronze statues of King Robert the Bruce and Sir William Wallace flanked the main Gatehouse Entrance. I assumed the one represented the same William Wallace portrayed by Mel Gibson in the movie *Brave Heart* and images of bloody battles and tyrannical kings were brought to mind as we stopped to witness the changing of the guard where, with incredible pomp and circumstance, one guard replaced another. Working from our souvenir guide, we selected areas of the Castle we thought would be of most interest including St. Margaret's Chapel built by King David I in 1124, the Great Hall built by King James IV in 1513, the castle vaults, prison, hospital, and Scottish National War Memorial. There was so much to see and we were rushing around so fast I didn't even notice Brennan had fallen asleep in the pack strapped to my front. He was always so amiable to all of our travels and I was thankful for his even temperament.

With time running short, we reluctantly left the Castle and walked down the hill to hail a cab back to the stadium. While we were waiting for the driver to arrive, we slipped into one of the many weaving companies selling souvenir Scottish Clans and Tartans merchandise, which represented Scottish family heritage. Jaime opted for a blanket representing a name found in her family. But, with no Scottish roots in my lineage, I wasn't picky about the fabric patterns and simply selected a kilted skirt based on the pattern and colors I liked best.

We arrived back at the stadium at the end of the third quarter and were very pleased with our decision to tour the Castle after we saw the dismal score of the game. When it was over, the Thunder lost 42-to-3. Packages in hand, we made our way onto the field to access the tunnel and the team's bus. While the guys were changing, I found a hamburger stand in the parking lot and bought four hamburgers.

Tony was always ravenous following a game and, in the NFL, he reminded me every week to grab him a hotdog for immediately after. On NFL game days, the players ate breakfast early and then had a snack before they made their way onto the field for pre-game warm-ups. But Tony never ate much before a game because, if he did, he would get sick by half time. So, by the end of game, he was often starving and couldn't wait to eat something. A hot dog always held him over until more substantial food was available.

When Tony emerged from the tunnel following the Claymore's game, I handed him two hamburgers. I ate one and put the other one up for grabs. The hamburger stand had closed and so many of the players wanted the remaining burger I handed it to Tony and told him to decide. I think the guys did ro-sham-bo, the rock/paper/scissors hand game, to see who would get it. Back in Glasgow, we ventured out for dinner and ate at a small Italian place with alfresco seating. The following day, Jaime and I took the team bus to the airport and awaited our flight to Berlin, which departed later than the team's.

Game five took us to Amsterdam, Holland. For a change, the team was traveling by train with additional tickets readily available. Jaime and I were relieved to travel with them following the previous week's fiasco in Scotland. When the ICE (Inter City Express) train stopped at the crowded Berlin platform, our little clique of players was fortunate enough to be standing directly in front of an opening door. Boarding first, offensive lineman Mike Edwards, safety Billy Gustin, Scott, Jaime, Tony, Brennan and I secured a comfortable six-seat private cabin with plenty of leg room and storage space for the bags of snacks the Thunder coaches suggested the players bring because of the limited food service on the train. With big appetites in our group, we packed sandwiches and hearty fare for the half-day ride.

We were moving at quite a clip and the noise from the train was surprisingly hushed. The rhythmic motion nearly rocked everyone to sleep until the train's pace suddenly slowed to a crawl. After nearly an hour at snail's pace, one of the Thunder's staff came back to our cabin. Tony and Scott had become team captains of sorts and so they were told the news first. Someone committed suicide on the tracks ahead forcing our train to be rerouted. The delay would force the team to miss the connecting train in Duisburg and there wasn't another one going into Amsterdam that night. All we could do was laugh and make jokes regarding the past weeks' unbelievable travel misfortunes. At the next train stop, the Thunder arranged for buses to pick us up and complete the remaining three-hour trip into Holland. On the way out of the train station, I stopped at a food stand and purchased additional sandwiches for Tony and me. But, with little time to board the bus, many of the guys didn't think about it.

After an hour on the bus, several attitude-prone players loudly voiced their displeasure with not having anything to eat. Coach Vaas ordered the buses to stop at a rest stop convenience store and gave the players ten minutes to get in and out. But, the two store clerks couldn't handle the sheer volume of two bus loads of hungry athletes and the ten minutes easily turned into twenty. Coach Vaas found the delay unacceptable and screamed from the bus doorway for the players to get on the buses. Some came running but the ones with attitude, which is probably what got them sent to NFL Europe in the first place, showed no mind. They were slowly and defiantly walking back to the bus. Very irritated, Coach yelled some expletives and gave the bus driver the order to go! I'm sure the defiant players were pretty surprised as our bus began to drive away. Everyone stood up for a better view of the players suddenly sprinting to catch the second team bus behind us. The moment was priceless and our bus roared with laughter. It took two full buses to accommodate everyone traveling and the only empty seats were on ours. Sitting on the second bus's floor for the remainder of the two-hour trip probably did little to improve their attitude but it did wonders for ours. Only every now and then did a player with such arrogance in the NFL, which tended to embrace such egotistical maniacs as long as they benefited the team, get their just rewards!

In Amsterdam, we met up with a friend and former exchange student from Tony's high school one evening and Annemeika and her fiancé walked us through some of the more historical areas of the city on our way to a wonderful Indonesian restaurant. After dinner, the personal tour continued by car. As we neared the famous Red Light District, we saw a number of the players touring the city on foot. Jon Blackman was standing on one of the corners and as we stopped at the red traffic signal, Tony yelled out his open window, "Hey, Blackman." Annemeika's fiancé freaked out. He thought Tony was yelling at the African-American players standing with Jon and calling them black men. He nearly drove through the red light thinking Tony was about to get in a fight. Bouncing around in the back seat of the speeding car, Tony and I questioned what was going on. A few blocks down the street, he slowed the car after we explained Blackman was Jon's last name. Once we all calmed down, we found the humor in the misunderstanding. Tony and I would have liked to take a closer look at the famous Red Light District but, with Brennan in tow, we made our way back to the hotel.

The next morning while the players were in pre-game meetings, Brennan, Jaime and I accompanied Annameika to the Keukenhof tulip fields. We were disappointed to learn the acres of fields, which supply much of the world's tulips, had been cut just two weeks earlier. However, the botanical flower garden, dated by drawings from 1830, was absolutely beautiful. With seven million bulbs planted, the Keukenhof was the biggest and most beautiful Spring Garden in Europe. I can't even describe the sheer beauty of the tulips, roses, daffodils, hyacinths, and freesias found in every color dominating the vast property. We spent so much time wandering the incredible gardens we missed our window of opportunity to visit the Anne Frank house made famous in her World War II diary.

We returned to the hotel just in time to board the team bus to Amsterdam's stadium.

The enormous stadium was an architectural marvel with a retractable roof and a concrete "moat" used to protect the soccer players whom usually played there from being mobbed by spectators on the field. Jaime and I were in awe of the facility and didn't notice several ladies had joined the team in Amsterdam. All season long, the football players' family members had arrived for visits for anywhere from five to fourteen days. On this particular trip, four or five wives/girlfriends arrived for the game. As we took our seats in the stadium, several of them relayed stories they'd heard about Brennan. He had become somewhat of the team mascot and all the girls wanted to play with him during the game. I was used to having him in my lap all the time so I took advantage of the rare break to really watch the plays. Over the past few weeks, Tony's individual play at right tackle was consistently good but, overall, the offense was struggling. Coach Vaas named Scotty the starting quarterback for the Amsterdam game and we hoped the change would bring about improvement.

Going into the fourth quarter, it looked as though the team would secure a much needed win. Scott and Tony were working together to keep the ball moving on the right side and they seemed to have a unique understanding of the offensive line's vulnerabilities on each and every play. They understood the dynamics of the entire offense and their past NFL experience was paying off as they correctly anticipated the defensive movement on the field. I thought we'd win right up to the end and then, with only minutes remaining, the Admirals pushed ahead to beat us 24-to-21.

We hoped the return trip from Amsterdam to Berlin would be on another fast-moving ICE train. But, the Thunder booked the team on a regular train, which made frequent stops and increased the travel time to about five-hours. The regular trains weren't nearly as nice as the Inter City Express trains and inside the un-air-conditioned cars, the air was hot and humid. We opened the windows but the excessive noise from the train was deafening and each time another train passed, the meeting created a severe vacuum, which popped our ears.

Back in Berlin, Coach Vaas announced the players would have two consecutive days off later in the week. Jaime, Scotty, Tony and I were dying to do something other than sit around the hotel and Tony suggested we rent a Mercedes, drive the Autobahn to a resort somewhere and get away from the always-noisy, team hotel. That sounded like a great idea and we were all into it. Jaime and I returned to the same travel agency we'd visited before and booked rooms at a resort they recommended about three hours away. Tony reserved a Mercedes through the Thunder front office. We had visions of screaming down the Autobahn in a beautiful S-Class Mercedes on our way to lobster by the beach.

The car was delivered to our hotel on the morning of the trip but it was no Mercedes. Outside the lobby awaited a newer blue, Jeep Grand Cherokee. Tony had specifically requested a Mercedes and was disappointed when the delivering agent told him, because he was with the Thunder, the rental agency had upgraded him to the Jeep at no additional charge. After seeing several Mercedes pulling horse trailers and boats over the past weeks, we should have realized requesting a Mercedes from the rental agency would be like requesting a Ford or Chevy in America; they were abundant and easy to come by. But, Tony failed to specify he was looking for a luxury Mercedes and it was likely the agency's entire fleet was made up of lower end Mercedes cars. They probably thought they were doing us a favor by upgrading us to a foreign SUV. I thought the Cherokee offered plenty of cargo space but Tony was disappointed in the choice nevertheless. When it started to rattle and shake at 95mph, he made fun of it even more. I, on the other hand, was glad it couldn't go any faster. I'd heard there were never accidents on the Autobahn, only fatalities and I thought it better the five of us arrive in the northern coastal town of Warnemunde alive.

During the three hour drive and over the noise of the rattling Jeep, we discussed, in great detail, all the seafood we were going to eat during the two-day hiatus. While the Italian restaurant in Teltow featured dishes with tiny shrimp, we were in search of fish, crab and lobster. As we neared the coast, the warm and sunny weather was a welcome change from the dreary clouds, which often encased Berlin. The tall, white buildings of the Hotel Neptun resort were easy to spot as we navigated the narrow streets of the small town. After checking in and dropping off our bags, we immediately left our rooms to see what the coastal town had to offer. Walking a short distance along the beach, we settled on a small restaurant overlooking the boats docked at the marina. With great anticipation we took the menus from our server and looked them over for seafood items to tempt the palate. To our disappointment, dishes identical to those offered in Berlin graced the menu. We inquired about the absence of prawns, crab and lobster and were disturbed to discover the only seafood available in Warnemunde was the same tiny shrimp found in Berlin. Extremely disappointed, we ordered the same mundane dishes repetitively served there.

The next day, we opted to go to the beach where we rented two cabanas. Jamie and I were in one facing the boys and the sun and Tony, Scott and Brennan were in the other facing us in the shade. For the longest time, the guys were very content sitting quietly, which was unlike them. Usually, they would have been complaining of boredom within half an hour. I only discovered the reason for their contentment when I stood up to look down the beach. Slightly behind us and directly in the guys' sight lines were two young twenty-something girls completely bare-assed; sunning themselves on the naked beach. No wonder they'd been so quiet and content. I winked at Jaime and nonchalantly asked Tony if he cared if I took off my top as I reached around and pretended to untie my swimsuit. He immediately sat up in his chair to protest. With their concentration on the girls broken, we chided them for their ogling and then made jokes about their negative influence on Brennan. Jaime then reminded me of the two very large women we'd seen on the nude beach in Spain. They'd been sunning themselves spread eagle offering a full view of their unmentionables and it wasn't a pretty sight. At least the two young girls behind us were being somewhat discreet as they lay face down on their blanket.

The nude beaches were just another product of the open attitude toward sex and nudity in Europe. Even the team hotel back in Teltow broadcast soft porn television shows every night after 10:00 p.m. They appeared on the regular stations following reruns of "Dateline" and "Jay Leno." Some of the shampoo commercials even featured naked women from the waist up. But for all the open sexuality, what we didn't see on television in Germany was violence. I watched the *Terminator* dubbed in German one afternoon while the guys were at practice and all the violent scenes were edited out. Surprisingly, the movie didn't lose too much without them. I thought the European openness to nudity and the aversion to violence was probably healthier than what we experienced in the United States. Somewhere in the middle of the violence vs. nudity conversation, we left the beach to walk along the tiny row of shops and ended up at an ice cream parlor. The Germans loved their ice cream and while beef was difficult to come by, ice cream was everywhere. We topped off the day with double-scoop cones and made one final pass along the water before calling it a night. Our stay in Warnemunde was over and the next morning we made the return trip to Berlin.

Back at the team hotel in Teltow, offensive lineman Jon Blackman set up a hair cutting station in his room. He was one of two players who had enough forethought to bring a set of clippers and many of the guys were in desperate need of haircuts, including Tony. For hours after our arrival, you could hear the constant buzzing of the clippers. Jon refused to charge a fee for the cuts but reluctantly accepted tips. I think he made about $200.00 that day.

After Tony's cut, I realized I was also looking a little shaggy. Jon offered to trim me up but I respectfully declined. Instead, I asked Tony to cut my hair with the tiny pair of scissors from my traveling sewing kit. At first, he absolutely refused afraid he would screw it up and never hear the end of it. But, after I promised I wouldn't say a word about the outcome, he relented. I trimmed my bangs, which were hanging in my eyes, and Tony set about trimming the back. I convinced him he really couldn't do much damage to my long, straight hair. I'd gone without a haircut for over two months and the blunt-cut bottom was already uneven. Nervously, Tony made the first cut and I told him to keep on going. When he finished, he surprised me and himself with how well he'd done. Desperate times called for desperate measures and while I doubted he would ever do it again, I thought he did a great job. I suppose I could have found a beauty salon somewhere in the city but the level of difficulty in finding a Laundromat alone, kept me from embarking on the search for a German hair salon.

The following week (May 21st) hosted game six, at home, against the Rhein Fire. Jon Blackman's wife, Cammy, arrived for a visit and Jaime and I filled her in on what it was like living in Berlin for the past seven weeks. We told her about the hoochies in the hotel and how one of them had knocked on our door at 10:00 p.m. one night looking for a player—any player. The girl was looking for no one in particular. I sent her packing and she ended up knocking on three or four more doors down the hall, until she disappeared into one of the rooms. Another night, our phone rang and a female voice with a thick German accent said she was looking for a Berlin Thunder player. Tony asked, "Which one?" and she replied, "It didn't matter." Tony told her she had the wrong room and hung up. It was like that all the time and the girls were so brazen they'd camp out in the hotel hallway waiting for the players to return from practice or meetings.

I noticed the girls on a regular basis because I kept our hotel door open into the hallway. The open door kept our room from feeling so small and the players and coaches would often stop in to say hello to me or Brennan, which helped break the daily monotony. Most days after practice, Coach Vaas returned to the hotel before the team bus and he would stop by to say hello or comment on the baby. He was the nicest head coach I'd ever met and I was so appreciative of him taking the time to get to know us. In addition, I especially appreciated him allowing us to be so involved with the team and our husbands during the season. Based on my previous NFL experience, I had anticipated Brennan and I would be left completely to our own devices, which made me initially reluctant to make the trip. I was, of course, pleased to be very wrong. Coach Vaas was a good coach and I hoped the team would make it to the play-offs and the World Bowl.

Game six ended with the Thunder beating the Fire in overtime after Jaret Holmes kicked a dramatic 52-yard field goal making the score 24-to-21 or something like that. With so many games and scores, sometimes the numbers got mixed up. In the end, the final scores never really mattered any way. The only important statistic was the team's win/loss ratio.

With four weeks of the season remaining and World Bowl hopes still alive, the team was informed they'd be changing hotels because the Thunder, for reasons they wouldn't disclose, hadn't been able to secure the Teltow Marriott for the team's entire stay. Most of the players were used to packing up their rooms each time the team left for an away game because the league wouldn't pay for the rooms when the guys were gone. But, we were lucky. Coach Vaas allowed our room to be one of the four the team kept when on the road in order to store everyone's luggage and personal belongings. We'd been traveling to the away games as well, so I never cared four or five bags were tossed into our room while we were gone. Not having to move had been really convenient but, with the whole team moving, we knew we didn't have a choice.

On our third wedding anniversary, Tony and I spent the morning packing up Brennan's portable playpen, his swing, the baby food jars lining the desk, the makeshift clothes line in the bathroom and the multitudes of clothing, shoes and baby accessories. But, before we loaded the bags onto the bus and headed for practice, I gave Tony a pair of onyx cufflinks I purchased weeks before at the Edinburgh Castle gift shop. He was very surprised and felt bad he hadn't gotten me anything. But, I didn't expect a gift. When he wasn't with the team, he was with me and I just wanted to show him how much his decision to bring us on the trip meant to me. I felt bad about the five weeks of complaining he endured when we first arrived in Berlin. But, I'd stuck it out and, with our time in Berlin on the downhill slide, I was really glad I changed my attitude and stood by Tony to make the best of the trip.

After the team's practice, we boarded the buses for the new hotels. Due to more unacknowledged planning errors, the team was temporarily separated into three different hotels. A few of the team members stayed at the Courtyard Marriott in Teltow. Others were put-up at a small bed and breakfast down the road from the second hotel, the Sol Inn Hotel in Potsdam-Michendorf, which would ultimately be the final destination for the whole team once space was available. Fortunately, Scott and Tony were assigned rooms at the Sol Inn Hotel right off the bat. I'm sure Coach Vaas had something to do with the fact we weren't going to have to move twice like the majority of players.

Many of the guys were already grumbling about the multiple moves and, once we all learned the Sol Inn would charge 60DM or $30.00 per day for any additional adults staying in the players' rooms, team morale took a serious hit. The Thunder staff had warned us, way back during our stay in Florida, the room charge would jump from 25DM ($12.50) per day in Teltow to 36DM ($18.00) per day in Michendorf-Potsdam. I could have lived with the slight increase. But, the increase to $30.00 per day was, without question, excessive. For Jaime and I to each pay $900.00 to stay with our husbands for the remaining month of the season was out of the question. We started making noise about it and other players with visiting girlfriends or family members jumped on the bandwagon to protest the ludicrous charges. No one important was really paying attention until a number of other factors began fueling a full-team uprising.

First, the players' rooms had only showers; no bathtubs. With no place to adequately bath Brennan, I was unhappy. But, the players were furious there were no tubs for soaking soar muscles. Second, the newly built hotel had no air-conditioning and the 90°F days and equally humid nights were stifling. We couldn't open the windows because there were no screens to keep out the huge mosquitoes and flying bugs, which were rampant in the agricultural fields surrounding the hotel. And, when the players discovered no trains or buses stopped within miles of the isolated hotel, located on the far outskirts of a small Berlin suburb, the shit

hit the fan. The grumbling turned into hostility and Head Coach Vaas, sick of listening to the gripes but understanding of the discontent, asked the Berlin Thunder General Manager Michael Lang to attend a meeting with the players to air out the problems. He especially wanted the players with visiting wives or girlfriends to attend.

The deputy general manager, a roly-poly American ex-patriot living in Germany, began the meeting by explaining the team had been forced to move into the three separate hotels for the week because the Thunder organization hadn't booked the rooms early enough to acquire the large block necessary for the whole team. He then addressed the issue of the large increase in the guest charge and that's when things really got interesting. He made the mistake of saying the team was doing the players a favor by allowing their wives to be there. Scott Milanovich would hear none of that nonsense and immediately piped up. Cutting the deputy GM short, Scotty said the team was doing him no favors by allowing his wife to be there. He was completely paying her way and if she wasn't in Germany, he wouldn't be either. And, without pause, Scotty continued by saying, "The food sucked, the bathrooms were ill-equipped without bathtubs and the hotel was out in the middle of fucking no where without air conditioning." He wanted to know how it was the team thought they were doing us a favor!

I applauded his courage to say it like it was and I realized all eyes in the room had turned to Scott and Tony. Following Scotty's lead, Tony brought up the lack of access to non-carbonated drinking water and pointed out the Coke fountain the organization was so proud of moving to the new hotel was not the beverage of choice for professional athletes trying to remain hydrated in 90° heat. And, it was great ice cream was available to the players 24/7 but the dinner entrees were neither nutritious nor palatable. The deputy general manager started to be a smart ass and Tony interrupted his comment to ask what would happen if players like him and Scotty went back to the U.S. and told other players or even the newspapers how miserable playing for the Berlin Thunder had been. The deputy GM immediately shut up. The freaky wife, sitting on the other side of the room, broke the uncomfortable silence to comment on the lack of beef and iron in the athletes' diets. As if we weren't aware of the players' dietary needs, she continued her diatribe by schooling us in the need for protein to build muscles. I was appalled by her entrance into the highly volatile conversation. It was one of those moments between the players and administration when the husbands should do all the talking. The inappropriate interjection only served to make her husband look spineless and her idiotic. When she finished making an ass out of herself and her husband, the dialog broke down and players started yelling out random complaints and insults at the administration.

General Manager Michael Lang stepped forward to ask Tony and Scotty what he needed to do in order to make the players happy. He suggested, because the team inadvertently quoted the incorrect room charge for additional guests, the Thunder pick up the difference in cost for any players with visitors during the remaining month of the season. There wasn't much he could do about the general lack of bathtubs, but the Thunder would provide us, personally, with a small rubber tub for bathing Brennan. And, twice-daily, a shuttle bus would make roundtrips into Berlin from the hotel. The concessions seemed to appease everyone and when the meeting was over, the players accepted the circumstances at the new hotel a little better. Tony and I and the Milanovichs' were certainly pleased with the resolutions and when Jaime and I stumbled on the lone self-service washer and dryer located at the end of our hall, we were just fine with the new accommodations.

Within a few days, game seven (May 28th), took the team to Rhein, Germany, to play the Rhein Fire. Jaime and I elected to stay behind. I liked the idea of taking a break from dragging Brennan to yet another game. He was always a good sport but after traveling to the games in Barcelona, Edinburgh and Amsterdam over the past few weeks, we both needed a little rest and relaxation. The team's absence gave us the chance to go to bed and wake-up to quiet instead of the sounds of blaring hip-hop or boisterous voices yelling up and down the hall and also afforded me the opportunity to utilize, at my leisure, the always-busy washing machine and dryer.

I liked the temporary break from the team. But, that's not to say I wasn't interested in the game. Jaime and I still wanted to know how the game was going and, on Saturday, we logged onto the Thunder website, which carried a live audio/visual link from the Rhein Stadium. For some reason, we couldn't get the visual link up and running to watch what was happening but from Scotty's microphone, in his helmet, we could hear everything going on, including the profanity and smack-talking on the line, which was something Jaime and I had never heard before. We chuckled at each "fuck," "shit," and "damn" muttered and expressed doubts about Scotty ever being wired for sound again. Following the action on the field was difficult based solely on Scotty's words and the background chatter but we heard enough to know the team lost the game 27-to-28.

While the team was away for the weekend, unbeknownst to Jaime and me, the hotel staff went through all the players' rooms looking for proof to back-up their claims additional guests were staying in the rooms without paying the guest fees. Based on items they found, they compiled a list of rooms, which they believed were subject to additional charges. I'm sure the front desk staff inadvertently assumed the significant number of groupies leaving the hotel each morning were regular player guests attempting to avoid the room surcharge. But, regardless of their motivation, the hotel staff should never have gone through the players' belongings. When the team returned from Rhein, the players were livid to find their personal belongings had been searched and their privacy violated. Rightfully so, they raised hell with Coach Vaas who promptly spoke with the hotel management about the improper activity. Jaime and I were shocked to learn of the invasions of privacy. Not once during the weekend did we see anyone entering or leaving the rooms on our hall. With our doors consistently open, the staff must have been very sneaky to avoid detection and that was kind of creepy. Jaime and I discussed how such actions would be interpreted in America and decided the hotel would have settled out of court.

With the loss to Rhein, only two home games and one away game remained of the season. Tony and Scotty, tired of relying on the team's limited shuttle service from the hotel, decided to rent a car for the remaining three weeks. The Thunder assisted with the coordination of the small four-door and we finally had the freedom to explore the city on our own terms.

On one such outing, we discovered a multi-level department store called the *Ka-De-Wa*. There were floors of house wares, linens, designer clothing lines and all the normal things you find in a U.S. department store with one exception; the entire sixth floor featured food from around the world. And, not just packaged food, but food stations with chefs who would cook up a delicious meal while you waited. It was a dream come true and, there, we finally found the seafood we'd been looking for. We sat down at a kiosk offering fresh lobster and prawns and ordered the chef to cook them up. We spent the whole day, eating and walking around the spectacle. There were wine and champagne bars, bakery areas with bagels and delicious pastries, pasta stations and virtually every type of gourmet food you could imagine. We thought we'd died and gone to heaven. Then, we stumbled on the American food section where we found Kraft macaroni and cheese, Chips Ahoy and Oreo cookies, ranch dressing, chips and salsa and all kinds of offerings from home. We were in such a buying frenzy we didn't even realize we paid $9.00 for a bag of Chips Ahoy cookies and $11.00 for a jar of salsa until we were in the car. Regardless, the price was irrelevant compared to the joy of having a small taste of home. We decided to drive around the area a little more and see what else might entice us.

Not far from the *Ka-De-Wa* building, we discovered another popular shopping area called *Marlene-Dietrich-Platz 3*. There, a Tony Roma's restaurant was located next door to a movie theatre showing American films in English. We'd heard bits and pieces about the movie theatre from some of the other players, but no one ever mentioned the food finds. We kicked ourselves for not renting a car and venturing across the city sooner. After shopping a bit, we ate dinner at Tony Roma's. Two nights later, we went back again.

Delicious meals, including a BBQ prepared by the Berlin Thunder Fan Club also known as the Bowlhunters, highlighted the entire week. We weren't sure what we were getting into when the Thunder asked us, Billy Gustin, Jon Blackman, Mike Edwards, Scott and Jaime Milanovich, and Jarett Holmes to attend a BBQ at the Bowlhunters' request. We agreed to attend the affair after GM Michael Lang said they were the same group of fans who raised such a ruckus at the airport upon our initial arrival in Berlin and he knew them personally. But, I don't think any of the players were prepared when the bus pulled up to an apartment complex and we were escorted into someone's private downstairs residence.

Inside the door, folding tables in a small hallway featured various homemade salads and breads. At the end of the hallway in a small multi-purpose room decorated with football pennants and flags, a boom box played background music and a u-shaped table was set. In the small attached courtyard, a man in a baseball cap was grilling pork steaks and brats and tubs of beer and soda were on ice; a nice American touch considering the Germans like their beer and soda relatively warm. We couldn't believe we'd actually been invited to a BBQ at someone's home and the Thunder simply dropped us off without anyone from the team to chaperone. That type of event would never have taken place in the NFL but in Europe everything was a little different.

For a while, there was very little conversation and we simply sat around drinking beers, nodding our heads and smiling at each other. I played with Brennan to fend off the awkwardness of the situation. Finally, one of the fifteen people in attendance from the fan club started a dialogue in broken English. Turns out he was the only one in the group who could speak English. He was a huge American football fan, proudly showed off his Green Bay Packers watch, and informed us he'd traveled to the United States to specifically attend NFL games.

After he broke the ice, the large group inundated him with questions for the players. The conversation took the form of a panel discussion with the English-speaking gentlemen translating each question to the recipient and then each answer to the crowd. There were several awkward pauses during the exchanges but the group was very sweet and genuinely interested in us. Very taken with

Brennan, they watched him and talked amongst themselves occasionally breaking into laughter at his funny faces and drool-dripping smiles. At six-months-old, he laughed at their tickles, smiled at their urging and in doing so eased the language difficulties. One of the fans inquired about our decision to come over as a family. They, excitedly, told us they were part of the welcoming group, which met us upon our arrival in Germany and were surprised when Tony came around the corner from customs with two gigantic carts of luggage and a baby stroller in tow. They weren't expecting any players to bring their family to Berlin and they were impressed by Tony's effort. One of the ladies in the group said she was responsible for giving Tony the stuffed bunny Brennan received at Easter. I thanked her for the gift and then the man at the grill motioned to the group it was time to eat.

They were so genuinely tickled to have us there, Tony and I regretted our own initial reluctance to attend. The initial invitation to the BBQ had been a week earlier and when the team reminded the players about the event the day before, several of the players rescinded their promises to attend. GM Michael Lang was not happy about the cancellations and strongly suggested Tony and Scotty persuade the guys to recommit because the fan club members purchased a large amount of steaks for the lunch and were really looking forward to the event. All of the invited players boarded the bus after hearing about the menu. Upon arrival, the players were disappointed to see the promised steaks at the BBQ were not beef but pork. Fortunately, the food was some of the best we'd eaten in Germany and the BBQ, which would never have happened between fans and players back in the NFL, turned out to be a very pleasant experience for everyone.

With the team still spread out at three separate hotels, Coach Vaas wanted to create a sense of unity before game eight on June 3rd. So, after the Friday practice, the entire team was bussed to a theatre for a private showing of the movie *Gladiator* in English. Morale was much improved and the players joked and laughed while ordering popcorn, ice cream, Coke and even beer at the concession stand. Tony, Brennan and I made our way to the stadium-style seating in the balcony section hoping Brennan wouldn't disturb the players as they watched the movie. To our surprise, he slept through the entire epic never even flinching during the resounding fight scenes. Following the movie, we were treated to dinner at a restaurant called Juleps, which called itself a New York Bar Restaurant. With only two weeks remaining of the season, the mood of the team was definitely lightening up.

The next day, we went down to the pre-game meal at 2:00 p.m. We'd eaten out so often over the past weeks, we'd forgotten how truly bad the team meals at the hotel were. At the start of the buffet, I set aside several plates smeared with remnants of something red and orange. I dug down through the entire stack and not one plate was free of dried food. The strength and conditioning coach, standing in line behind me, summoned the catering staff to take the dirty plates away. Minutes later, a dripping wet stack, looking very similar to the one taken away, was placed back on the buffet and I tried hard to convince myself they didn't just rinse them off to appease us. I could probably have lived with the dirty plates but the first entrée of slightly bloody, obviously under-cooked chicken legs and thighs was grossly disgusting and I uttered a few profanities out loud as, simultaneously, the infuriated strength coach yelled for the chicken to be taken away and something else to be served.

It took thirty minutes for them to bring out a single pan of lasagna. Tony and I placed some lasagna, along with a little salad, on our plates and headed back into the banquet room to fill what was left of our appetites. But, after taking the first bite, I realized the lasagna was still frozen in the middle. I indignantly pushed my plate away as a player at another table gasped when he found tiny, red bugs in his salad. In a simultaneous burst, nearly everyone eating threw down their silverware and groaned at the meal. Scott, Jaime, Tony and I elected to leave immediately and grab something to eat on the way to the game.

With little time before the guys had to report to the stadium, we went through the McDonald's drive-thru for hamburgers and fries. Tony and Scott bantered back and forth regarding the nutritional value of their meals and how it happened they were actually looking forward to eating McDonald's before stepping onto the field for one of the most physically demanding sports out there. Their comments about the potential protein found in the salad bugs only served to completely squelch my appetite until half-time when I broke down and ate a stadium brat.

I'd like to think the pre-game meal contributed to the Barcelona Dragons beating us 22-to-9. But, the breakdown of the offensive line probably had more to do with it. I think that's also the game when Scotty suffered abuse from the left side of the offensive line all day. Flat on his back, with the football in his hand after the third or fourth sack, he pointed to the defending player and asked, "Can someone please block that Mother Fucker?" Tony laughed hysterically as he described the riotous moment in the lousy game.

The next day, the team was invited to a party at a new dance club called the House of Entertainment, The New World. I was nervous about entering with Brennan after metal detectors marked the entrance. But, inside, the enormous club featured a bowling alley, rooms for live music, rooms with a DJ and huge dance floors. We were led through the entire complex on our way to the outdoor disco, which featured an above-ground pool, additional dance floors, several bars and a fantastic buffet set-up just for us. No one blinked an eye when we made ourselves comfortable with Brennan. We ate and drank and took advantage of the unique atmosphere. Food had become a central issue for the team and anytime we got away from the hotel for a decent meal the mood was up. When the shot girls came around and convinced several players to slam multiple drinks, we knew the party guys on the team were there for the night. Before things got too crazy, we boarded the first bus to the hotel. Only three other players joined us and it was a quiet ride back as we discussed our final week in Berlin. We decided to see as much as we could by touring the city every day after football practice.

The next day, we visited the Sanssouci Palace, which dated back to 1745 when Prussian kings and emperors ruled in absolute power. Built as the summer residence of Frederick II of Prussia, the grounds encompassed seven palaces and 717 acres. *Sanssouici*, meaning "without cares," was one of the largest and most significant parks in Europe. The grounds were spectacular and Tony, Brennan, Jaime and I spent the afternoon touring lavish rooms and stately gardens.

I could hardly believe our twelve weeks overseas were coming to an end. I'd shot one roll of film each week to document everything from our adventures traveling to Spain, Scotland and Holland for games to foot-stomping the laundry in the bathtub. But, I also shot one entire roll of film simply walking through the tranquil residential streets of Michendorf. One afternoon, Jaime, Brennan and I, bored while awaiting the team's return from practice, went exploring on foot. The old buildings and homes around the hotel were full of charm and character; reminiscent of the old world and a simpler time. In front of a faded clap-board house, a little old lady sat contently on a blue, wooden bench. Her hands were clasped in her lap and her gray hair was disheveled. She was wearing a faded red, floral dress and her stockings had wrinkled around her ankles. She was looking down at her tiny flower garden when I asked to take her picture. She looked up sweetly and smiled as she nodded her head yes. Giddy at capturing her quiet moment of contemplation, I knew the photo would make a wonderful addition to my scrapbook detailing our stay. As eager as I was to return home to the U.S., I was already feeling nostalgic about our crazy adventures and mishaps in Europe.

The June 10th game against the Amsterdam Admirals would officially mark the end of our stay in Berlin and I didn't want to miss the goodbye. As difficult as the trip sometimes was, I knew we'd never again have an experience like NFL Europe. The stories, both good and bad, would stick with me forever and I looked forward to sharing them with Brennan when he was old enough to find the humor in travel snafus and the Thunder's theme song, AC/DC's *Thunderstruck*, which was played loudly over and over again at the beginning of every home game.

Jaime and I arrived at the stadium with the team early as usual. But this game, the fans were already there and poised to close out the season with a big party. *Thunderstruck* was rocking the house and fans were throwing around footballs, toasting beers and a few even had their faces painted with the team's multi-colored logo. As part of the Berlin Thunder, I realized Tony and I had grown from the experience. He and I were closer than ever and our support system was stable and nurturing. As for Tony's football career, he played very well during the last eight games of the season and started loving the game again. He continually talked about how fun it was to play and the change in approach made a big difference in his game and attitude. Obviously, we both hoped the experience would parlay itself into a return to the NFL, but I got the feeling if it didn't, he would be okay with it.

We beat Amsterdam 28-to-15 and, even though five previous losses had already eliminated us from World Bowl contention, the win was uplifting. Following the game, Brennan and I joined Tony for the unusual celebration taking shape on the field. Usually, the players left the field immediately but, that night, they were standing around talking to each other and to the fans in the stands. Rare to be on the field with Tony still in uniform, I tried to preserve the moment by having Brennan sit on Tony's knee for a picture. But, dripping with sweat and looking like the Incredible Hulk in his football uniform and pads, Tony's appearance upset Brennan and he would having nothing to do with it. We gave up so Tony could respond to the hundreds of Thunder fans lining the stadium wall and repeatedly calling to the players. During the interaction, I captured Tony signing autographs and shaking hands with one hand while holding Brennan in the other. The heart-warming scene was picture perfect and an ideal depiction of our time spent in Berlin.

With only days remaining until we departed Berlin for the final game of the season in Frankfurt, we paid our final visits to the Berlin Wall and Brandenberg Gate. We ate at Tony Roma's for the last time, where Brennan enjoyed his first cracker, and met our circle of friends at the beer garden for one last authentic German meal of beer, brats, and pretzels. Jon Blackman set up shop for one last round of haircuts and we hosted one final late night party in our room.

During our month-long stay at the Sol Inn, our room was the nightly place to be. With Brennan asleep in the crib by 9:00 and Tony and I tied to the room, several ball players started congregating in our room on a nightly basis. Drinking, laughing or just talking, they'd be sitting on our bed and on the floor. I loved just hanging out like that and despite the difficulties of living in a hotel room for three months, I was going to miss the nightly ritual.

Jaime left a day later and I was sad to see her go. We'd spent nearly 24 hours a day together for months on end and Tony and I counted her and Scotty among our closest friends. We promised to stay in touch and I truly hoped we would. The rest of us departed Berlin for Frankfurt soon after.

In Frankfurt, Brennan came down with a nasty cold and so he and I didn't attend the Thunder's final game. I thought it better we take it easy before the long international flight home. Besides, in my mind, the season was over and I was already concentrating on getting back to the States as soon as possible. When the Thunder lost to the Frankfurt Galaxy 17-to-24 resulting in a 4-and-6 record, I really didn't care. I just wanted to get home to separate bedrooms, home cooked American food, and peace and quiet.

But, not all the ball players felt the way I did. Some of them planned on attending the World Bowl game featuring the Rhein Fire versus the Scottish Claymores. A few even made arrangements to stay yet longer and tour other cities and countries. We'd seen everything in and around Berlin and part of me would have liked to continue touring Europe in a way Tony's limited time off and rigorous away game schedules hadn't permitted. But, after being away for fourteen weeks, it really was time to go home. Tony received his return airline ticket the day after the final game and we paid $150 to change mine and Brennan's ticket to be on the same next day flight. Departing without regrets, NFL Europe certainly was a season to remember.

The Rhein Fire, led by quarterback Danny Wuerffel, went on to win the 2000 World Bowl.

Chapter XIV

Politics As Usual

2000

Tony started all ten games in NFL Europe and, while the talent pool overseas was relatively inexperienced, he proved to himself he could still play the game. He was physically ready to take on the challenge of any NFL training camp and by completing the short season without any injuries, he felt he'd successfully dismissed any concerns the NFL teams had about his health. But, more importantly, he felt emotionally redeemed from the turmoil of the previous season in Denver. He looked forward to playing the game and once again being part of an NFL team.

Arriving back in the United States one month before the start of most camps, we anticipated Tony being immediately courted by an NFL team looking for depth and experience on their offensive line. Neil assured us Tony would be picked up relatively quickly and we waited for the calls to come in. But, June quickly turned into July and with the opening of most training camps just weeks away, Neil was finding little interest in Tony.

Once again, each passing day without a contract offer ate away at Tony's faith in his athletic abilities. We'd gone through a lot just to prove he was still a viable athlete and it was beginning to look as though the season in Europe made little difference in his career. Tony analyzed all the decisions he'd made leading up to that moment and his anguish started to get the best of him. More and more, he talked about football being over.

I thought we'd done everything right to get his career back on track. But, the lack of interest in Tony certainly clouded our future. My frustration with the system turned to anger and I wanted to know why Tony couldn't catch a break. Only three years earlier, he was practically the second coming. As a team player always dedicated to the sport, he was honest, committed and a good person. He never turned down a charitable request or appearance, showed no propensity for violence on or off the field and never mouthed off about the team or coaches in the media. He could play the game and he was one of the good guys. Why couldn't one of the teams find value in his character and his talent? The NFL was full of shit heads whose antics off the field were criminal and commitment on the field slight at best. They always seemed to get so many chances. Surely, Tony deserved the same opportunities.

I started to hate the game and its driving politics. Tony had become just a number like the one he wore on his back; a commodity with no value. The teams never saw people, just dollar signs. I used to think professional athletes were over-paid and, when they refused to go to camp or play unless they made more money, I ridiculed them and their greedy tantrums. But, after seeing the system up close and personal, I felt differently. Professional football wasn't really about the game; it was about money and power and who controlled or commanded it. For every $30 million paid in players' salaries, owners made $300 million and they were never at risk for torn ligaments, broken bones, or the early onset of arthritis. After seeing behind the shroud of glitz and glamour, I felt strongly players deserved to command as much as they could from the sport.

I finally understood the nature of the beast and it wasn't pretty. Naïve about it all only until we no longer wielded any power and were trying desperately to claw our way back in, I realized we had to be ruthless and cold toward the game. To find our own success, we had to hope other players would be cut or get hurt and we had to work the system to our benefit no matter what. Losing our innocence was sad but necessary for our survival. Bitter and jaded, I wanted nothing more than to screw them at their own game and prove them wrong for making Tony expendable.

Over the next few weeks, Tony pushed himself to work-out and condition every day and I encouraged him because I wasn't ready to give up. But, each day closer to the opening of the NFL training camps, he drifted further away from the idea of playing again. His workouts got progressively shorter and, finally, I was out of mundane words of encouragement and tired of analyzing the possibilities. We were both sick to death of talking about football. Perhaps it was time we both accepted the notion Tony wasn't the same caliber of player as he used to be.

By mid-July, he could no longer muster the fight and relinquished the idea of returning to the NFL. The bastards broke his spirit and it broke my heart. We talked about retirement and what it would mean to our family financially and emotionally. Tony had played football since he was nine years old and worked toward the goal of becoming a professional football player for so long, he never saw past it. As much as we hated to admit it, football was our life and we always thought we'd worry about what came after, ten years down the road. We always thought there would be plenty of time to make commitments and plans for life after the game. It sounds ridiculous but football completely defined us. It provided most of our social circle and our every move over the previous five years had been dictated by the regular season, mini-camp and training camp schedules. Without the game, everything familiar was suddenly gone and we weren't sure how to begin life without it.

I understood Tony's feelings of loss but my own sense of bereavement caught me off guard. Having my own persona was always very important to me but I had to concede, the minute I left my life in Denver to join him in California, football began defining me too. Like it or not, my identity and Tony's were directly linked to who he was and what he did for a living. Sure, I could have created a separate identity in San Diego by seriously re-entering the business world and keeping quiet about Tony's job. But, instead, I chose to work a flexible, part-time job in the marketing department at SeaWorld just to pass the time while Tony was at work. My new friends and co-workers at SeaWorld learned about

Tony playing for the Chargers five weeks into my job after one of them asked why I always took Tuesdays off. From that moment on, I was forever linked to the game and whenever the topic arose, I was always brought into the conversation. It didn't bother me too much until mere acquaintances at SeaWorld began seeking me out to ask for game tickets, comment on Tony's play or the outcome of a game. To keep from always being associated with Tony and the Chargers, I limited the people with whom I engaged in a football-related conversation to my very close friends in the marketing department. But even so, during the season, football was all-encompassing and everything revolved around it.

During the off-season, we tried to get a break from it by leaving San Diego and visiting family and friends in Colorado and Florida. But, it was still a huge part of our lives and everyone wanted to talk about it. We took grand vacations with our financial advisor and other football players and, of course, we spent much of the trips discussing our individual teams and football in general. It was never out of our minds because Tony was always readying for the next mini-camp or mandatory team work-out and we were always working around the NFL schedule.

In early 1998, when we decided to spend much of the off-season in Nevada, I left my position at SeaWorld and willingly let go of my remaining shred of individualism. Left with nothing but football and football-related activities, I was simply "Tony Berti's wife," which certainly wasn't a bad thing. But, it meant football was all I had. The next two football seasons took us from San Diego to Seattle and finally to Denver. Along for the ride, I bought into the lifestyle hook, line and sinker. Football was as much a part of my life as Tony's and I felt equally lost without it.

Don't get me wrong, we both expected football to end some day; we just weren't prepared for an abrupt transition. Being a professional football player is about as unique a profession as you'll find and, when you lose your job as a professional athlete, you can't exactly look in the newspaper for another position in the same field. Tony had never held a real job outside of football and his college degree in Psychology was relatively worthless without additional schooling, which he had no interest in pursuing. He had no idea what he wanted to do and we were truly at a loss.

In our late twenties, we couldn't exactly do nothing for the rest of our lives. I had a taste of that after leaving SeaWorld and it wasn't very rewarding or satisfying. I felt confident I could return to advertising and probably land a job in Vegas. But, Brennan was only seven-months-old and Tony and I agreed long before we had children, I'd be a stay-at-home mom for the benefit of our kids. Tony didn't want the end of his football career to change that ideal and, just getting a handle on being a new mom, neither did I. Tony half-heartedly suggested he might have an interest in the real estate field and quickly followed that comment with another about potentially playing in Vince McMahon's XFL if he could play for the team in Las Vegas. The second comment surprised me because when we first heard about the founding of the XFL, Tony shrugged it off as the minor leagues. Obviously, the unexpected crossroads was forcing both of us to do some serious soul-searching and, unfortunately, the gut-wrenching conversation only served to raise more questions about our future.

The next morning, we took the boat out for a day on the lake. We thought we'd try to relax and take our minds off our dilemma but the minute we were on the water the conversation resumed where it had left off the night before. We realized all those off-seasons should have been spent laying a foundation for when football was over. We should have pursued business opportunities more heavily during Tony's football tenure, which would have offered additional financial stability and, more importantly, a focus when the game was done. We rehashed all our missed opportunities including the scuba shop we considered opening in San Diego after diving became Tony's passion in 1998. The store never came to fruition because the deal fell apart soon after we drafted partnership papers and selected a possible location in Del Mar, just north of San Diego. One potential partner, an experienced diving buddy, attempted to hide financial problems and, then, a second potential partner wouldn't fully commit to running the store. With football, Tony could only be actively involved six months of the year and we weren't willing to stake any money without someone we trusted at the helm.

After the scuba shop idea fell apart, we next had Ken confidentially contact, on our behalf, the owners of a family-owned restaurant chain in San Diego called Oscar's to inquire about potential franchise opportunities. I loved their Greek salads and gyros and Tony was a big fan of their pizzas and wings. We thought their casual dining and catering business would have great success in a business complex south of Denver called the Denver Tech Center. We had plenty of friends in the restaurant business and management candidates were plentiful. Unfortunately, they weren't interested in franchising and we never pursued it further.

We also laughingly re-visited Berti's Backyard BBQ, a cable television show concept we outlined a few years earlier. In addition to diving, Tony was passionate about food and cooking. While he watched little sports programming on television, he was always engrained in the food channel. His cooking abilities were well received by his teammates and our Monday night cookouts during football season always drew big crowds and generous accolades. We often talked about pitching a cable television show showcasing backyard cooking with special celebrity guests sharing their favorite recipes. There certainly would be no shortage of guests among the professional athletes we knew. But, once again, we got busy with other things and the idea was relegated to a back burner until we had more time to actually outline a proposal and get serious about contacting networks or producers, which never happened because the next football season was always around the corner.

The scuba shop, restaurant and television show ideas all stemmed from our personal hobbies and preferences. But, there were other opportunities too. A former teammate once inquired about us partnering in a fiber-optic company. But, we weren't familiar with the technology and declined. Between 1996 and 1999, we half-heartedly considered several things but committed to nothing out of fear of risking everything. We were always certain the perfect opportunity was just around the corner. Fortunately, while we did nothing in the way of actually purchasing a business, we did manage to put away much of Tony's salaries in anticipation of someday buying into something. Overseen by Ken Ready, the money was diversely invested with his high-profile securities firm and for that we were thankful.

Discussing the positive financial situation reduced our anxiety over Tony's impending retirement. The panicked conversation from the night before gave way to calmer, more realistic notions of what life after football might be like. We agreed it would feel good to get off the emotional roller coaster. The instability of never knowing what would happen next was very stressful for both of us. With the initial flood of emotions released, we realized how nice it would be to stop worrying about injuries, training camps, roster spots and other people's agendas. I especially liked the idea of not moving again, especially with Brennan. We could settle into a stable life of normalcy. By the end of the day on the lake, Tony and I concluded his retirement might be the best thing for us.

Ironically, when we got home, there were two messages waiting; One from Neil and one from Reggie McKenzie of the Green Bay Packers. Green Bay wanted to sign Tony to a one-year deal for the League minimum of around $450,000. Tony and I were numb. We'd spent the previous 24 hours coming to terms with the notion he was done with the NFL and then there was another carrot dangling in front of us. It was the ultimate emotional yo-yo and we were both too burned out to get emotional or excited.

With training camp opening in just a few days Tony simply told Neil and Reggie he'd be there. The Packers provided flight information and told Tony the contract could be signed upon his arrival in Green Bay. We didn't like the idea of not having a signed contract but Neil assured us it was no big deal. After the phone calls, Tony and I agreed Brennan and I would not move to Green Bay until after training camp, if at all. Tony, then, started packing.

Two days later, Brennan and I took Tony to the airport at 6:00 a.m. He was unusually reserved as we sat at the gate waiting for his flight to begin boarding. Convinced he wasn't going to be picked up by an NFL team again, the last minute call from Green Bay surprised him and psychologically he was struggling. There'd been no time to flip the mental switch from accepting the notion football was over to the aggressive nature needed to go into another training camp. In a state of excessive emotional turmoil, he hesitantly boarded the flight.

When I returned home from the airport at 7:30 a.m., there was another message from Reggie and the Packers. Once again, I was absolutely blindsided. Reggie's message suggested Tony put off going to Green Bay because they'd incurred some salary changes and there was no room to sign him under the salary cap. I immediately returned Reggie's call and informed him Tony was already on the flight, provided by the team, bound for Green Bay. There was no way I could stop him.

Feeling enormous anxiety and on the verge of tears, my voice cracked when I next phoned Neil. I told him of my conversation with Reggie and he was immediately in an uproar. He said he'd call the Packers and get back to me. I was sick to my stomach. Tony was already reticent about going and the meaningless trip would just destroy any remaining amount of professional confidence in him. I hated the idea he was going to step off that plane in Green Bay only to find out from some team assistant at the airport they didn't really want him after all.

The Chargers and the Broncos each had a hand in wearing him down but this final jab by the Packers would finish the job. It broke my heart for his career to end this way and I hated them all for it. I had to do something to remove the element of surprise and give him some advance warning as to what he was walking into. I knew during his layover in Minneapolis, he would call me or at the very least check his cell phone messages so I left a message, without detail, to call me the minute he landed. I tried to make it sound urgent but not daunting.

When he finally phoned, I gave him an abridged version of the situation. He didn't need to know the ugly reality of it, yet. If Neil worked out the salary cap problem, I didn't want Tony going into camp knowing the Packers had dismissed him so easily. He would never put himself through the emotional rigors of another training camp if he thought for a second they didn't want him. So, I told him there were some issues with Green Bay's salary cap and Neil was addressing them. But, the sugar-coating didn't fly. He already suspected something was up because he had two additional messages from Reggie and Neil.

The money problem arose after Green Bay signed one of their top draft picks, a tight end they anticipated would hold-out but didn't, and his salary ate up much of the cap room needed to accommodate Tony. To solve the money problem, Neil said he had another Green Bay player willing to renegotiate his contract, if necessary, to free up additional cap money, which could be used for Tony. The solution was complicated and Tony was fully prepared to abort his trip to Green Bay and catch a return flight to Las Vegas from Minneapolis. But Neil told him to continue on to Green Bay and he'd have it worked out by the time Tony got there.

Tony arrived in Green Bay expecting little except a return ticket home. But, miraculously, Green Bay found the necessary salary cap room and Neil didn't even have to renegotiate anyone's contract to get Tony signed to his minimum deal. On the first day of practices, Tony spent the day observing the Green Bay system. Most of the players new to the team began learning their playbook during the spring mini-camps and summer school. Tony had no such luxury signing so close to training camp. But, he was experienced, smart and usually able to grasp a system relatively quickly. One day of watching would be sufficient for him to pick up the mix.

On the second day of practices, Tony was thrown into the play rotation, which was a good sign. But, he had major concerns even though the Packers' starting right tackle, Earl Dotson, was suffering from a back injury and his starting position was potentially up for grabs. Green Bay had drafted an offensive lineman in the first round. He wasn't in camp yet but Tony wasn't sure how long he might hold-out or refuse to report. When and if that guy signed, his contract would be worth big money, which would further affect the salary cap. In addition, one of the players vying for the tackle position with Tony was a rookie free-agent and his cap money (or salary) would be one-third of Tony's as a vested veteran. And if that wasn't enough, Green Bay had an abundance of linemen in camp with some of the line positions three and four players deep. But, despite the competition, Neil believed Tony had a good shot at making the team. With Dotson injured and the first rounder holding out, Green Bay needed experience on the line.

By the third day of practices, Tony was getting fed up with one of the Green Bay traditions. The players practice field was located across the street from Lambeau Field and each day kids from the community waited outside the locker room to lend the players their bikes. Players rode the kids' bikes across the stadium parking lot to the practice fields while the kids carried the players' helmets. After practice, the kids were waiting and the players rode the bikes back to the locker room at the stadium. The problem with that tradition was all the kids wanted the big name players to ride their bikes. When Tony asked several of the kids to ride theirs', they all told him they were waiting for someone else. Most were waiting for quarterback Brett Favre who ironically was one of the few players who got a ride across the lot because of the sheer volume of fans trying to get to him. But regardless, four times a day, Tony faced the humiliation of being rejected by little kids who were pretty sure he wasn't worthy of riding their bikes. The two roundtrip walks across the stadium parking lot in cleats each day gave Tony time to reflect on just how honest and mean little kids could be. He liked the idea of Green Bay's community involvement and traditions, but he thought the daily bike custom was rather cruel and embarrassing.

On the fourth day of camp, Tony walked across the parking lot to the morning practice not even stopping to ask any of the kids for a bike. Their lack of interest in him was no big thing but it was part of a bigger picture. By the end of practice, he'd decided he was done and went to see the team's general manager. He couldn't put himself through the paces any longer. He didn't have the fight to continue and his heart wasn't in it. Deep down, he felt it was time to retire.

The general manager shook Tony's hand and wished him good luck. Then, the offensive line coach stepped out of a meeting and did the same. Only when the goodbyes were done did he call Neil. Surprised by the uncharacteristic decision, Neil expressed disappointment in Tony's failure to consult with him before making the announcement. But, Tony explained he didn't want anyone talking him out of it; the decision was made. Following the brief exchange with Neil, he next phoned me.

"Do you want me to come home?" he asked immediately after I answered the phone. Confounded, I hesitantly asked if he'd been cut. Very matter-of-factly, he responded he couldn't go through another training camp, couldn't bare the emotional burden of being cut again and felt it was better to leave on his own terms rather than theirs. Based on what he'd seen in camp, he elected to retire.

Chapter XV

Walking Away

2000

Tony's words hit me like a ton of bricks. We'd talked retirement but never once discussed the option of walking away. He said he didn't discuss it with me because, like Neil, I would have tried to talk him out of it. And, he was certainly right.

Instead of being happy, I was angry with him for making such a huge decision without at least discussing it with me first. I feared we would always wonder what would have happened if he'd stayed and played it out. And, even though I was profoundly aware of just how arduous the previous two seasons had been on him, I couldn't understand walking away from even the slightest possibility of making the roster. I wanted to believe he was capable of not only making the team, but starting and playing another five seasons. But, Tony never wanted to be the veteran player hanging on to his glory days too long and he couldn't stand the thought of being cut after spending five weeks as camp fodder. I conceded being used and abused by Green Bay would have been a terrible finish to a reasonable stint in the NFL. But, rather than accept he ended his own career by unceremoniously walking away, I still preferred to blame the teams' poor decision making for forcing him out of the game.

As I waited at the Las Vegas airport for Tony's flight to arrive, it occurred to me by him choosing to leave the game on his own terms, he didn't gain anything but he didn't lose either. Staying in

Green Bay might have continued the dream but getting cut would have blown it all to hell. I realized his solitary decision to walk away was probably one of the most difficult of his life. Always the competitor, he must have found it very challenging to succumb to the notion the risks outweighed the rewards. By admitting he couldn't do it anymore, he was being completely honest with himself and, with that kind of fortitude, I had no right to be angry with him. The back-to-back shoulder surgeries had taken a physical and mental toll and wallowing in the negative aspects of his decision would only cause Tony and I to be swallowed up by what should have or could have been. I reminded myself I wasn't the one out there dealing with the physical and emotional demands of the game. If he truly believed football was over then I had to accept it and support his decision to walk away.

That evening, Tony and I worked together to compose an e-mail to alert our friends and family to the news before they read it in their local papers the next morning. The message read, "The past three seasons of injuries, instability, uncertainty and political bureaucracy have taken a toll on us. Somewhere along the way, the fun disappeared from the game. It's difficult to let go of something which has been so much a part of Tony's life. When you've done something for twenty years, it can't help but shape who you are. But when your heart just isn't in it anymore, it's time to make a change. So, yesterday, Tony officially announced his retirement and walked away from the NFL. The transition will be slow and the void large. But we take great pleasure in all the wonderful friendships we've established along the way. You've always shown encouragement, support and enthusiasm and we can't thank you enough. Like the song says, 'Every new beginning is some other beginning's end.' So, with a smile and a tear we embark on a new beginning."

I cried as we put the words to paper. In the brief paragraph, we summed up the good, the bad and the ugly of life in the NFL. We knew some of our non-football friends wouldn't understand Tony's decision. They were, after all, the same people who incessantly teased us about the ease of NFL life and often commented on how one

NFL paychecks would ease all their burdens. Having never been in similar circumstances, I didn't really expect them to get it. I did, however, hope our NFL friends would appreciate the difficulty of the situation.

Immediately, we began receiving replies from other ball players affirming some of them were all too familiar with our recent struggles. One wrote, ". . . as another football family, we understand the many lows can outweigh the few highs and it is usually the paychecks which keep us hanging in there. That is not the way to enjoy life and it's not money that governs happiness and life quality. We all face the idea of retirement differently but we all face it ultimately and we wish you all the peace in knowing your decision was the right one."

The simple reply offered support and encouragement and, even though every NFL family's experience is different, I found a sense of serenity in the words, which so eloquently offered understanding of our heavy hearts. To move on, Tony and I both needed to make peace with the decision.

Chapter XVI

XFL Extreme Football

2001

By the end of August, Tony and I, more or less, came to terms with his NFL career being over. But, each of us still harbored ill will toward the team we individually held responsible for the downward turn in his career. The Chargers and Kevin Gilbride, in particular, bore the brunt of my hostility, which had abated little since 1998, when the organization placed Tony on IR (Injured Reserve), even though he was healthy to play, and then screwed around long enough to impact his opportunity in Seattle. Even Gilbride's firing the same year didn't weaken my contempt for the Chargers organization. Despite wanting the best for our friends still playing there, I always liked for the team to lose.

Tony, on the other hand, felt the writing was on the wall in San Diego and he wasn't bothered by Gilbride or the IR sham. Instead, his animosity lay with the Broncos. He believed he was signed in 1999 strictly as an insurance policy for Matt Lepsis and once Lepsis proved he could handle the starting right tackle position, Tony's contribution became costly and unnecessary. The Broncos never gave him the opportunity promised and they added insult to injury by dangling the starting right tackle position in front of him, inviting him to their high-brow Super Bowl ring ceremony and then cutting him lose after what he believed was a productive pre-season. His ire for them, although reserved, often culminated in cheerful gloating when he stumbled across the weekend sports scores highlighting another Broncos loss. He was amused by their lack of success but preferred to focus his attention on the Colorado Buffs.

Early in the fall, we were invited to Boulder, Colorado, for the Tenth Reunion of the 1990 CU National Championship football team. Excited to be involved in the nostalgic weekend and see Coach McCartney and his former college teammates, Tony jumped at the chance to attend. Ken Ready invited us to spend the weekend at his home in Denver and we accepted his gracious offer.

Departing Las Vegas late Friday afternoon, our Denver-bound flight was delayed and it was nearly 1:00 a.m. before Tony, Brennan and I settled in at Ken's for the night. At 6:00 a.m. the next morning, Tony's cell phone rang several times. He let it go to voicemail. But, within minutes, the phone rang again. Agitated by the early morning interruption, Tony answered it abruptly and, then, immediately sat up in bed shaking his head to clear his sleepy daze. From the look on his face, I knew the call was bad news. He spoke little but from the fragmented conversation, I gathered someone suffered a heart attack. When he finally hung up the phone, what he said absolutely stunned me.

During the night, John Parrella's father, Joe, had been murdered. Someone broke into his home in Grand Island, Nebraska and when the alarm went off, Joe went downstairs to investigate. He fired a shot at the intruder inside the living room and then followed the person outside where police believed there was a struggle and Joe was shot in the chest with his own gun.

Tony and I were devastated by the news and made arrangement to drive north on Sunday to join John and his family in Grand Island. We attended Saturday evening's CU reunion and then, on Sunday, met Leigh Parrella at Denver International Airport to offer assistance with her three boys during their layover en route to Grand Island. We brought toys and coloring books for the kids and provided Leigh with a little relief during the stressful trip from San Diego. Once she and the boys were on their flight, we embarked on the six-hour drive to Grand Island in a rental car. We elected to drive because Tony hated the small, puddle-jumper airplanes used to ferry passengers between Denver and Grand Island and we also wanted the flexibility of staying in Grand Island however long necessary.

In a testament to John's emotional strength and faith, he played on Sunday despite the shocking news of his father's death. He was certain Big Joe would have expected nothing less and John planned to travel to Grand Island immediately following the Chargers away game. In a surprisingly compassionate gesture, Dean Spanos, the Chargers owner, flew John, teammates Mike Mohring, Raylee Johnson, Darren Bennett, Kurt Gouveia and a few others directly from the game to Grand Island in his private jet.

The scene was emotional for everyone involved and we spent the next several days consoling the Parrella family, showing support and offering assistance. To ease our sorrow, we eulogized Big Joe in our own way. Over beers, we recalled his humorous stories and antics and laughed at his prolific words of wisdom and John's impeccable impersonation. We helped with the task of accepting, organizing and distributing the hundreds of floral arrangements and houseplants arriving from every flower shop within 150 miles of Grand Island. As a cohesive group, we tried to buffer the family from the media contingent following the story. But, the murder was big news in the small town and everyone was talking. All kinds of speculation and ridiculous rumors suggesting suicide, mafia affiliations and bad business deals came of it. The banter only served to heighten the family's anxiety, but we hoped the local and national media circus might garner leads or a suspect. Unfortunately, the case went cold within days. Following the funeral and John's return to San Diego, we drove back to Denver to catch our flight home to Vegas.

The unusual turn of events in September, gave Tony and I plenty of time to reflect on our past and discuss our future. We needed a direction and Tony, still uncertain of his ideal post-football career, decided to actively pursue his interest in real estate by enrolling in the Real Estate School of Nevada. The extremely active Las Vegas market with its unlimited income potential appealed to his competitive side and his knack for being a mediator and desire to work for himself made real estate a reasonable choice. Never complacent, Tony was a licensed real estate agent by the end of October and had his first clients—us.

Deciding to make Nevada our year-round home was easy. We liked the city's attractions, favorable tax climate and weather. But, our town home was a little too small for our growing family and we decided it was time to buy a bigger house with a kid-friendly yard for Brennan. Our town home sold within seven days of listing and we purchased a new, larger home under construction on the other side of town. Over the next month, through referrals and friends, Tony picked up a couple additional clients. He enjoyed the challenge and success of real estate but soon admitted he missed football. Not necessarily the game itself, but the interaction and locker room banter with the guys.

So, when Vince McMahon of the World Wrestling Federation announced Las Vegas would definitely be home to an XFL team, Tony was eager to check it out. We discussed the opportunity to play again and Tony became more interested in the new league when Don Gregory, a friend and former talent scout for the San Diego Chargers, was named the Las Vegas Outlaws' Director of Player Personnel. Without uprooting our lives and leaving the city, the team affiliation would fill the football void in Tony's life. We also thought the connection might garner some positive PR and help build his real estate business. Playing in the XFL seemed like an ideal scenario.

Tony signed the required contract outlining his intent to enter the XFL draft. There was no need for Neil to look over the paperwork because it was the same for all potential XFL players. Besides, Tony was pretty certain Neil, convinced Tony would have made the Packer's roster, was miffed at him for leaving Green Bay's camp after only a few days.

As for the XFL, we weren't sure what to expect. We knew there would be eight teams initially including the Los Angeles Xtreme, Chicago Enforcers, Orlando Rage, Las Vegas Outlaws, New York/New Jersey Hitmen, San Francisco Demons, Memphis Maniax and Birmingham Thunderbolts and the ten-game-season would be played from February to May with four teams attending training camp in Las Vegas and four teams attending in Orlando. To even the talent pool, teams were supposed to be able to protect players from certain colleges within their geographic areas meaning each team would have a priority opportunity to sign and retain certain players based on their former college. For example, the Las Vegas Outlaws would have the first shot at signing any eligible player who attended the University of Nevada, Las Vegas (UNLV), Brigham Young University in Utah (BYU) or the University of Nebraska. We were also told players already residing within a team's home city could be protected. Based on those initial guidelines, we thought Tony was a shoe-in for the Vegas team. But, the guidelines were soon changed and the teams were no longer allowed to protect players just because they were living within a particular team's vicinity. If the XFL was intending to lure NFL veterans to the new league, we thought the change was a big mistake because few vets, including Tony, would be willing to move to another city to participate in an unproven, start-up league.

A few weeks before the XFL draft, the teams began calling the house to discuss Tony's interest in playing for them. He adamantly told the Chicago Enforcers, San Francisco Demons, Memphis Maniax and Birmingham Thunderbolts he would only play for the Las Vegas team. When asked why, he explained the $4500 salary paid per week for a loss and the $5500 paid per week for a win, wasn't enough over the ten-week-season to warrant shelving his new real estate business and moving to another state. Playing in the XFL outside of Las Vegas simply wasn't an option and he told Don Gregory and the Las Vegas Outlaws Head Coach Jim Criner, the very same thing. He would only play for the Las Vegas franchise.

During the weeks leading up to the draft, the XFL held much publicized tryouts all over the country and had thousands of applicants. But, the tryouts were primarily publicity stunts to generate hype about the league. The majority of talent was coming from a pool of former college and NFL players, Arena League players and other semi-pro venues. There were a few Cinderella stories but most of the guys had a decent athletic resume to their name.

January 2001 ushered in the XFL draft and Tony was unhappy when the New York/New Jersey Hitmen, who never contacted us to inquire about his interest in playing for them, drafted him. Head Coach Rusty Tillman phoned Tony after the selection and was understandably frustrated when Tony said he was flattered but wanted to be traded to Las Vegas.

On the flip side, Tony was frustrated with the Las Vegas Outlaws for not drafting him right away. They obviously assumed because of Tony's strong outspoken opposition to playing outside of Vegas, none of the other teams would draft him. Our big mouths got us into trouble again and the Outlaws took advantage of the situation thinking Tony would still be sitting on the draft board whenever they got off their butts to pick him up. In the mean time, New York thought they landed a big fish.

All XFL players reported to training camp in February. But, even after repeated phone calls from the Hitmen, Tony refused to report to the New York camp in Orlando. Coach Criner and Don Gregory kept telling Tony they were working on a trade for him. But, Criner was being a prick about it. He was so sure Tony wouldn't play for New York he kept offering them bad trades including players he was going to cut anyway. New York didn't buy it and they understandably refused to trade away their high-round pick unless they got something in return. Criner thought he had New York over a barrel and he was going to get Tony for free. But, Rusty Tillman and his New York Hitmen just got more and more resolute about letting Tony go.

Because we were unaware the New York team could hold Tony's rights for the entire season even if he was a no-show at camp, Tony stood his ground and demanded to be traded. But, doing so gave the Hitmen the upper hand. In retrospect, Tony should have gone to New York's camp in Orlando, which would have forced the Las Vegas Outlaws to either trade for him or the New York team to cut him. Instead, training camp came and went and we were stuck in limbo.

Refusing to join the New York team, Tony made a point of visiting the Outlaws practices. His reasons were two-fold. First, he hoped to cash in on any real estate opportunities which might present themselves. The Outlaws' coaching staff signed two-year contracts and many of them were moving to the Las Vegas area. In addition, he and I worked with a local apartment finding service to put together housing packages for the players. Tony would receive a small referral fee if any of the players moved into one of the recommended complexes. Intending to protect the players, we required the participating apartments to outline specific financial terms if a player was cut or traded during the season. We didn't want any of the guys forced to cover a full-lease term like we were Denver. The complimentary packets were designed to provide immediate information and recommendations for players temporarily moving to the city and included sections on furniture rentals, city maps, shopping and such. And, if one of the players decided to relocate permanently, the packets highlighted Tony's real estate tie-in.

The second reason Tony attended the practices was to watch the team and learn their system from the sidelines so when the trade was finally complete, he'd be ready to play. Unfortunately, New York got wind of his practice visits. They cried foul and told Coach Criner and the Outlaws to go screw themselves. They'd simply keep Tony on their no-show list and he would play for no one. Tony blamed himself for being stubborn and coach Criner for screwing around with the trade for so long.

Don Gregory kept us abreast of the situation. We were disappointed in the dick measuring contest but we were a little taken aback by the league's direction anyway once the regular season started. The kick-off ball scramble and on-field cameramen were unique innovations to the game but the stripper-like cheerleaders and mid-game player interviews were more spectacle than sport. Football fans weren't buying into the sideshow and the mediocre play was sending once promising television ratings plummeting.

Five games into the season, Vince McMahon's pro wrestling-inspired antics turned a great idea into a running joke on late night television. As ratings floundered and the backlash grew, the league back paddled. Former NFL players, interested in playing but sidelined by their refusals to relocate to other XFL cities, were being contacted to play and the Director of Player Personnel for the entire league ordered teams to empty their no-show lists to improve the talent pool. College affiliations and residential geography no longer mattered. The XFL just wanted the most talented players on a team, on the field, improving the quality of the game and, hopefully, the television ratings.

But, New York still refused to trade Tony to Las Vegas and Tony still refused to play anywhere else. Finally, someone at the top of the XFL organization ordered New York to make it happen. So, New York traded Tony to San Francisco and, in turn, San Francisco traded him to Las Vegas. The necessity of the three-way trade was all about egos but it put Tony in Vegas where he wanted to be. In addition, he found himself playing with former teammates Kurt Gouveia from the San Diego Chargers, Werner Hippler from the Chargers and the Frankfurt Galaxy, and Jon Blackman from the Berlin Thunder. Officially joining the Outlaws gave Tony the football fix he needed and the first thing he did was invite all the guys to our house for a barbeque. They sat around eating, drinking and swapping football stories until the wee hours of the morning. Tony was once again in his element.

Within four days of joining the team, he secured the starting right guard position and played in his first game. The talent was average but the teams had heart. Everyone made the same amount of money so there were no big contracts dictating who got opportunities and who didn't. Pay for play meant winning earned each player an extra $1000 for the week, which had the potential to generate a reasonable annual salary in only ten weeks and offered quite an incentive to some of the younger guys on the team.

Once we learned to ignore all the stupid shenanigans surrounding the league, we decided the XFL was pretty cool. Tony liked the guys he was playing along side and the variations in the rules gave the game a new twist. He said it was the most fun he'd had playing since college and I could see in his play and on his face his love of the game had returned. He was having a good time, which made watching him and the games so much more fun. Win or lose, there was chemistry and cooperation between the players and pleasure in the endless rehashing of plays and calls. During the final five games of the season, Tony found his redemption and I knew he'd never look back again.

The Outlaws finished their season with four wins and six losses and failed to make the play-offs. But quarterbacks Scotty Milanovich and Tommy Maddox led the Los Angeles Xtreme to the April championship, The Million Dollar Game, where they defeated the San Francisco Demons 38-to-6. In May, the XFL suddenly announced its demise following the 2001 inaugural season. Tony and I learned about the league's collapse on the evening news.

In July, the NFL's Jacksonville Jaguars contacted Tony about reporting to their training camp. He respectfully declined.

Chapter XVII
Financial Yardage

Financial gains from even a few seasons in the NFL can be substantial and the most important decision Tony made, prior to the NFL draft, was enlisting the services of a reputable money manager to provide advice in handling his future finances. Though not every player makes millions each season, even the average NFL salary is exceptional and requires the oversight of investment and tax professionals. Early in Tony's career, Ken Ready made us realize the money Tony would make in the NFL could last our lifetime if spent and invested wisely. So, during Tony's six professional football seasons, we worked closely with Ken setting budgets and controlling our spending to ensure the money would last long after football was over. Of course, Tony's big salary jump in 1998, contributed significantly to our financial security. But, even before his million dollar season, we took saving seriously.

Prior to Tony's entry into football, I never truly thought about the negatives effects money could have on relationships. But, at Dr. Bucky's monthly luncheons for the Chargers Women's Association, several of the wives regularly discussed the pressures and problems they experienced when their husband's family members expected and constantly asked for money. Most of the time, but not always, the affected players came from lower socio-economic backgrounds and the expectations often went well beyond the players' means. Their mothers wanted new houses and cars, their siblings wanted cars, clothes and jewelry, and their friends borrowed money they couldn't pay back. It was often difficult for the players to say no and if they did, their refusal often strained the relationships and fostered animosity and jealousy. Sometimes, the wives were blamed for the action and found themselves caught in the middle. The financial fall-out caused a lot of grief and the wives openly discussed the difficulty in trying to balance their own family's future with the needs and expectations of other loved ones.

Obviously, the extended family members making over-the-top monetary requests and demands weren't aware of the costs involved in earning a six- or seven-figure salary. After listening to some of the wives' stories, I understood how professional athletes occasionally ended up penniless at the end of their careers. I could see how a player might give away the store if he gave in to everyone asking for money or if he, himself, wasn't familiar with the hidden costs associated with high-dollar salaries. For example, players in San Diego were not only subject to the highest federal tax bracket but also to an additional 10% tax levied by the state of California. So, a million dollar salary on paper automatically dropped to $500,000 in take-home pay. Players were also required to file income tax returns in every state where they played a football game and pay the associated percentage of taxes on their salary in accordance with however many days they were in that state. In 1997, we filed nine state tax returns. Not only did we have to pay the taxes, but we had to hire a highly competent accountant to figure out all those individual returns.

In addition to tax liabilities, players also have to pay their agents between two and four percent of the overall contractual amount for negotiating their contract. Money managers also charge fees to set up accounts and handle financial matters. While the adage "money makes money" still holds true, it also costs money to make money and those fees have to be taken into consideration when determining disposable income. Those kinds of details were often lost on the families. But, the families weren't always responsible for dwindling a player's savings.

Sometimes, the players themselves were responsible for financial predicaments. Unfortunately, it wasn't uncommon to see players spending indiscriminately or living beyond even their substantial means. One player bought multiple diamond-encased custom watches costing close to $100,000. A few bought luxury cars and tricked-out SUVs on a regular basis, often making the change simply because of a vehicle's color and, still more, bought big houses with even bigger price tags. Tony and I, personally, loved the idea of having a big house overlooking the beach in La Jolla, but buying a multi-million dollar home with a 30-year mortgage didn't seem prudent when we considered the average life span in the NFL was only four seasons. But, I don't think those guys ever really thought about the possibility of their careers being over or the NFL paychecks going away. Otherwise, they certainly would have been more conservative with their spending. Wouldn't they?

One of the starting defensive ends with the Chargers made a lot of money during his multiple seasons in San Diego but he lived the lifestyle. He went out all the time, always had an entourage on his tab and liked fancy cars and limousines. He epitomized the professional athlete persona and he was obviously unconcerned with managing his money. I often wondered how even *he* could afford such frenzied spending and I got my answer soon enough.

On the last year of his contract, he walked into training camp with only the shoes on his feet. He'd blown through the sizeable six-figure signing bonus he received at the beginning of the contract as well as the subsequent seasons' salaries and literally walked into camp with nothing. His unfortunate but self-deserving situation only served to encourage our continued budgeting of money for the off-seasons, when the players didn't receive paychecks, as well as the time when the much-anticipated paychecks stopped all together.

His extreme financial failure was a great example of what not to do with an NFL salary regardless of its size. Given guidance and a few seasons of even minimum salaries, there's no reason most NFL players shouldn't leave the game with a respectable financial portfolio. Unfortunately, my guess is there will always be a small percentage of professional athletes unable to handle their finances responsibly.

However, on the other end of the financial spectrum were the players who made more money than they needed. During one of

Ken Ready's annual travel escapes, Tony and I were asked to join Ken and his wife, Linda, on a scenic drive around the Hawaiian island. But first, Ken had to a make a stop at the local Prudential Securities office. When we experienced difficulty finding the building, he became anxious. Eventually, we located the office and he went in to conduct his business. Upon returning to the car, he was much more relaxed. It turns out one of the ball players on the trip signed a big money deal just before leaving for Hawaii and shoved his signing bonus check in his pocket to give to Ken. All morning, Ken had been walking around with a crumpled up multi-million dollar check in his pocket and he couldn't wait to make the deposit and forego the responsibility of keeping it safe. Ken had never encountered a situation like that before and he was understandably uncomfortable. But, who could blame him? He would have had to call the issuing NFL team and inform them a replacement check was necessary because the first one had been lost, which would not have sat well with anyone involved. Although the guy who nonchalantly shoved the check for that much money into his sweat suit pocket before embarking on a cross-country trip to Hawaii, obviously, wasn't too concerned with his finances.

We never reached that level of compensation in the NFL. But, several good seasons guided by Ken's financial expertise, allowed us to leave the game with assets somewhere between the broke partier and the unconcerned multi-millionaire.

Chapter XVIII

The Final Score

Recently, I asked Tony if he would do it all over again. Despite the wear and tear on his body and the early onset of arthritis, the emotional roller coaster and the mental anguish of the politics, he unequivocally said yes.

He was very proud of his accomplishments in college and his free education. Financially, the NFL allowed him to reach goals, by the age of 25, which some people work their entire lifetime to achieve. But, the primary reason he'd do it all again wasn't for the money. He said his years as an athlete gave him unique once-in-a-lifetime experiences and endless stories, funny anecdotes and fond memories. And most importantly, the people he met forever changed his life. When I pressed him about whom some of those people might be and why they had such an impact on him, I was truly surprised by his candor and ability to articulate why they made such a difference in his life.

The first person he mentioned was Bill McCartney, the former head coach of the University of Colorado. He praised Coach Mac as a great leader and motivator. He said, "Coach Mac could make you believe and then push you to achieve. He was a self-evaluator and surrounded himself with people to compliment his strengths and supplement his weaknesses. He was a man of conviction and it didn't matter if you were the starting quarterback or the third-string kicker; he treated all his players the same regardless of their standing on the team."

Coach Mac took personal responsibility for each and every one of his players. In 1990, when Tony was a senior in high school and being recruited by CU for football, Coach McCartney personally went to Tony's house to visit with his parents. He told Tony's mom he would be taking Tony out of her house, but would make sure Tony would still become the young man she wanted him to be. CU, in a way, would become his surrogate family and he would not only play for a top-notch college but also earn a degree.

Coach Mac stayed true to his word. He met with every player individually twice a year to make sure they were on the right track. He implemented programs to assist them academically if necessary and they were not permitted to play if their academics fell short. In 1992, when Tony decided to leave the University of Colorado football program, Coach Mac promised changes on the field and proclaimed Tony would be a great CU player. He also assured Tony his scholarship, ensuring him an education, would remain in place regardless of his decision. Convinced to stay by the conversation, Tony did become an outstanding collegiate athlete and did earn a degree in Psychology just as Mac promised.

In another instance, Coach Mac stayed true to his word when he made sure, in 1994, Tony's mom was aware and approved of Tony and me moving in together. He would not let it happen until Tony's mom called him and said it was okay. Coach Mac indeed felt responsible for Tony and wanted to make sure he was making good decisions with proper oversight. He was an inspiration to Tony both on and off the field and the qualities and standards he set forth in his football program, made Tony integrally aware of the importance of respect, fairness, guidance and leadership.

The second person Tony mentioned was Stan Brock. I knew Stan would be in the mix somewhere. From the moment Tony met him, he was drawn to his character. Stan's older brother, Willie, played in the NFL for twelve years and Stan used to jokingly call him a quitter. Tony always got a kick out of that. But seriously, after fifteen seasons in the League, Stan could have sat back and refused to help the younger guys like a lot of the veterans. But, he didn't. Instead, he was always willing to share his knowledge and assist the younger players. He had an aura about him and the younger guys responded to his work ethic. He set the standard by being the first to arrive for meetings and always learning more about his opponent even if he'd played against the guy over and over. When the team ran wind sprints, Stan had the opportunity to sit out and watch. His years in the League afforded him that luxury. But instead, the 37-year-old, ancient by football standards, led the charge and made the younger guys work at it just to keep up.

Stan always put the team first. In 1995, midway through the season, offensive tackle Vaughn Parker replaced Stan on the line. Instead of being an egotistical jerk about the demotion, Stan embraced the opportunity to maintain his role as a team leader and mentor the younger guys. "In that one year, I learned volumes about football, life and how to be a man," Tony said. Stan helped instill in him the importance of being a mentor and having a strong work ethic and positive attitude.

Tony loves a quote attributed to Tiger Woods, "I out work them, I out think them, therefore I intimidate them." He said every facet of that quote applies to former San Diego Chargers linebacker Junior Seau. He out worked other players in the weight room where he was one of the strongest players on the team and at practice, he practiced as if every day were game day. Tony was intimately familiar with Junior's intensity because, when he was with the Chargers, he was forced to block him in practice every day. Junior could out think his opponents because of his acute knowledge of the game and coaches relied on him for his input as to what was happening on the field. He was always calculating how to be better at what he did. On game days, he was in the training room with the opposing offense's formations and tendencies on the wall so he could study them. And, because Junior knew his "enemies" so well, he could predict their movements. That ability intimidated them and opposing teams often changed their game plans based on where he was on the field. His knowledge was power and he used it to succeed not with words but with action. Junior had heart and dedication to the art of the game. He taught Tony it's not what you say; it's what you do that makes a difference.

Coach Mac, Stan Brock and Junior were each responsible, in their own way, for helping Tony ascertain attributes and characteristics which he wanted to emulate in his own life. While football only lasted a few years, those people had an impact to last a lifetime. So, it's no wonder, Tony would do it all again.

I'm often asked if I think my sons, Brennan and Easton, will play ball. I suppose it's likely they will to some degree whether in Little League, high school, college or the pros. They've been exposed to their dad's past and, like all boys, have a propensity to like rough and tumble sports. They're also most certainly taking after Tony physically and are consistently taller and bigger than other children their age. So, given they have a desire to play, I'll certainly give them my blessing. Sports participation at any level encourages discipline, teamwork and goal-setting; all fine qualities on and off the field. College ball has the obvious reward of education and the NFL has much to offer young men straight out of college. And, if by chance and hard work, they someday end up playing in the pros, then, I think they'll benefit from our experiences and understanding of the inner workings of the game. Because when it's all said and done, I wouldn't want to deprive them of their very own NFL experience.

And, truth be told, I'd love to be a face in the crowd again.

BVG